Parallels

Brent Davis Reid

TEACHER'S ANNOTATED EDITION

Second Edition

TAKING A STAND IN ENGLISH

PEARSON
Longman

DISTRIBUTED IN CANADA BY ERPI
5757, RUE CYPIHOT, SAINT-LAURENT (QUÉBEC) H4S 1R3
TELEPHONE: **514 334-2690 ext. 232**   FAX: **514 334-0448**
infoesl@erpi.com   **w w w . l o n g m a n e s l . c a**

ACKNOWLEDGEMENTS

Many thanks to:
- Sharnee Chait, Lucie Turcotte and the entire ERPI team for their matchless professionalism;
- Anne Villeneuve for her fantastic illustrations;
- friends and family members for their continued support.

The following colleagues provided constructive feedback for the first edition:

Geraldine Arbach (Collège de l'Outaouais)
Maria Askerow (Collège François-Xavier-Garneau)
Audrey Blair (Cégep de Drummondville)
Diane Boisvert (Cégep de Saint-Laurent)
Carol Broderick (Cégep André-Laurendeau)
Angelika Brunel (Collège Ahuntsic)
Jason Brunwald (Cégep de Lévis-Lauzon)
Alexandre Daigle (Cégep de Trois-Rivières)
Susan Frame (Cégep Marie-Victorin)
Catherine Lamontagne (Cégep de Chicoutimi)
Suzanne Pavelich (Collège de l'Outaouais)
Kay Powell (Collège Ahuntsic)
Claudia Rock (Consultant and author)
Kathleen White (Cégep de Sainte-Foy)
In memory of Sandra Seggie.

Managing Editor
Sharnee Chait

Editor
Lucie Turcotte

Copy Editors
Jeremy Lanaway
Katie Shafley

Proofreader
Katie Shafley

Art Director
Hélène Cousineau

Graphic Design Coordinator
Karole Bourgon

Book Design
Dessine-moi un mouton
Sylvie Morissette

Cover Design
Sylvie Morissette

Page Layout
Talisman illustration design

Illustrations
Anne Villeneuve   pp. 1, 18, 48, 83, 113, 145
Vincent Régimbald   pp. 31, 45, 88, 99, 157, 171

CREDITS

Unit 1, p. 6 "The Truth Is, I've Been Guilty of Lying" by Susan Schwartz, reprinted with the express permission of National Post Company, a CanWest Partnership. p. 10 Audio text "Commentary" © Canadian Broadcasting Corporation.

Unit 2, p. 19 Photograph © Sune Falk / Lorenzo Mondo / Shutterstock. p. 22 "Hey Music Industry: Sharing Is Good" by Lindsay Jones reprinted with permission of *The Daily News*. p. 26 Audio texts "Downloading Tape" and "Is Music File Downloading Killing the Music Industry" © Canadian Broadcasting Corporation. p. 34 Photograph © Elena Ray / iStockphoto. p. 37 "Cloning Becomes Freakshow" by David Suzuki reprinted with the permission of the David Suzuki Foundation. p. 41 Video segment "Cloning Wish" © Canadian Broadcasting Corporation.

Unit 3, p. 49 Photograph © vikki martin / Alamy. p. 52 "A New Family Man" by Lisa Fitterman reprinted with the express permission of the National Post Company, a CanWest Partnership. p. 56 Video segment "Love and the Law" © Canadian Broadcasting Corporation. p. 66 Photograph © newphotoservice / Shutterstock. p. 69 "They Aren't Just Babies Anymore, They're Products" by Susan Ruttan reprinted with the express permission of Edmonton Journal Group Inc., a CanWest Partnership. p. 73 Video segment "Policing Reproduction" © Canadian Broadcasting Corporation.

Unit 4, p. 84 Photograph © James Steidl / Shutterstock. p. 87 "I Am, Therefore I Sell" by Ronald Bailey reprinted with the permission of *Reason* magazine. p. 91 Audio text "The Organ Trade" © Canadian Broadcasting Corporation. p. 99 Photograph © Dmitriy Shironosov / Shutterstock. p. 102 "Pigs May Become Man's Best Friend" by Michael Fumento reprinted with the permission of the author. p. 106 Audio text "Controversy over Xenotransplantation" © Canadian Broadcasting Corporation.

Unit 5, p. 114 Photograph © Bork / Shutterstock. p. 117 "Disabled Are Not Dogs" by Tom Koch reprinted with the permission of the author. p. 122 Audio text "Essay on Euthanasia" © Canadian Broadcasting Corporation. p. 129 Photograph © Bork / Shutterstock. p. 132 "Liability Issues Beset Ultrasound Technology" by Anne Marie Owens reprinted with the express permission of National Post Company, a CanWest Partnership. p. 137 Video segment "Measuring Up" © Canadian Broadcasting Corporation.

Unit 6, p. 146 Photograph © Cristi Matei / Shutterstock. p. 149 "Business or Big Brother" by Richard Foot reprinted with the permission of the author. p. 153 Video segment "Spying on Kids" © Canadian Broadcasting Corporation. p. 160 Photograph © Scott Bowlin / Shutterstock. p. 163 "The Dark Side of Gene Patenting" by Timothy Caulfield and Richard Gold reprinted with the permission of the authors. p. 167 Audio text "Medical Ethics Column: Gene Patents" © Canadian Broadcasting Corporation.

Photograph of files in filing cabinet, pp. 2, 19, 34, 49, 66, 84, 99, 114, 129, 146, 160 © Dariusz Sas / Shutterstock.

Photograph "Bee at Work," pp. 2, 20, 35, 50, 67, 85, 100, 115, 130, 147, 161 © Sándor F. Szabó / iStockphoto.

Photograph of open book, pp. 5, 21, 37, 52, 69, 86, 101, 117, 131, 148, 162 © zimmytws / Shutterstock.

Photograph "Good News" (detail), front cover, pp. 10, 26, 41, 56, 73, 91, 106, 122, 137, 153, 167 © Cristian Ardelean / iStockphoto.

Photograph of pencils, pp. 12, 29, 43, 59, 76, 94, 108, 124, 139, 155, 169 © Photothèque ERPI.

Photograph "Be Heard" (detail), pp. 13, 30, 44, 60, 77, 95, 109, 125, 140, 156, 170 © iStockphoto.

Photograph of go word, front cover, pp. 15, 31, 45, 61, 78, 96, 110, 126, 141, 157, 171 © kd2 / Shutterstock.

Photograph "Duet of the Puffins," front cover, pp. 16, 31, 45, 63, 79, 97, 111, 127, 143, 158, 172 © Scott Hunt / iStockphoto.

© 2009 Longman Published and distributed by

ÉDITIONS DU RENOUVEAU PÉDAGOGIQUE INC.

Registration of copyright: Bibliothèque et Archives nationales du Québec, 2009
Registration of copyright: Library and Archives Canada, 2009
Printed in Canada

ISBN 978-2-7613-3038-1   123456789 SO 13 12 11 10 09
                  133038   ABCD 0F10

Parallels: Taking a Stand in English, Second Edition is a comprehensive four-skills textbook aimed at intermediate to high-intermediate learners of English as a Second Language (ESL) studying in science and humanities programs.

There are six units in the textbook. Everyone should start with the first unit: it introduces the notion of ethics and sets the stage for the kinds of activities involved in the rest of the book. Each of the remaining five units (Units 2–6) is divided into two sections: Section A is aimed at humanities students and Section B is aimed at science students. Many sections are appropriate to either field of study. You can pick and choose sections to complete in the order you deem appropriate.

The title of the book merits a brief explanation.

The title, *Parallels*, is significant because:

- Selected Canadian articles, radio and television segments *parallel* the students' courses of study, focusing on program-related vocabulary.
- Students, regardless of their programs, have *parallel* learning experiences in that they are asked to accomplish similar tasks in *parallel* sections.
- The accompanying eleven-unit grammar workbook (*Parallels: Taking a Stand in English—English Grammar*) *parallels* the topics covered in the eleven sections of this textbook.

The subtitle, *Taking a Stand in English*, underscores the controversial character of the thought-provoking subjects dealt with in this book: personal morality, music downloading, human reproductive cloning, gay and lesbian families, commercial surrogacy, the human organ trade, xenotransplantation, voluntary active euthanasia, wrongful life, electronic surveillance and human gene patenting.

Throughout the book, helpful reading and writing strategies are included as well as pertinent listening and speaking suggestions. Two comprehensive appendices dealing with essay writing and public speaking are included to help structure student productions.

New to the second edition are:

- notes relating to commonly used expressions;
- eleven cooperative projects;
- five additional readings;
- a companion website including forty-four additional reading, listening, writing and speaking exercises.

On a personal note, the writing of *Parallels: Taking a Stand in English* has been a positive experience *without parallel* in my professional life, and it is sincerely hoped that teachers and students using the textbook will participate in a rich and highly educational experience *beyond parallel* in their academic lives.

Warmest regards,

Brent Davis Reid
Montreal, April 2009

HIGHLIGHTS

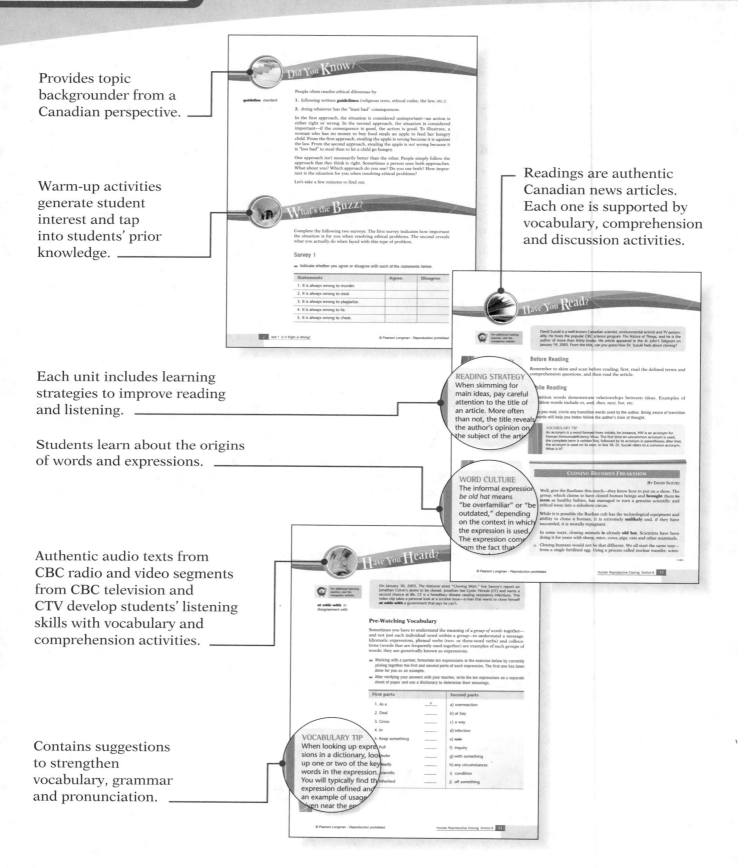

Provides topic backgrounder from a Canadian perspective.

Warm-up activities generate student interest and tap into students' prior knowledge.

Readings are authentic Canadian news articles. Each one is supported by vocabulary, comprehension and discussion activities.

Each unit includes learning strategies to improve reading and listening.

Students learn about the origins of words and expressions.

Authentic audio texts from CBC radio and video segments from CBC television and CTV develop students' listening skills with vocabulary and comprehension activities.

Contains suggestions to strengthen vocabulary, grammar and pronunciation.

Students choose topics to develop in free-form or essay assignments.

Provides hints to improve writing and speaking skills.

A companion website provides additional reading, listening, writing and speaking practice.

Students can choose to discuss issues in a small group, give a presentation or participate in a debate.

Interactive activities facilitate the acquisition of new vocabulary.

Each unit ends with an activity that encourages cooperative learning.

• Supplementary articles provide students with further reading practice.

• Appendix A provides students with instructions and a model persuasive essay. Appendix B outlines the essentials of a presentation and gives detailed instructions on a debate.

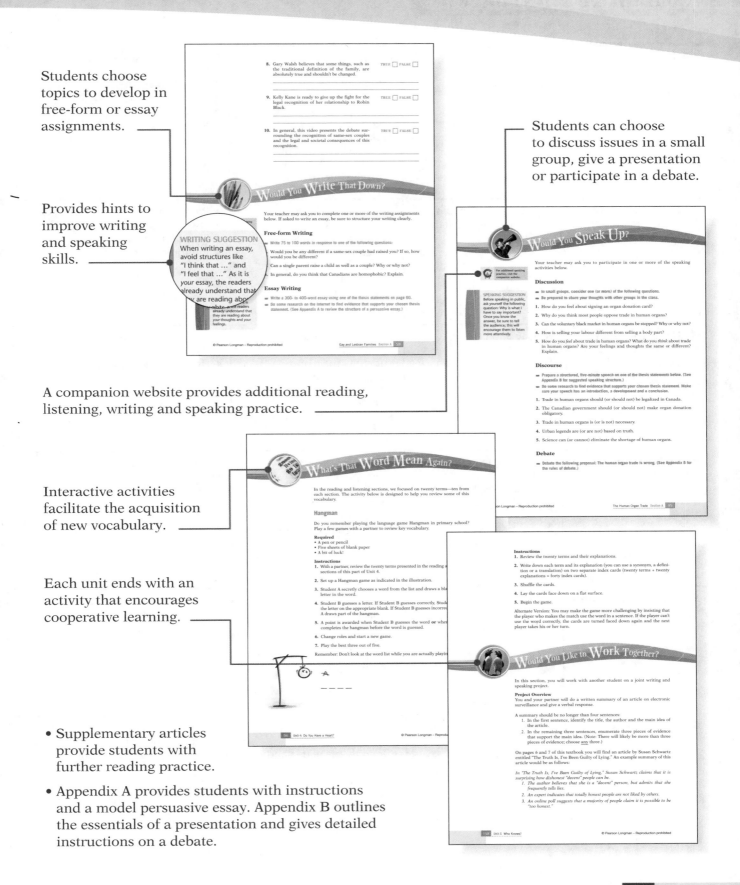

SCOPE AND SEQUENCE

Unit	Section	Reading	Listening/Watching
1. Is It Right or Wrong?	Personal ethics	• Identify main and secondary ideas • Recognize common idioms • Skim and scan for specific information • Research information on the Internet	• Identify main ideas • Listen for details • Recognize gender-neutral vocabulary
2. Is a Copy Right?	A. Music Downloading B. Human Reproductive Cloning	• Consider divergent viewpoints • Identify main and secondary ideas • Identify transition terms • Research information on the Internet	• Identify main ideas • Listen for details • Listen for transition terms • Interpret messages
3. Have You Heard about Adam and Steve and Their Daughter Eve?	A. Gay and Lesbian Families B. Commercial Surrogacy	• Consider divergent viewpoints • Identify main and secondary ideas • Use metacognitive cues • Understand anecdotes • Research information on the Internet	• Identify main ideas • Listen for details • Use verbal and nonverbal cues
4. Do You Have a Heart?	A. The Human Organ Trade B. Xenotransplantation	• Consider divergent viewpoints • Identify main and secondary ideas • Read actively • Research information on the Internet	• Identify main ideas • Listen for details • Listen actively
5. Can We Come and Go as We Please?	A. Voluntary Active Euthanasia B. Wrongful Life	• Consider divergent viewpoints • Identify main and secondary ideas • Prepare optimal reading environment • Research information on the Internet	• Identify main ideas • Listen for details • Listen for collocations • Optimize listening comprehension
6. Who Knows?	A. Electronic Surveillance B. Human Gene Patenting	• Consider divergent viewpoints • Identify main idea and understand details • Chart ideas • Research information on the Internet	• Identify main ideas • Listen for details • Draw on previously acquired knowledge

Writing	Speaking	Vocabulary	Critical Thinking
• Express opinions • Write a short paragraph • Write an individual or a group essay • Support opinions with research • Learn academic essay structure	• Participate in a group presentation • Resolve an ethical problem in a small group • Evaluate personal ethics	• Use context clues to understand new words • Complete word definitions and synonyms • Know etymology of common idioms	• Create, revise and discuss ethical scenarios
• Express opinions • Support opinions with research • Write a short paragraph • Write an essay • Apply correct referencing techniques • Use sequencers	• Express opinions • Support opinions with research • Discuss issues in small groups • Give a presentation • Participate in a debate • Use transition terms	• Use words in context • Learn idioms, phrasal verbs and collocations • Complete expressions • Use acronyms • Know etymology of common idioms	• Construct, ask and answer questions • Evaluate website credibility
• Express opinions • Support opinions with research • Write a short paragraph • Write an essay • Apply correct referencing techniques • Write concisely	• Express opinions • Support opinions with research • Discuss issues in small groups • Give a presentation • Participate in a debate • Illustrate opinions with anecdotes	• Use collocations in context • Recognize "false friends" • Know etymology of common idioms	• Prepare and conduct an opinion poll • Compile and analyze results • Write a report
• Express opinions • Support opinions with research • Write a short paragraph • Write an essay • Apply correct referencing techniques • Explain significance • Write legibly	• Express opinions • Support opinions with research • Discuss issues in small groups • Give a presentation • Participate in a debate • Use outlines	• Identify terms • Verify vocabulary usage • Know etymology of common idioms	• Write questions to summarize an article • Ask and answer questions
• Express opinions • Support opinions with research • Write a short paragraph • Write an essay • Apply correct referencing techniques • Write credibly	• Express opinions • Support opinions with research • Discuss issues in small groups • Give a presentation • Participate in a debate • Increase speaking credibility	• Use terms in context • Infer collocation meanings • Know etymology of common idioms	• Construct, complete and present a K-W-L chart
• Express opinions • Support opinions with research • Write a short paragraph • Write an essay • Apply correct referencing techniques • Write persuasively	• Express opinions • Support opinions with research • Discuss issues in small groups • Give a presentation • Participate in a debate • Strengthen argumentation	• Use synonyms • Explain expressions • Know etymology of common idioms	• Write a summary • Give a verbal defense

TABLE OF CONTENTS

UNIT 1 · Is It Right or Wrong?

Have you ever done anything wrong? Now I don't mean getting a wrong answer on a test. Have you ever cheated, stolen or plagiarized? If you say you have never done anything wrong, you have lived an exceptional life—or you have just told a lie!

For some people, lying is always wrong. For others, it is always right. For most of us, however, the truth about lying sits somewhere in the middle: lying is sometimes right (or at least necessary) and sometimes wrong. It all depends on the situation—and whether or not we can get away with the lie! The same is true for other ethical questions, such as cheating, stealing and gossiping.

In this unit, we are going to take a look at some common ethical issues that individuals face on their own. In subsequent units, we will shift our focus to more complex issues that society faces as a whole.

Did You Know?

guideline standard

Personalize the introduction for students: first, ask them whether stealing is wrong; then ask them whether they would steal food to feed a starving child; finally, ask them whether they did the "right thing" by stealing (or by not stealing).

People often resolve ethical dilemmas by

1. following written **guidelines** (religious texts, ethical codes, the law, etc.);

2. doing whatever has the "least bad" consequences.

In the first approach, the situation is considered unimportant—an action is either right or wrong. In the second approach, the situation is considered important—if the consequence is good, the action is good. To illustrate, a woman who has no money to buy food steals an apple to feed her hungry child. From the first approach, stealing the apple is wrong because it is against the law. From the second approach, stealing the apple is *not* wrong because it is "less bad" to steal than to let a child go hungry.

One approach isn't necessarily better than the other. People simply follow the approach that *they* think is right. Sometimes a person uses both approaches. What about you? Which approach do you use? Do you use both? How important is the situation for you when resolving ethical problems?

Let's take a few minutes to find out.

What's the Buzz?

Complete the following two surveys. The first survey indicates how important the situation is for you when resolving ethical problems. The second reveals what you actually do when faced with this type of problem.

Answers will vary.

Verify student understanding of the words *murder*, *steal*, *plagiarize*, *lie* and *cheat*. If students disagree with the statements, ask students to describe situations in which it is right to murder, steal, plagiarize, lie or cheat.

Survey 1

▬ **Indicate whether you agree or disagree with each of the statements below.**

Statements	Agree	Disagree
1. It is always wrong to murder.		
2. It is always wrong to steal.		
3. It is always wrong to plagiarize.		
4. It is always wrong to lie.		
5. It is always wrong to cheat.		

Interpretation

Find out what the survey indicates about you.

- Determine the number of statements with which you agreed.
- Examine the chart below.

somewhat to a certain point

If you agreed with ...	The situation is ...
All five statements	Unimportant
Three or four statements	**Somewhat** unimportant
One or two statements	Somewhat important
None of the statements	Important

- Compare your results to those of your classmates. Then do the next survey about everyday ethical problems.

Answers will vary.

If students say, it "depends," make sure they explain themselves!

Survey 2

- Indicate your response—Yes, No or Depends—to each of the questions below.
- You may wish to use a dictionary for this exercise.
- Be prepared to discuss your answers with the rest of the class.

mall shopping centre

Questions	Yes	No	Depends
1. Your father lends you his new BMW with one condition: you must be home by 1 a.m. If you're late, he'll never lend you his car again. You get home at 2 a.m., and your father is asleep. The next morning, he asks you what time you got home. Do you tell him you got home at *about* 1 a.m.?	☐	☐	☐
2. You're shopping in a busy **mall** when nature calls. The lineup for the men's room/ladies' room is quite long. Do you quietly slip into the washroom reserved for people with a handicap even though you don't have a handicap?	☐	☐	☐
3. You park too close to another car in the school parking lot. When you open your car door, you make a dent in the car next to you. The car belongs to one of your teachers. Do you quickly drive away and not leave a note on the windshield?	☐	☐	☐
4. You miss an English test because you slept in. Your teacher asks you why you're late. Do you make up an acceptable excuse so that you can take the test another day?	☐	☐	☐

© Pearson Longman – Reproduction prohibited

Is It Right or Wrong? Unit 1   3

Questions	Yes	No	Depends
5. You're failing a physics course for the second time. You need this course to get into medical school. A classmate is selling copies of the final exam. Do you purchase a copy?	☐	☐	☐
6. Your best friend suspects her boyfriend is cheating on her. Her suspicions are correct: you see her boyfriend kissing another girl. Do you pretend you didn't see anything and say nothing to your friend?	☐	☐	☐
7. You're walking down a city street. Gangs of **rowdy** teenagers are walking in front of you. One of the teens drops a twenty-dollar bill. No one is behind you. Do you pick up the bill, turn around and walk the other way?	☐	☐	☐
8. A good friend tells you some great gossip about your ex-boyfriend/ex-girlfriend. The story is embarrassing. You don't believe it, but you **can't stand your ex**. Do you share the gossip with friends of your ex?	☐	☐	☐
9. You invite your latest romantic interest over for supper. He/She compliments you on your cooking abilities. A good friend made the entire meal for you. Do you accept the compliment and take credit for the meal?	☐	☐	☐
10. You have a summer job delivering pizza. A drunken customer gives you a one-hundred-dollar bill and says, "Keep the change." The bill for the pizza only comes to twenty dollars. Do you keep the eighty-dollar tip?	☐	☐	☐

rowdy noisy and disorderly

not stand someone/ something be unable to tolerate someone/ something

Interpretation

Find out what the survey reveals about you.

- Count the number of times you answered *Yes*, the number of times you answered *No* and the number of times you answered *Depends*.
- Determine which answer you chose the most.

If you mostly answered *Yes*, your honesty is *rather* doubtful. If you mostly answered *No*, your honesty is *fairly* admirable. If you mostly answered *Depends*, your honesty is *somewhat* selective.

Have You Read?

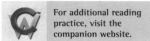
For additional reading practice, visit the companion website.

Susan Schwartz is a columnist. While she writes about many different subjects, her columns are frequently about people. In the article below, which appeared in the St. Catherines Standard on October 25, 2003, Ms. Schwartz addresses an intriguing subject: individual honesty—and dishonesty.

Before Reading

- Before reading the entire article, skim for the main ideas and scan for specific information.

How do you skim and scan? First, examine the ten words in bold and their definitions in the margin. Then look over the reading comprehension questions at the end of the article. Finally, scan the text and underline the answers to the questions. This is one way to skim and scan.

READING STRATEGY
Reading for pleasure and reading for information are two very different activities. When reading for pleasure, it is OK to read the first paragraph first, the second paragraph second and so on until the entire text has been read. When reading for information, it is better to read the entire first paragraph, the first sentence of each subsequent paragraph and then the entire last paragraph. Afterwards, you can go back and reread the entire text. When you read in this way, you are using a very effective skimming technique.

While Reading

As you read, pay particular attention to how the words in bold are used.

- Try to read the whole article once without using a dictionary. Circle any unfamiliar words and try to understand their meanings from the context.
- Reread the article and use a dictionary to look up any words that you couldn't understand.

VOCABULARY TIP
The author uses many *idioms* in her article. Idioms are expressions used by native speakers of a language. When the author writes that lies "roll off her tongue" (line 1), she means that she lies easily. It is good to use idioms in your writing, as they create images in the minds of your readers.

THE TRUTH IS, I'VE BEEN GUILTY OF LYING

BY SUSAN SCHWARTZ

MONTREAL – I am shocked by the fluidity with which lies sometimes roll off my tongue.

They're insignificant lies, mostly: I say I have read a book that I have not; or that I am not free for lunch when the truth is I just don't care to have it
5 with the person asking.

On occasion, the lies are darker and more **nefarious**, gilded with the knowledge that people could be hurt by my actions. Still, I think of myself as a decent person, so why do I lie at all? Why do any of us? A lot of reasons. We lie to make ourselves look good—have you never taken credit for
10 a cake you bought?—and to save ourselves **bother**.

At times, we're uncomfortably conscious that we're lying. Other times, we're merely polishing or embellishing the truth, which hardly seems to count as lying anymore: You know that way some stories have of evolving as you repeat them, so that your age or what you earn don't always
15 remain constant figures?

To try to make it all right, we tell ourselves our lies don't **matter**. In *Good Housekeeping* [magazine] recently, Joanne Kaufman declared that people who insist on being completely honest are quite likely to be just as completely friendless. "Who wants to be **buddies** with someone who unhesi-
20 tatingly says: 'Yes, that dress does make you look fat'?"

Robert Feldman, a professor of psychology at the University of Massachusetts, observed in the magazine's September issue that "there are lies of omission that grease the wheels of social interaction." The sugges-tion, then, is that we lie because sometimes it's perfectly acceptable to lie.

25 The line between what she calls a white lie and a regular lie is clear to her, Kaufman writes: "I'm secure in the belief that I know the difference between lying about my weight and lying on my income-tax return."

Fair enough. Only one is against the law. But is the other really acceptable? Does the truth have gradations? Is something not either true or untrue?

30 In an online poll by *Good Housekeeping*, respondents agreed that honesty is important. Yet there was an interesting elasticity to their views. Fully 75 per-cent said it is possible to be too honest—even though 70 percent said they'd told a lie they later regretted and 94 percent said they'd been hurt by a lie.

Asked whether they think people are less honest than a decade ago,
35 76 percent said yes.

Certainly we hear more about people lying—from Jayson Blair, the former *New York Times* reporter who made stories up out of whole cloth, to Martha Stewart, who may or may not have done anything **dreadful** in how she dumped her Imclone shares, to too many business executives
40 wearing handcuffs.

---

nefarious immoral (formal)

bother trouble

matter be important

buddy friend

dreadful very bad

The danger, it seems to me, is that as lying becomes a currency in transactions of daily life, people have come to see it as acceptable—even necessary.

Based on a survey of 12,000 high-school students, the Josephson Institute for Ethics found the number of young people who said they'd lied to their
45 parents and teachers at least once was 93 percent in 2002—up from 83 percent a decade before. That's only 7 percent who don't lie.

And 37 percent said they would stretch the truth to get a good job, up from 28 percent two years before, *The New York Times* reported recently.

thief bandit

"The scary thing," Michael Josephson, president of the Los Angeles-
50 based institution, told writer Abby Ellin, "is that so many kids are entering the work force to become corporate executives, politicians, airplane mechanics and nuclear inspectors with the dispositions and skills of cheaters and **thieves**."

scoff laugh derisively

There is a passage Jews recite several times during prayer services on
55 Yom Kippur [holy day] in which we list the myriad ways we have done wrong—lied and corrupted, **scoffed** and provoked, gone astray and led others astray.

stunned surprised

Each time I read that passage, I'm **stunned** by the scope and the manner in which we can do wrong, by how easy it can be.

deed action
unwitting unintentional

60 Then we ask to be granted atonement—for having lied or breached trust, hardened our heart or spoken foolishly. We ask forgiveness for wrongs of word and of **deed**, those which were deliberate and those which were **unwitting**.

We ask a merciful God to wipe the slate clean, for the opportunity to
65 begin again, to try to be kinder, better. More honest.

731 words

WORD CULTURE
The expression *wipe the slate clean* means "make a fresh start." The expression comes from nineteenth-century schoolrooms and taverns where slate blackboards were used to record exercises and debts, which were later erased to allow students and customers to "start over again."

Reading Comprehension

▬ **Respond to each of the questions below.**

1. In the third paragraph, the author suggests three separate reasons why people lie. List the three reasons.

   a) to protect others (from being hurt)

   b) to make ourselves look good

   c) to save ourselves bother (or trouble)

2. In line 12, the author uses the expression "to embellish the truth." What does she mean by this expression? Give an example of embellishing the truth.

   to add false details to something or to exaggerate the truth. Examples will vary.

© Pearson Longman – Reproduction prohibited

Is It Right or Wrong? Unit 1   7

3. According to *Good Housekeeping* magazine, lying is a social necessity: to get along in society, you sometimes have to lie.

TRUE ☑ FALSE ☐

4. What is a "white lie"? Provide an example to demonstrate your understanding.

a harmless lie. Examples will vary.

_____

5. According to a poll conducted by *Good Housekeeping* magazine, most respondents claimed that
  a) it is possible to be too honest.
  b) they regret a lie they have told.
  c) they have been hurt by a lie.
  d) people are less honest now than a decade ago.
  e) All of the above

6. According to a survey conducted on high-school students, only 7 percent of respondents claimed they have never lied to their parents or teachers.

TRUE ☑ FALSE ☐

7. *The New York Times* has reported that 37 percent of people would "stretch the truth" to get a good job. What is the meaning of the expression "to stretch the truth"? What other expression from the article has a similar meaning?

to exaggerate the truth. Similar expression: to embellish the truth.

_____

8. In line 61, the author uses the expression "to harden one's heart." Explain this expression in your own words.

to become unfeeling

_____

9. In line 64, the author writes that we ask God "to wipe the slate clean." What does this expression mean in the context in which it is used?

to forgive us

_____

10. The main idea of Susan Schwartz's column is that
  a) everybody is a hopeless liar.
  b) lying is a social necessity.
  c) it is surprising how dishonest "decent" people can be.
  d) society is increasingly dishonest.

Discussion

- In small groups, discuss your answers to each of the questions below. Try to arrive at a group consensus.
- Be prepared to share your group's ideas with the rest of the class.

1. In the article, the author indicates that people lie for many different reasons. In your opinion, does the reason for the lie influence how you feel about the lie? For example, is a lie told to protect someone's feelings better than a lie told to impress others? Explain.

2. Is it possible to be "too honest"? Explain.

3. Describe a situation in which it is OK to stretch or embellish the truth.

Word Work

In the article (pp. 6–7), ten terms are defined for you:

Adjectives	Nouns	Verbs
1. dreadful	5. bother	9. matter
2. nefarious	6. buddy	10. scoff
3. ~~stunned~~	7. deed	
4. unwitting	8. thief	

Each of the sentences below contains a term in italics.

- Choose a term from the list above that could replace the italicized term without changing the meaning of the sentence. The first one has been done for you as an example.
- If you replace a verb, make sure to conjugate correctly.

1. Everyone was *surprised* when she left her husband for a younger man; they seemed to have the perfect marriage.   *stunned*

2. He was involved in several *immoral* activities, including drug trafficking and money laundering.   nefarious

3. Honesty *is important* to most people.   matters

4. If you perform a good *action* every day, you will feel good about yourself.   deed

5. John is a good *friend* of mine; we've known each other for more than ten years.   buddy

6. She committed a *very bad* crime—she killed her neighbour in a fit of rage.   dreadful

7. She *laughed derisively* when he told her the price; it was far too much to pay for such an insignificant work of art.   scoffed

8. She was an *unintentional* accomplice; she had no idea he had hidden the stolen money in her home.   unwitting

9. Taking care of young children can be a lot of *trouble*.   ____bother____

10. That politician is a real *bandit*; he stole more than 100,000 dollars from taxpayers.   ____thief____

Have You Heard?

For additional listening practice, visit the companion website.

VOCABULARY TIP
The use of gender-neutral terms such as *ombudsperson* rather than *ombudsman* or *ombudswoman* promotes gender equality. Instead of using the terms *policeman*, *mailman* and *fireman*, why not use the terms *police officer*, *mail carrier* and *firefighter*?

An *ombudsperson* is someone who investigates complaints against various private and public institutions. Universities have an ombudsman or an ombudswoman to ensure that complaints are dealt with and resolved satisfactorily. Deborah Eerkes is an ombudsperson at the University of Alberta in Edmonton. Let's listen to what she has to say about academic dishonesty in a radio segment originally broadcast on CBC's *Commentary* on September 5, 2003.

Pre-Listening Vocabulary

The following is a list of ten terms used in the radio segment:

• ~~CEO~~	• to cut corners
• grade	• to fib
• plagiarizing	• to fudge
• slippery slope	• to throw the first stone
• to cook the books	• tuition

▬ **Working alone or with a partner, write each term beside its proper description in the space provided. The first term has been done for you as an example.**

Descriptions	Terms
1. Acronym for Chief Executive Officer, the president of a company	*CEO*
2. Expression based on the biblical quote, "Let he who is without sin cast the first stone." (John 8:7)	to throw the first stone
3. If a builder does this when building your house, you won't have a very good house!	to cut corners
4. If you're on this, you're likely to "slip" into a dangerous situation.	slippery slope
5. Synonym of "to falsify"	to fudge
6. What a dishonest accountant does	to cook the books
7. What a teacher gives a student after marking a test	grade

© Pearson Longman – Reproduction prohibited

Descriptions	Terms
8. What students pay	tuition
9. What you will be accused of if you present somebody else's work as your own	plagiarizing
10. Synonym of "to tell a white lie"	to fib

While Listening

LISTENING STRATEGY
When listening for information, skim and scan as you do when reading for information. The first time, listen for the main idea. The second time, listen for the details.

You will hear the segment twice. Before listening the first time, read through the comprehension questions.

■ Take notes as you listen and then respond to the comprehension questions.

Listening Comprehension

■ Referring to your notes, respond to each of the questions below.

1. Fill in the blank. "One in _____three_____ university students admits to plagiarizing."

2. Deborah Eerkes claims that society has come to accept a bit of cheating when done for the "right" reasons.　　TRUE ☑ FALSE ☐

3. Eerkes lists many reasons why students cheat. Which of the following reasons does she list?
   a) Society puts a lot of pressure on students to get good grades.
   b) Universities emphasize achievement over learning.
   c) Students are under more pressure today than they were in the past.
   d) Society doesn't discourage cheating and plagiarism enough.
   e) Students don't think cheating is a big deal.
   f) All of the above.

4. Why does Eerkes think that student cheating is a big deal?
   Because students of today are the CEOs, doctors, lawyers and engineers of tomorrow. If students cheat now, they will cheat later on in life, with more serious consequences (implied).

The answer to question 5 is "false" because Ms. Eerkes asserts that "… it is up to all of us (all of society) to set this right."

5. Only students can solve the problem of student cheating.　　TRUE ☐ FALSE ☑

6. What can parents do to help stop student cheating?
   teach children the value of integrity

7. What does Deborah Eerkes mean when she says that "… grades are only a by-product of learning …"?
   The focus should be on learning, not grades.

8. Fill in the blanks. Educators "... need to teach them (students) proper _____research_____ and _____citation_____ techniques and help them understand why it's important ..."

9. Deborah Eerkes believes that educational institutions must set, model and apply high standards of integrity.

TRUE ☑ FALSE ☐

Question 10 tests the student's ability to identify the main idea of the segment.

10. The main idea of the commentary is that
   a) nothing can be done to reduce academic dishonesty.
   b) students must face the consequences of academic dishonesty.
   c) society must work together to end a culture of academic dishonesty.
   d) None of the above.

Would You Write That Down?

You have read and heard a lot about what others think about dishonesty; now it is *honestly* time for you to write about what *you* think.

The proposed writing assignments in this textbook are of two types: free-form and essay. In free-form writing, you aren't required to follow any particular structure. In essay writing, you *are* required to follow a specific structure. An essay should have an introduction with a well-defined thesis statement, a development and a conclusion.

There are many kinds of essays; descriptive, narrative and persuasive are three examples. Given the subject matter of this text, your teacher will likely ask you to write a persuasive essay. If so, you can find a detailed explanation and example of how to write a persuasive essay in Appendix A (p. 182).

Free-form Writing

 Write 75 to 100 words in response to one of the following questions:

1. Is it true that "cheaters never prosper"? Briefly explain your point of view.

2. Society is comprised of many age groups: children, teenagers, young adults, middle-aged adults and senior citizens. Is any one age group more dishonest than another? If so, which one is more dishonest? Why?

3. American statesman and inventor Benjamin Franklin once said, "Honesty is the best policy." Do you agree with this statement? Is honesty *always* the best policy? Explain.

For additional writing practice, visit the companion website.

GRAMMAR TIP
Many adverbs of manner are formed by adding "ly" to the corresponding adjective: *honest* ➡ *honestly*. For more information on adverbs of manner, consult Unit 11 of the companion volume *Parallels: Taking a Stand in English—English Grammar.*

Answers will vary. In free-form writing, no specific structure is required; however, the student is asked to write 75 to 100 words.

You may wish to increase or decrease the number of words required. The free-form writing assignments are great for "sampling" student writing ability.

WORD CULTURE
The expression *the ends justify the means* means "all actions are acceptable if they lead to successful results." The expression dates back to antiquity: the Greek playwright Sophocles wrote in *Electra*, "The end excuses any evil …" and the Roman poet Ovid wrote in *Heroides*, "The result justifies the deed."

Essay Writing

- Write a 300- to 400-word essay using one of the thesis statements below.
- Do some research on the Internet to find evidence to support your chosen thesis statement. (See Appendix A to examine the structure of a persuasive essay.)

1. It is (or is not) always wrong to lie.

2. It is (or is not) necessary to be dishonest in today's society.

3. Students are (or are not) more dishonest today than in the past.

4. A student caught plagiarizing should (or should not) be expelled from school.

5. The ends justify (or do not justify) the means.

Your teacher may ask you to work in small groups of two or three so that you can help one another learn the essay structure. If your teacher asks you to write a persuasive essay in a group, divide up the work as follows:

- All members write the introduction and the conclusion together.
- Each member writes one of the three remaining paragraphs individually. (If there are only two members, both members work on the remaining paragraph together.)
- All members revise the completed essay together.

WRITING SUGGESTION
When researching on the Internet, type key words into search engines such as http://www.google.ca, http://ca.yahoo.com or http://www.ask.com

Would You Speak Up?

 For additional speaking practice, visit the companion website.

As this is your first unit, it is likely that you don't know the other students very well. Because this textbook constantly challenges you to "take a stand in English," it is important for you to feel comfortable with your classmates. To help you feel more comfortable, two group speaking activities are suggested. Your teacher may ask you to participate in one or both of these activities. Either way, you are certain to practise your spoken English *and* get to know other students at the same time. To use an English proverb, you will "kill two birds with one stone"! In later units, the suggested speaking activities will be more varied: individual, small group and large group.

WORD CULTURE
The expression *to kill two birds with one stone* means "to achieve two goals with a single effort." The expression dates from the 1600s.

Activity 1: Lie Detector

This activity tests your ability to tell a lie and get away with it.

Have you ever heard the expression, "Truth is stranger than fiction"? It means that sometimes the strangest things in life are true!

■ Take a couple of minutes and think about a strange (but true) story that actually happened to you, for example, meeting a famous person, breaking your leg, seeing someone shoplifting, winning a special award, etc.

■ Select one story that you think might interest your fellow classmates and write down a few details—what happened, where it happened, who was there, when it happened, etc.

Your teacher will

1. number the class members off, creating small groups of three (or four) members;

2. ask group members to meet together and select *one* of the members' true stories;

3. ask each group to go to the front of the class and present the story as if the story actually happened to him or her;

4. ask the class to question the group members to discover who is telling the truth and who is lying;

5. give you feedback on your grammar—and your lying abilities!

Activity 2: Shoot or Die!

In this unit's What's the Buzz? section, you indicated whether or not it is always wrong to murder (see Survey 1, page 2). To use yet another English expression, it is now time to find out whether you "practise what you preach." Do you actually do what you say you do? Let's find out!

■ Read through the scenario below.

You are the owner of a bed and breakfast (b&b) in the country. There are eight people (including yourself) in the establishment. One evening, one of your guests overpowers the rest, tying up everyone but yourself. He hands you a gun and informs you that if you murder one of the six hostages, you and the remaining five hostages will be spared. If you don't do as he asks, he informs you that he will murder everyone—including you. The hostages include

1. an English teacher;

2. a ninety-year-old woman;

3. a convicted wife-beater who has served his time and been released from prison;

4. a young man with a terminal disease;

5. a fashion model;

6. a world-famous scientist.

The "ideal" option is arguably to hand the gun back to the sadistic guest, especially for those students who believe it's "always wrong to murder." Why? Because the sadistic guest is unlikely to keep his promise to spare "your" life and the lives of the other guests, as you would all be witnesses to his sadistic game. What's better? To die a murderer or to die an "innocent" person? (Also, it is doubtful as to whether the gun is actually loaded!)

■ **What do you do? Your choices do not include committing suicide or shooting the maniac!**

Your teacher will

1. number the class members off, creating small groups of five (or six) members;

2. ask group members to meet together and decide what to do in the scenario above;

3. ask each group to present its decision (and explanation for the decision) to the rest of the class;

4. ask the rest of the class to react to the group's decision;

5. give you feedback on your spoken grammar—and your murderous tendencies!

What's That Word Mean Again?

The Global Language Monitor estimates that as of February 1, 2009, there were 998,773 words in the English language. Our objective in this textbook is not to focus on all of them—but to focus at most on 220 of them (or ten words from each of the eleven reading and listening sections). Two hundred and twenty words doesn't seem like that much, does it?

In the reading and listening sections of this unit, we studied nouns, verbs, adjectives, acronyms and expressions. Do you still remember all of these terms? If you don't, you are probably not alone. Most people need to use a word at least three times to remember it; as the saying goes, "Use it thrice, and it's yours for life!" This section gives you another opportunity to use the terms that you have studied, helping you remember the new vocabulary. Activities here are always presented in the form of a game. Remember: Just because you are having fun doesn't mean you aren't learning anything!

Word Tic-Tac-Toe

Answers will vary. This game-like activity is a supplementary activity appropriate to some, but not all, academic contexts.

Everybody knows the game "tic-tac-toe" or "Xs and Os." Two players compete against each other, alternating turns, trying to get three Xs or three Os in a row inside a nine-cell grid. The first player to get three in a row wins the point. This very simple game can be used to help review vocabulary. Do you want to give it a try?

Required
- One sheet of blank paper
- One pen or pencil
- One dictionary

© Pearson Longman – Reproduction prohibited

Is It Right or Wrong? Unit 1   15

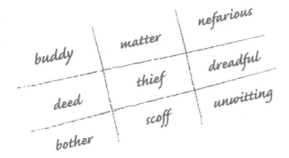

Instructions

1. Draw two tic-tac-toe grids.

2. In the first grid, write one vocabulary term from the reading section of this unit in each of the nine cells. (Note: You will have one word left over.)

3. In the second grid, write one vocabulary term from the listening section of this unit in each of the nine cells. (Note: You will have one word left over.)

4. Begin playing tic-tac-toe using the first grid—X goes first. In order for a player to put an X or an O in the cell, he or she must first explain the word. If the player's opponent challenges the explanation, a dictionary may be consulted to settle the challenge. The first player to get three Xs or Os in a row wins.

5. Continue playing tic-tac-toe using the second grid. Proceed as in the first game. (Note: The player who took the Xs in the first game now takes the Os and vice versa.)

Would You Like to Work Together?

In this section, you will work with another student on a joint two-part project: Part A is a writing project and Part B is a speaking project.

Answers will vary. This paired project encourages cooperative learning.

Project Overview
In this unit, you responded to ten ethical questions (see Survey 2, pages 3–4). For this project, you and your partner are going to create your own questions and challenge two of your classmates to respond to the questions you created.

Writing Ethical Questions
A good ethical question is one based on reality. Think of ten ethical dilemmas you and your partner have faced in the past. Common ethical dilemmas involve lying, cheating, stealing, gossiping, taking undeserved credit, etc.

Required
- A hat (or small container)
- Index cards
- A pen or pencil
- Sheets of paper
- Slips of paper

Procedure

Part A

1. Working individually, write three ethical scenarios on a sheet of paper using the simple present tense and/or the present continuous tense. Refer to Unit 2 of the companion volume *Parallels: Taking a Stand in English— English Grammar* to review these tenses. Use the second person singular (*you*) when writing your scenarios, and end each scenario with a yes/no question. The scenarios in Survey 2 (pp. 3–4) serve as models. Write 40 to 50 words for each scenario.

2. Working together, exchange your scenarios and revise one another's work. Verify spelling, grammar and word choice. Use reference materials: a dictionary, a thesaurus and/or a grammar book.

3. Rewrite your six scenarios on a single sheet of paper and submit them to your teacher for correction. (Don't forget to write both your names at the top of the sheet!)

4. Copy each of your six teacher-corrected ethical scenarios on a separate slip of paper. Fold your slips of paper.

Part B

1. Pair off with another group of two and sit around a desk facing one another.

2. Take out ten index cards. On five of the cards write the words *tell the truth*, and on five of the cards, write the words *tell a lie*.

3. Shuffle the index cards and place them face-down in the middle of the desk.

4. Place all twelve folded slips of paper (six from each group—see Part A above) into a hat (or small container), and place the hat (or small container) in the middle of the desk beside the index cards.

5. The person whose first name starts with a letter closest to the letter A begins. He or she selects a slip of paper and reads it aloud.

6. Each of the other three group members selects an index card and must respond to the ethical question asked as indicated on the card (i.e., either by *telling the truth* or by *telling a lie*). Note: The ethical question must be responded to with either a "yes," a "no" or a "depends"—and all answers must be fully explained.

7. The person who read the card declares whom he or she thinks is telling the truth and/or whom he or she thinks is telling a lie. The group members then turn over their index cards and show their true colours!

8. The index cards are returned to the deck, the deck is reshuffled and the cards are returned face-down to the middle of the desk.

9. The turn now passes to the person seated to the right of the person who read the ethical scenario aloud. He or she selects a slip of paper and reads it aloud.

10. Repeat steps 6, 7, 8 and 9 until all slips of paper have been selected, read and discussed.

WORD CULTURE
The expression *show one's true colours* means "to reveal oneself honestly." The expression has nautical origins and refers to the practice of deceiving the enemy by sailing an unfriendly boat under a friendly flag.

UNIT 2 | Is a Copy Right?

The title of this unit is a play on the word copyright—*the legal right to be the only producer or seller of a work. The title raises the question as to whether making a copy of something is morally right.*

Writer Charles Caleb Colton said that "imitation is the sincerest form of flattery," and since he first made this statement, many others have made it too. In fact, so many people have repeated Mr. Colton's maxim that it has become a common expression in the English language. While imitation may indeed be flattering, in certain contexts it may also be wrong. Two such contexts are music downloading and human cloning; the morality of both will be discussed in this unit.

GRAMMAR TIP
Sincerest is the superlative form of the adjective *sincere*. The comparative form is *sincerer*. Use comparative adjectives to compare two people or things; use superlative adjectives to compare three or more people or things. For more on comparative and superlative adjectives, see Unit 11 of the companion volume *Parallels: Taking a Stand in English—English Grammar*.

SECTION A
Music Downloading

Examines the morality of sharing music online.

SECTION B
Human Reproductive Cloning

Examines the morality of replicating humans.

Music Downloading

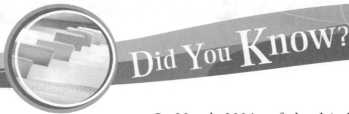
Did You Know?

swapping exchanging or sharing

In March 2004, a federal judge in Canada found that neither downloading music for personal use nor **swapping** music via the Internet violates Canadian copyright law.

Following the lead taken by the Recording Industry Association of America, the Canadian Recording Industry Association (CRIA) attempted to sue a number of people who had used online services to swap music. In order to sue, the CRIA needed to know the real names of the users—not just their online nicknames. Unfortunately for the association, the judge ruled that Internet Service Providers (ISPs) couldn't be forced to reveal the music swappers' identities since the CRIA was unable to prove that copyright had been violated. An appeal launched by the CRIA in 2005 was dismissed.

lawsuits legal battles

However, Canadian music swappers shouldn't be too quick to celebrate their victory over the record companies. International **lawsuits** are a real possibility, and well-known Canadian musicians and music industry representatives have been lobbying Canadian politicians to update copyright laws in an attempt to stop music downloading, also known as file-swapping and peer-to-peer networking. The lobbying seems to have been successful: the federal government may amend Canada's Copyright Act so that it would force ISPs to reveal the names and records of those who swap large numbers of files.

Consequently, the legality of music downloading remains as uncertain as its morality, and we are likely to hear much more about this highly controversial topic in the years to come.

Let's take a look at some of the arguments surrounding this debate.

Music downloading is right because it	Music downloading is wrong because it
1. promotes artists and their work.	1. is a form of stealing.
2. makes music more easily available to the fans, cutting out the "middleman."	2. causes record companies and artists to lose money.
3. reduces the record companies' control over the artists and their fans.	3. results in job losses within the music industry.

While young people are far more likely to download music than older people, it is typically older people who make the laws. This is a curious state of affairs, don't you think?

What's the Buzz?

Are you hip? Do you know what's "in" in music and music **paraphernalia**? Let's take a moment to find out.

paraphernalia
equipment

Cosmic 2 is a type of skateboard.

■ **Alone or in pairs, choose the best answer for each question below. (After class, give this quiz to a few people over the age of forty and see how they do.)**

1. If someone gave me an MP3, I would
   a) see a doctor.
   b) wear it.
   c) listen to it.

2. The abbreviation "MP3" stands for
   a) Multilink Point-to-Point-to-Point.
   b) MPEG-1 Audio Layer-3.
   c) Miniature Portable Productive Player.

3. Which of the following is *not* a portable audio player?
   a) Cosmic 2
   b) Apple iPod
   c) SonicBlue Rio

To expand student vocabulary and introduce today's youth to an American icon, why not play Nat King Cole's "Route 66" and have students complete a fill-in-the-blanks exercise? Complete song lyrics can easily be found on the Internet.

4. On which of the following sites can you download music?
   a) Napster   **c)** Puretracks
   b) Kazaa   **d)** All of the above

5. A "mash-up" is
   a) a meal made of potatoes.
   b) the combination of elements from two separate recordings.
   c) a new dance.

Discussion

Answers will vary. Encourage students to arrive at a consensus in their groups. After the groups present their viewpoints, encourage the class to arrive at a consensus.

- **Get into small groups.**
- **Consider the questions below as a group and arrive at a consensus.**
- **Present your findings to the rest of the class.**

Note: As one group is presenting, be prepared for your teacher to intervene and ask you if you agree or disagree with what has been said.

1. Modern music is generational. While you might enjoy listening to rapper Choclair, your grandparents might not! And while they might like Tony Bennett, you might not feel the same way. Why do you think music is generational?

2. A Canadian judge has compared downloading music to using a photocopy machine in a public library. Is this a fair comparison?

3. Do you download music? If so, do you feel guilty about downloading? Why or why not?

Have You **Read?**

For additional reading practice, visit the companion website.

Lindsay Jones is a journalist whose article "Hey Music Industry: Sharing Is Good" appeared in the *Halifax Daily News* on April 11, 2004. From the title of her article alone, you can deduce Ms. Jones's opinion on music downloading. Do you think she agrees or disagrees with music downloading?

Before Reading

READING STRATEGY
When skimming for main ideas, pay careful attention to the title of an article. More often than not, the title reveals the author's opinion on the subject of the article.

Remember to skim and scan before reading; first, read the defined terms and comprehension questions, and then read the article.

While Reading

Transition words demonstrate relationships between ideas. Examples of transition words include *so*, *and*, *then*, *next*, *but*, etc.

As you read, circle the transition words used by the author. Being aware of transition words will help you better follow the author's train of thought.

HEY MUSIC INDUSTRY: SHARING IS GOOD

BY LINDSAY JONES

I was always taught that sharing is good. So I'm not surprised that the Federal Court of Canada ruled in favour of music downloaders. I think it's great that we can freely share songs on the Internet for our own personal use without the looming **threat** of being sued as **scapegoats** for a **greedy**
5 record company.

And really, when you think about it, music has been copied and replayed since the player piano.

Then there was home-taping. I can fondly remember **taping** the Top 40 countdown off the radio and dubbing Whitney Houston off my sister in
10 the '80s.

Next, there were CD burners and online sharing sites. Unfortunately, record companies think this is piracy.

But the Federal Court of Canada has decided that downloading for personal use doesn't amount to copyright infringement. Mr. Justice Konrad
15 von Finckenstein wrote that he cannot see the difference between a library that places a photocopy machine in a room full of copyrighted material and a computer user that places a personal copy on a shared directory.

This all came about because the Canadian Recording Industry Association
20 (CRIA) **sought** a court order to identify music uploaders so CRIA could in turn **file** lawsuits against them. The Recording Industry Association of America has sued 1,977 people for sharing music files.

Now, it's understandable that the record companies would feel threatened by downloaders; trading music over the Internet is way easier and
25 way faster than music rolls and tape decks. But maybe record companies have to reinvent themselves because technology and communications is only going to get better, more innovative and higher **speed**.

My friend Sara Jane just got an MP3 player for her birthday and says she doesn't buy CDs anymore; she downloads music off the Internet.

30 It's too expensive to buy CDs, she says. The last concert I went to cost me $65—see, there's all kinds of ways for them to make money. I don't see the

threat menace
scapegoat victim
greedy wanting more (money or possessions)

tape record

seek (sought) pursue
file submit

speed rapidity

difference (in downloading versus taping) other than I don't have to sit by the radio with my tape recorder to tape my song.

She says the only way she'd start buying CDs again is if they were
35 cheaper.

I'd pay about $5, she says.

Mark Mullane plays in the band North of America, and is a music, graphics and field producer for Street Cents. He says as long as people get to hear his music, downloading can't hurt.

40 I'm sure a lot of people that download it, buy it too, he says. If the band is worth the money, they'll pay for the CD. It's just there's so much music out there and it's so expensive to afford it all.

Ten bucks is a reasonable price for a CD, he adds.

Mullane and his friends have been buying records, taping them and shar-
45 ing them for years. And he downloads music, too, but says if he's going to listen to it for the next two years, he buys it.

trendy fashionable

But sharing music files only affects **trendy** pop music, because the people who listen to it are not true music fans, he adds.

For years they were the ones getting suckered into buying the whole thing
50 when they just wanted that one song. Does anybody really have any pity for Britney Spears and her handlers? Please, people would rather see her **fail** anyway, like Martha Stewart, says Mullane.

fail not have success

The big question is: Are music companies even losing money as a result of sharing music files?

55 Universal Music cut one of its two staff representing Atlantic Canada last year, and Warner Music axed a part-timer in Newfoundland and Labrador last week, wrote Sandy MacDonald in *HFX*.

layoff dismissal of employees

But are these **layoffs** as a result of file-sharing? A new study by econo-mists at Harvard University and University of North Carolina shows there
60 is no connection between decreased sales and downloads. It's well known that anyone who wants to promote themselves, their art or their business does so online now. In fact, many artists have their music on their web-sites. Britney Spears has her new CD, *Toxic*, completely downloaded on her website, as do Beck, Ludacris and the Liars.

65 Record companies may be important for the distribution and promotion of an artist and their album, but if one person can now do four people's jobs because of the Internet, I don't think that calls for crime bosses to start suing music downloaders.

So, thanks Federal Court of Canada for allowing us to share and share
70 alike.

744 words

Reading Comprehension

— **Indicate whether each of the following statements is true or false. If the statement is false, explain why it is false.**

1. In the first paragraph, the author indicates that the record industry's opposition to music downloading is motivated by money.

   TRUE ✓   FALSE ☐

2. Music copying began with the emergence of the Internet.

   TRUE ☐   FALSE ✓

   Music copying has been around since the player piano.

3. The author argues that taping and downloading music are "one and the same" (identical actions).

   TRUE ✓   FALSE ☐

4. Sara Jane and Mark Mullane justify downloading by claiming that CDs are too expensive; they suggest that an acceptable price would be about five dollars.

   TRUE ☐   FALSE ✓

   Sara Jane believes $5 to be a reasonable price; however, Mark Mullane's suggestion is $10.

5. Mark Mullane never buys CDs—he only downloads.

   TRUE ☐   FALSE ✓

   Mark Mullane buys CDs, and he downloads music.

6. According to Mullane, music downloading only affects pop music.

   TRUE ✓   FALSE ☐

7. According to Mullane, downloading allows a music fan to buy the song that he/she is interested in instead of having to buy the entire CD.

   TRUE ✓   FALSE ☐

8. The article states that no studies have ever demonstrated a connection between decreased CD sales and music downloading.

   TRUE ☐   FALSE ✓

   The article mentions that one study conducted jointly by Harvard University and the University of North

   Carolina found no connection between decreased sales and downloads.

9. The author suggests that downloading music is a more efficient way of promoting artists and their work than the methods used by record companies.

TRUE ✓ FALSE ☐

_____

_____

Question 10 tests the student's ability to identify the main idea of the text.

10. In general, the author claims that downloading music is right.

TRUE ✓ FALSE ☐

_____

_____

Discussion

Answers will vary.

■ In small groups, discuss your answers to each of the questions below.

■ Be prepared to share your group's ideas with the rest of the class.

1. Is CD burning a form of stealing? Why or why not?

2. Record players were replaced by audiocassette players; audiocassette players were replaced by CD players. Do you think CD players will be replaced by MP3 players? Explain.

3. How long do you typically listen to a new CD—a week, a month, a year? Is the enjoyment you get from a CD worth the price you have to pay?

Word Work

In the article, ten terms are defined for you:

Adjectives	Nouns	Verbs
1. greedy	3. layoff	7. fail
2. trendy	4. scapegoat	8. file
	5. speed	9. seek
	6. threat	10. ~~tape~~

■ Reread the definitions provided for these words. Then reread the sentences in which the words are used to ensure that you understand how each word is used in context.

■ Fill in the blanks using the words above. Remember to conjugate the verbs as required. The first one has been done for you as an example.

1. Be sure not to change the channel on the TV—I _____*am taping*_____ my favourite show because I don't have time to watch it right now.

2. Computer technology is advancing with frightening _____speed_____; three years after you buy a new computer, it is considered "old" technology.

3. Have you _____filed_____ your income tax report? It's due tomorrow!

4. Recording artists are _____greedy_____; they earn millions of dollars a year—and it's still not enough money!

5. Do you think that music file-swapping is a _____threat_____ to the record industry?

6. Poor sales resulted in a _____layoff_____ at a local factory; more than 500 people lost their jobs.

7. Never fear to _____fail_____—we can always learn from our mistakes.

8. She's so concerned about her image that she only wears _____trendy_____ clothes and won't be seen with anyone who's not popular.

9. Timothy Leary (a controversial American psychologist) once said, "Women who _____seek_____ to be equal with men lack ambition."

10. When I was young, I was always the family _____scapegoat_____; whenever any of my brothers broke something, they would say that I did it!

Have You Heard?

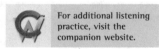

For additional listening practice, visit the companion website.

> *The Current* and *Cross Country Checkup* are two popular CBC radio programs. Shortly after the March 2004 court decision that found it legal to share music online for personal use, these programs interviewed Canadians about their opinions on music downloading. You will hear four famous Canadian singers' reactions followed by an "average" Canadian's reaction. The first segment from *The Current* aired on April 6, 2004. The second segment from *Cross Country Checkup* aired on April 4, 2004.

In the second part of this exercise, students are asked to use a dictionary to determine the meanings of the expressions. Suggested meanings are listed in the Additional Notes in the Teacher Section of the companion website.

Pre-Listening Vocabulary

Sometimes you have to understand the meaning of a *group of words* together—and not just each individual word within a group—to understand a message. Idiomatic expressions, phrasal verbs (two- or three-word verbs) and collocations (words that are frequently used together) are examples of such groups of words; they are generically known as expressions.

- Working with a partner, formulate ten expressions in the exercise on the next page by correctly joining together the first and second parts of each expression. The first one has been done for you as an example.

- After verifying your answers with your teacher, write the ten expressions on a separate sheet of paper and use a dictionary to determine their meanings.

First parts		Second parts
1. Be a real	_i_	a) a doubt
2. Be a double-edged	_c_	b) of something
3. Feel the brunt	_b_	c) sword
4. Figure	_f_	d) board
5. Flog the	_h_	e) a living
6. Get left	_g_	f) something out
7. Get on	_d_	g) behind
8. Have one's head	_j_	h) wrong horse
9. Make	_e_	i) ~~drag~~
10. Without	_a_	j) in the sand

While Listening

You will listen to each segment twice.

- The first time you listen, try to understand whether each speaker is for or against music downloading.

- The second time you listen, try to identify the reasons each speaker gives to support his/her opinion, taking brief point-form notes to help you remember the information.

Listening Comprehension

- Referring to your notes, respond to the questions for both segments below.

Segment 1: *The Current*

1. You will hear singers Sarah McLachlan, Tyler Stewart (*The Barenaked Ladies*), Jim Cuddy (*Blue Rodeo*) and rapper Choclair voice their opinions on music downloading. As you listen, indicate with a check mark whether each speaker is for or against music downloading.

Name	For Music Downloading	Against Music Downloading
Sarah McLachlan	✓	
Tyler Stewart		✓
Jim Cuddy		✓
Choclair		✓

2. What does Sarah McLachlan think about the music industry charging people for downloading?

She thinks it's ridiculous and that the industry has realized too late that things need to change. She claims

that the industry "has had its head in the sand."

3. What does Tyler Stewart hope will happen with the judge's decision?

He hopes the decision will change; he hopes the decision can be appealed.

VOCABULARY TIP
Do not confuse the adjective *affected*, meaning "influenced" or "touched," with the past-tense verb conjugation *effected*, meaning "caused" or "resulted in." The singer was directly *affected* by the court decision. The judge's ruling *effected* a change in the law.

4. How has Jim Cuddy been personally affected by music downloading?

He says that many people in the industry have lost their jobs due to music downloading.

5. What has happened to Choclair at HMV?

Fans have asked him to sign "burnt" CDs.

Segment 2: *Cross Country Checkup*

6. Is the caller for or against music downloading?

He is for music downloading.

7. What does the caller, who works in a second-hand CD store, think about the price of new CDs?

He thinks that new CDs are too expensive, and he agrees with the host that the prices of new CDs are

inflated and exaggerated.

8. According to the caller, how many corporations control about 85 percent of the music produced worldwide?

only four corporations

9. Is the caller worried about the impact of music downloading on second-hand CD sales? Why? Why not?

No, he's not worried. Many of his regular clients download music, but they continue to buy used CDs to

get "the whole package" at a fair price.

10. What does the caller say about money spent on "manufacturing" celebrities?

He says the industry should stop manufacturing (young) celebrities "from one song"; instead, the

companies should put money into "real" artists. (He thinks the music industry is misspending money by

manufacturing celebrities.)

Would You Write That Down?

 For additional writing practice, visit the companion website.

There are two types of writing assignments below. While free-form writing has no specific structure, essay writing does. If your teacher asks you to write an essay, be sure to follow the format requested.

Free-form Writing

- **Write 75 to 100 words in response to one of the following questions:**

1. Define the words *sharing* and *stealing*. Explain whether music file-swapping is sharing or stealing.

2. If music downloading is stealing, is it less wrong to steal from an industry than it is to steal from an individual? Why or why not?

3. In your opinion, is the CD an outdated technology? Justify your response.

Answers will vary. In free-form writing, no specific structure is required; however, the student is asked to write 75 to 100 words. You may wish to increase or decrease the number of words required. The free-form writing assignments are great for "sampling" student writing ability.

Essay Writing

- **Write a 300- to 400-word essay using one of the thesis statements below.**
- **Do some research on the Internet to find evidence that supports your chosen thesis statement. (See Appendix A to review the structure of a persuasive essay.)**

1. Music downloading should (or should not) be criminalized.

2. Music file-swapping can (or cannot) be stopped.

3. Music downloading is (or is not) good for the music industry.

4. Music fans should (or should not) boycott recording artists opposed to music downloading and file-swapping.

5. Imitation is (or is not) the sincerest form of flattery.

Answers will vary. The recommended essay format for *Parallels: Taking a Stand in English* is the persuasive essay (see "Appendix A: The Persuasive Essay" on page 182), but you may opt for another essay structure. The student is asked to write 300 to 400 words. You may also wish to increase or decrease the number of words required.

Refer to page 18 of this textbook for the etymology of the expression "imitation is the sincerest form of flattery."

WRITING SUGGESTION
A sequencer is a special type of transition word. Examples include *first*, *second*, *third*, etc. When writing an essay, consider using sequencers to help the reader follow the sequence of your ideas.

Would You Speak Up?

For additional speaking practice, visit the companion website.

Answers will vary. As indicated in the Speaking Suggestion, encourage students to use transition terms (*so, then, next*) when speaking; transition terms help listeners "follow along." It might be interesting to have students research celebrity incomes and net worth prior to discussing question 2.

Answers will vary. Discourse structure is outlined in "Appendix B: Discourse and Debate" (p. 192). Given the polemic nature of *Parallels: Taking a Stand in English*, a persuasive discourse structure is recommended. The suggested speaking time is five minutes; you may wish to increase or decrease the required speaking time.

Answers will vary. Debate structure is outlined in "Appendix B: Discourse and Debate" (pp. 194–198). Arguments "for" and "against" the proposal are listed on page 20. For more information on running small group or whole class debates, refer to the Additional Notes in the Teacher Section of the companion website.

Your teacher may ask you to participate in one or more of the following speaking activities.

Discussion

- In small groups, consider one (or more) of the following questions.
- Be prepared to share your thoughts with other groups in the class.

1. On the topic of music downloading, hip-hop artist Jay-Z said, "The record industry is in trouble, but the music industry is not" (as cited by Chuck D in *Disclosure*). What do you think the artist meant by this statement?

2. Some recording artists make more money in one year than most of their fans make in an entire lifetime. Is this disparity fair?

3. What is a fair price for a CD?

4. Have you ever bought a CD for just one song? If so, do you think you overpaid?

5. If you were a recording artist, how would you feel about music downloading?

Discourse

- Prepare a structured, five-minute speech on one of the thesis statements below. (See Appendix B for a suggested speech structure.)
- Do some research on the Internet to find evidence that supports your chosen thesis statement. Make sure your speech has an introduction, a development and a conclusion.

1. File-sharing sites such as Napster should (or should not) be shut down.

2. The music industry exploits (or does not exploit) teenage music fans.

3. Music fans should (or should not) boycott CD sales to force companies to lower CD prices.

4. Internet Service Providers (ISPs) should (or should not) be required to reveal the names of music downloaders.

5. Music should (or should not) be treated like a business.

Debate

- Debate the following proposal: Music downloading is wrong. (See Appendix B for the rules of debate.)

What's That Word Mean Again?

In the reading and listening sections, we focused on twenty terms—ten from each section. When learning vocabulary, you have to "use it or lose it." Let's use some of that vocabulary now.

Draw Me a Picture!

It is said that "one picture is worth a thousand words." How many words do you think one of your pictures is worth? Let's find out in a game of "Draw me a picture!"

Required
- Ten slips of paper, each one about the size of an index card
- One hat (or other small container)
- Ten sheets of blank paper
- One pen or pencil
- A little bit of artistic ability

Instructions
1. In teams of four, review the twenty terms studied in the reading and listening sections of this unit.

2. Select ten of these terms and write each one down on a slip of paper.

3. Fold the slips of paper, mix them up and place them in a hat (or other small container).

4. Divide into two teams of two, Team A and Team B.

5. One member (Student A) from Team A takes a slip of paper and draws a picture of the selected term on a sheet of blank paper. His/Her teammate can make one guess as to which term has been drawn. If the teammate guesses correctly, the team gets a point and Student A takes another slip of paper. If the teammate doesn't guess correctly, the team gets no point and the turn passes to Team B.

6. The first team to reach five points wins.

Have one's head in the sand

Would You Like to Work Together?

In this section, you will work with another student on a joint two-part project: Part A is a writing project, and Part B is a speaking project.

For a trivia game activity focusing on the simple past tense in the active and the passive voices, see pages 93–94 of the companion volume *Parallels: Taking a Stand in English—English Grammar.*

Project Overview

In the warm-up section of this unit (pp. 20–21), you responded to five multiple-choice trivia questions about music and music paraphernalia. Trivia questions are factual questions about general topics such as sports, literature, history, etc. In this project, you and your partner will challenge another pair of students to a game of music trivia.

Writing Trivia Questions

A good trivia question must be factually accurate. To write factually accurate questions (and persuasive essays!), you must first do some research using *credible* sources. To judge website credibility, ask yourself the following ten questions suggested by the School of Journalism and Library Science:

1. Who is responsible for the web content?

2. Is the person responsible qualified?

3. What are his or her academic credentials?

4. Are the creation and editing dates indicated?

5. Is the content up-to-date?

6. What is the focus of the site?

7. Is the site well-organized?

8. Is the content of the website biased?

9. Are sources listed?

10. Are sources varied and verifiable?

Required

- A computer
- Internet access

Procedure

Part A

1. Working individually, "surf the Net," looking for credible music websites. Browse through these sites, looking for factual information that could be used to write good trivia questions. For example, you could go to the Rock and Roll Hall of Fame Museum website and learn that Elvis Presley was born on January 8, 1935 and that he died on August 16, 1977. A good multiple-choice trivia question would be the following:

   How old was Elvis Presley when he died?
   a) 39 years old
   b) 42 years old
   c) 48 years old

   The correct answer is (b).

   Be sure to record your references using the format suggested in the chart on page 185. For the example cited above, the reference is as follows:

   Rock and Roll Hall of Fame Museum. "Elvis Presley." Retrieved: 6 September 2008. http://www.rockhall.com/inductee/elvis-presley

You may wish to have students refer to "Appendix A: Common Information Question Words" (p. 130) in the companion volume *Parallels: Taking a Stand in English—English Grammar*.

2. Working with your partner, write five multiple-choice trivia questions based on your individual research. (Don't forget to indicate the correct answer for each question!) Use a word processor. Run a spell-check and submit a printout of your questions to your teacher for correction. Save a copy of your work.

3. Correct your saved copy and print out your work.

Part B

1. Pair off with another group of two and sit facing one another.

2. Team 1 reads its first question aloud to Team 2. (Either team may start.) The members of Team 2 may not read the question: they may only hear the question. Should the members of Team 2 have difficulty understanding, they may ask for clarification using one or more of the following expressions:

   Could you repeat that?
   How do you spell …?
   I'm sorry; I didn't understand. What does … mean?

   If Team 2 answers correctly, the members are awarded a point. If not, no point is awarded.

3. Team 2 reads its first question aloud to Team 1. The members of Team 1 may not read the question: they may only hear the question. Should the members of Team 1 have difficulty understanding, they may ask for clarification using one or more of the expressions listed in step two. If Team 1 answers correctly, the members are awarded a point. If not, no points are awarded.

4. Repeat Steps 2 and 3 until all ten multiple-choice trivia questions have been asked and answered.

tie equal score

5. The winner is the team that scores the most points. In the case of a **tie**, each team creates an additional "tie-breaking" question. In the case of a disputed answer, return to the original source and re-evaluate website credibility!

Human Reproductive Cloning

Did You Know?

GRAMMAR TIP
The noun *ovum* is of Latin origin. The plural of *ovum* is *ova*. Words of Latin or Greek origin form their plurals according to the rules of those languages. For more information on plural noun forms, see Unit 9 of the companion volume *Parallels: Taking a Stand in English—English Grammar*.

A *clone* is an asexually reproduced genetic duplicate of its parent.

Clones have long existed in nature—organisms as simple as a geranium or as complex as identical twins have been cloned.

In the laboratory, clones are artificially produced through a process known as nuclear transfer. In simple terms, nuclear transfer occurs when an ovum is emptied of its deoxyribonucleic acid (DNA), which is then replaced with DNA from another cell. Cell division is either chemically or electrically induced, imitating the cell division that occurs naturally when an egg is fertilized by a sperm cell.

When applied to humans, nuclear transfer technology might best be categorized as:

1. Therapeutic

2. Reproductive

More Canadians support therapeutic human cloning than reproductive human cloning.

harvest collect

In therapeutic human cloning, a cloned human embryo is allowed to develop 250 to 300 cells before cell division is stopped. These undifferentiated cells are known as stem cells; they can be **harvested** and used to treat a variety of human diseases like lupus, multiple sclerosis, Parkinson's, Alzheimer's, diabetes, heart disease and Acquired Immune Deficiency Syndrome (AIDS). Many scientists even claim that stem cells could one day be used to create cloned organs such as hearts, livers and kidneys.

In reproductive human cloning, the human embryo is allowed to develop into a fetus and then into a human being. However, reproductive human cloning remains a hypothetical concept, and in Canada, it has been illegal since the government's adoption of *The Human Reproduction Act*.

Dr. Barnard's patient was grocer Louis Washkansky. Mr. Washkansky died from double pneumonia eighteen days after the transplant.

While many people have ethical concerns about human cloning, it is important to remember that many people also had ethical concerns when Dr. Christiaan Barnard performed the world's first human heart transplant on December 3, 1967. Are people concerned about human cloning simply because it is a new technology? Or do they have fundamental problems with artificially replicating a human being?

Let's take a look at both sides of the issue.

Human reproductive cloning is right because it would	Human reproductive cloning is wrong because it would
1. advance the science of human genetics.	1. reduce genetic diversity.
2. help infertile people reproduce.	2. be unsafe.
3. make it possible for society to replicate "important" individuals.	3. increase social inequity and discrimination.

It is a difficult yet fascinating topic to argue. Why is it difficult? It is difficult because arguments on both sides of the debate are hypothetical: no human clone has ever been created. Do you think one ever will? It is an interesting question, isn't it?

What's the Buzz?

Scientists normally experiment on animals before experimenting on humans, and the results of animal experiments are then applied (or misapplied) to humans. A great number of successful and unsuccessful animal cloning experiments have been conducted. How much do you know about animal cloning?

> **VOCABULARY TIP**
> Synonyms of the expression *conduct experiments* include *do experiments, run experiments* and *carry out experiments*: Scientists *conduct* (or *do*, or *run* or *carry out*) *experiments* on lab animals every day.

1. Dolly, the first mammal to be cloned, was a
   a) sheep.
   b) pig.
   c) cow.

2. Which of the following statements is true?
   a) It took 27 attempts to clone Dolly.
   b) It took 277 attempts to clone Dolly.
   c) It took 2,777 attempts to clone Dolly.

Dolly was euthanized because she was suffering from a lung disease associated with premature aging.

3. Dolly died at the age of
   a) two.
   b) four.
   c) six.

4. In which city were the world's first cloned goats produced?
   a) Toronto
   b) Boston
   c) Montreal

5. Which of the following animals had been successfully cloned by 2005?
   a) A monkey
   b) A cat
   c) A pig
   d) A horse
   e) All of the above

Discussion

Answers will vary. Encourage the students to arrive at a consensus in their groups. After the groups present their viewpoints, encourage the class to arrive at a consensus.

■ **In small groups, consider the questions below and arrive at a consensus.**
■ **Present your findings to the rest of the class.**

Note: As one group is presenting, be prepared for your teacher to intervene and ask you whether you agree or disagree with what has been said.

1. People are always afraid of emerging technologies. Arguing that scientists shouldn't proceed with a technology because "they don't know enough" is an unacceptable argument. Do you agree or disagree with this statement?

2. A human clone would be like a reproduction of a great work of art: the clone would look the same but would be worth much less than the original. Is this analogy fair?

3. Human cloning is illegal in Canada, but is it immoral as well?

For additional reading practice, visit the companion website.

READING STRATEGY
When skimming for main ideas, pay careful attention to the title of an article. More often than not, the title reveals the author's opinion on the subject of the article.

Before Reading

Remember to skim and scan before reading; first, read the defined terms and comprehension questions, and then read the article.

While Reading

Transition words demonstrate relationships between ideas. Examples of transition words include *so, and, then, next, but,* etc.

- **As you read, circle any transition words used by the author. Being aware of transition words will help you better follow the author's train of thought.**

In the vocabulary tip, students are asked to go to line 38 of the reading that follows and identify the acronym. The acronym is DNA, which stands for Deoxyribonucleic Acid.

VOCABULARY TIP
An acronym is a word formed from initials; for instance, HIV is an acronym for Human Immunodeficiency Virus. The first time an uncommon acronym is used, the complete term is written first, followed by its acronym in parentheses; after that, the acronym is used on its own. In line 38, Dr. Suzuki refers to a common acronym. What is it?

WORD CULTURE
The informal expression *be old hat* means "be overfamiliar" or "be outdated," depending on the context in which the expression is used. The expression comes from the fact that hats go out of style quickly.

bring to term give birth to

unlikely improbable

be old hat be outdated

CLONING BECOMES FREAKSHOW

BY DAVID SUZUKI

Well, give the Raelians this much—they know how to put on a show. The group, which claims to have cloned human beings and **brought** them **to term** as healthy babies, has managed to turn a genuine scientific and ethical issue into a sideshow circus.

5 While it is possible the Raelian cult has the technological equipment and ability to clone a human, it is extremely **unlikely** and, if they have succeeded, it is morally repugnant.

In some ways, cloning animals **is** already **old hat**. Scientists have been doing it for years with sheep, mice, cows, pigs, cats and other mammals.

10 Cloning humans would not be that different. We all start the same way— from a single fertilized egg. Using a process called nuclear transfer, scientists

prodding encouragement

WORD CULTURE
The expression *be a red herring* comes from the training of hunting dogs: smoked herrings could be used to train dogs to follow a scent, or smoked herrings could also be used to put dogs off a scent. It is from the latter that the expression derives its meaning. (See definition below.)

be a red herring be a misleading distraction

dismal very poor or inadequate

miscarry abort spontaneously

researcher scientist

offspring descendants

inherit receive from an ancestor

can remove the nucleus taken from the cell of an adult and insert it into an egg that has had its nucleus removed. With a little **prodding**, cell division starts and the egg, it is hoped, develops normally into an
15 embryo, which is then transplanted into the uterus of a surrogate mother. This "reproductive" cloning procedure produces a genetically identical but much younger version of the original person.

Another type of cloning already takes place in human beings—identical twins. Indeed, the Dionne quintuplets were clones of a fertilized egg that
20 divided three times before the cells fell apart and grew into separate individuals. They are genetically identical, yet do they feel somehow less human because of it? Are they ostracized for not being genetically unique? Do they fight over who the "original" person is? I think not.

Unfortunately, these are the sorts of concerns most often brought up
25 when reproductive cloning is discussed in the media. Though valid questions, such concerns **are** ultimately **red herrings** at this point. There are much more disturbing issues associated with the technological procedure of reproductive human cloning that need to be addressed before such an endeavour should ever be attempted.

30 First, cloning mammals has a **dismal** success rate. More than 97 percent of all such attempts fail. Many fail at the start. Others develop into embryos that are implanted into a female surrogate mother, only to be quickly **miscarried**. Some die shortly after birth. Some suffer from serious abnormalities. Because of these technical problems alone, we
35 cannot seriously consider trying to clone a human at this time.

Even if a healthy birth was assured, we would still have other problems to face. Dolly the sheep, the first cloned mammal, was born with shortened "telomeres"—little bits of DNA that cap our chromosomes. Our telomeres shorten as we age, and Dolly's were far shorter than her young age sug-
40 gested—more in line, in fact, with the age of her donor. That could help explain why Dolly has developed arthritis at an early age.

Last fall, **researchers** also discovered that seemingly healthy cloned mice suffer from abnormalities. Analysis of genes in the livers and placentas of one group showed that up to 4 percent of them were malfunctioning.
45 Other research has found that some cloned mice die far younger than those reproduced sexually, while others become obese.

Scientists have also had difficulties cloning successive generations of mammals. Clones of clones become less and less likely to be able to produce a successive generation of clones. What would that mean for cloned
50 humans? Would their **offspring**, cloned or sexually reproduced, **inherit** defects that would accumulate through successive generations?

When there are so many questions arising from the work already performed with other mammals, it is outrageous that any group would ignore the known risks and proceed with such experiments.

55 There are all sorts of ethical issues raised by the prospect of reproductive human cloning. But to have a truly informed debate, we need to focus on what is most relevant to the current reality. Right now, too much of the discussion is focused on the presumed psychological effects of being a cloned human and not enough on the health risks.

688 words

Reading Comprehension

— Indicate whether each of the following statements is true or false. If the statement is false, explain why it is false.

1. In the first paragraph, David Suzuki is highly critical of the Raelians. TRUE ☑ FALSE ☐

_____

2. The author admits it is possible that the Raelians have successfully cloned a human being. TRUE ☑ FALSE ☐

_____

3. Cloning animals is cutting edge (modern and advanced) technology. TRUE ☐ FALSE ☑
The author refers to cloning as being "old hat."

_____

4. Human and animal cloning are quite different. TRUE ☐ FALSE ☑
The author claims that cloning humans would not be that different.

_____

5. Suzuki is a proponent of the argument that human clones would feel like unimportant "copies." TRUE ☐ FALSE ☑
He refers to the Dionne quintuplets and doubts that any one of the five ever felt "less human" for being a "clone."

_____

6. The problems associated with human cloning procedures are serious and merit society's consideration. TRUE ☑ FALSE ☐

_____

7. Most mammal cloning procedures succeed. TRUE ☐ FALSE ☑
The author claims that cloning mammals has a dismal success rate.

8. Dolly is physiologically older than her chronological age. TRUE ☑ FALSE ☐

_____

9. Cloning the clone is as easy as cloning the original. TRUE ☐ FALSE ☑
The author states that scientists have had difficulty cloning successive generations of mammals.

Question 10 tests the student's ability to identify the main idea of the text.

10. In general, the author claims that the debate surrounding human cloning should focus on the associated health risks and not the presumed psychological effects. TRUE ☑ FALSE ☐

_____

_____

Discussion

- In small groups, discuss your answers to each of the questions below.
- Be prepared to share your group's ideas with the rest of the class.

1. Would you clone your pet? Why or why not?

2. Would you clone your child? Why or why not?

3. Is there a difference between cloning animals and cloning humans? Explain.

Word Work

In the article, ten terms or expressions are defined for you:

Adjectives	Expressions	Nouns	Verbs
1. dismal	3. be a red herring	6. offspring	9. inherit
2. unlikely	4. be old hat	7. prodding	10. miscarry
	5. ~~bring to term~~	8. researcher	

- Go back and reread the definitions for these words in the margin of the reading. Then reread the sentences in which the terms occur to ensure that you understand how the word is used in context.
- Fill in the blanks using the terms above. Remember to conjugate the verbs as required. The first one has been done for you as an example.

1. She will _____ *bring* _____ her baby _____ *to term* _____ in May.

2. Do you have any _____ offspring _____? Yes, I have two sons and one daughter.

3. Do you know how much Bill Gates's children will _____ inherit _____ when he passes on?

4. I enjoy playing Scrabble, but I'm a _____ dismal _____ player. Last night, my opponent beat me by almost 200 points!

5. I'm on a diet, but it's _____ unlikely _____ I will keep off the weight—I love chocolate, and I hate to exercise!

6. My sister was afraid she would _____ miscarry _____, so she was relieved when she gave birth to a healthy seven-pound baby boy.

7. My son needs a little _____ prodding _____ to do his homework, but after he finally gets started, he always finishes it.

8. The authors of detective stories often give the reader a clue that later turns out to _____ be a red herring _____.

9. Do you think that a _____ researcher _____ will one day create a human clone?

10. It's time for a change in leadership. The current prime minister has been in office for years and his policies _____ are _____ rather _____ old hat _____, don't you think?

For additional listening practice, visit the companion website.

at odds with in disagreement with

On January 30, 2003, *The National* aired "Cloning Wish," Eve Savory's report on Jonathan Colvin's desire to be cloned. Jonathan has Cystic Fibrosis (CF) and wants a second chance at life. CF is a hereditary disease causing respiratory infections. This video clip takes a personal look at a societal issue—a man that wants to clone himself **at odds with** a government that says he can't.

Pre-Watching Vocabulary

Sometimes you have to understand the meaning of a *group of words* together—and not just each individual word within a group—to understand a message. Idiomatic expressions, phrasal verbs (two- or three-word verbs) and collocations (words that are frequently used together) are examples of such groups of words; they are generically known as expressions.

In the second part of this exercise, students are asked to use a dictionary to determine the meanings of the expressions. Suggested meanings are listed in the Additional Notes in the Teacher Section of the companion website.

- Working with a partner, formulate ten expressions in the exercise below by correctly joining together the first and second parts of each expression. The first one has been done for you as an example.
- After verifying your answers with your teacher, write the ten expressions on a separate sheet of paper and use a dictionary to determine their meanings.

First parts		Second parts
1. As a	_e_	a) overreaction
2. Deal	g	b) at bay
3. Gross	a	c) a way
4. In	c	d) infection
5. Keep something	b	e) ~~rule~~
6. Pull	j	f) inquiry
7. Under	h	g) with something
8. Deadly	d	h) any circumstances
9. Scientific	f	i) condition
10. Inherited	i	j) off something

VOCABULARY TIP
When looking up expressions in a dictionary, look up one or two of the key words in the expression. You will typically find the expression defined and an example of usage given near the end of the entry. You will need a good dictionary for this type of exercise.

While Watching

You will watch the video clip twice.

- **The first time you watch, try to understand the speakers' various positions on reproductive human cloning.**
- **The second time you watch, listen for the details of what each speaker has to say, taking brief point-form notes to help you remember the information.**

Watching Comprehension

- **Referring to your notes, respond to the questions below.**

1. **Does Jonathan Colvin see his clone as a mere copy of himself?**
   No, he says he doesn't like to look upon the potential clone as a "copy."

2. **Why does Jonathan want to clone himself?**
   to give himself a second chance at life (to give himself a second chance to continue)

3. **According to Jonathan, his clone wouldn't necessarily have CF. How would this be possible?**
   CF has one small gene that no longer functions; it's possible to fix CF in a test tube, producing a cell without the genetic mutation. The clone would be made from the "fixed" cell.

4. **Does Jonathan picture his clone as looking exactly like him?**
   He sees his clone as himself as a 3- to 4-year-old (healthier, taller, chubbier) child.

5. **Geneticist Judith Hall states that cloned animals suffer from various abnormalities. Name two of the abnormalities that she mentions.**
   Potential abnormalities include growth (undergrowth and overgrowth), survival and behaviour.

6. **Jonathan rejects the idea of criminalizing reproductive human cloning. What does he propose instead?**
   He favours a moratorium on reproductive human cloning until cloning is proven safe.

7. **Does Dr. Hall believe that therapeutic and reproductive human cloning are fundamentally unethical? Briefly explain her point of view.**
   No, she does not believe reproductive human cloning to be unethical on principle. As a scientist, she sees value in scientific inquiry. As a doctor, she knows cloning human embryonic cells may one day save lives.

8. **What are the potential benefits of cloning human embryonic cells?**
   Cloning human embryonic cells may save lives by creating replacement organs for people in need.

9. What does the term *pro-choice* mean as applied to reproductive human cloning?

In this context, pro-choice means that if you want to be able to clone yourself, you should be able to do so, and if you don't want to clone yourself, you don't.

10. Does reporter Eve Savory take a personal position, one way or the other, on the issue of reproductive human cloning?

No, she makes an attempt to present both sides of the issue. She never takes a personal stance.

Would You Write That Down?

For additional writing practice, visit the companion website.

WRITING SUGGESTION
A sequencer is a special type of transition word. Examples include *first*, *second*, *third*, etc. When writing an essay, consider using sequencers to help the reader follow the sequence of your ideas.

There are two types of writing assignments below. While free-form writing has no specific structure, essay writing does. If your teacher asks you to write an essay, be sure to follow the format requested.

Free-form Writing

■ **Write 75 to 100 words in response to one of the following questions:**

1. If given the opportunity, would you have yourself cloned? Why or why not?

2. Do you think that society will one day clone a human being? Explain.

3. In your opinion, would clones experience psychological difficulties because they are "copies"? Justify your response.

Essay Writing

■ **Write a 300- to 400-word essay using one of the thesis statements below.**

■ **Do some research on the Internet to find evidence that supports your chosen thesis statement. (See Appendix A to review the structure of a persuasive essay.)**

1. Animal cloning is relatively safe (or is extremely unsafe).

2. Experimenting on human embryos is (or is not) ethical.

3. Society should (or should not) limit scientific inquiry.

4. Scientists should (or should not) be allowed "to play God."

5. Human therapeutic cloning should (or should not) be banned.

Would You Speak Up?

SPEAKING SUGGESTION
Use transition words (*so*, *then*, *next*) when you are speaking to help the listener follow along.

Answers will vary. As indicated in the Speaking Suggestion, encourage students to use transition terms (*so*, *then*, *next*) when speaking; transition terms help listeners "follow along."

Answers will vary. Discourse structure is outlined in "Appendix B: Discourse and Debate" (p. 192). Given the polemic nature of *Parallels: Taking a Stand in English*, a persuasive discourse structure is recommended. The suggested speaking time is five minutes; you may wish to increase or decrease the required speaking time.

Answers will vary. Debate structure is outlined in "Appendix B: Discourse and Debate" (pp. 194–198). Arguments "for" and "against" the proposal are listed on page 35. For more information on running small group or whole class debates, refer to the Additional Notes in the Teacher Section of the companion website.

Your teacher may ask you to participate in one or more of the following speaking activities.

Discussion

■ In small groups, consider one (or more) of the following questions.

■ Be prepared to share your thoughts with other groups in the class.

1. If it were possible, which historical figure would you most like to see cloned? Explain your choice.

2. Would a clone be *you, your twin brother or sister,* or *your child*?

3. Is human cloning one way to live forever? Justify your response.

4. Does a copy have less value than an original? Explain.

5. In his article "Cloning Becomes Freakshow," David Suzuki suggests that a lack of safety is the main reason why Canadians should oppose reproductive human cloning. Given what you have learned so far, what do you think? Is safety the central issue of this debate?

Discourse

■ Prepare a structured, five-minute speech on one of the thesis statements below. (See Appendix B for a suggested speaking structure.)

■ Do some research to find evidence that supports your chosen thesis statement. Make sure your speech has an introduction, a development and a conclusion.

1. Animal cloning experiments exploit (or do not exploit) animals.

2. People should (or should not) have the right to clone themselves.

3. The results of animal cloning experiments can (or cannot) be applied to humans.

4. Society should (or should not) be worried about human cloning.

5. Human cloning research is necessary (or unnecessary).

Debate

■ Debate the following proposal: Human reproductive cloning is wrong. (See Appendix B for the rules of debate.)

What's That Word Mean Again?

In the reading and listening sections, we focused on twenty terms—ten from each section. When learning vocabulary, you have to "use it or lose it." Let's use some of that vocabulary now.

Draw Me a Picture!

It is said that "one picture is worth a thousand words." How many words do you think one of *your* pictures is worth? Let's find out in a game of "Draw me a picture!"

Required
- Ten slips of paper, each one about the size of an index card
- A hat (or other small container)
- Ten sheets of blank paper
- A pen or pencil
- A little bit of artistic ability

Instructions
1. In teams of four, review the twenty terms studied in the reading and listening sections of this unit.

2. Select ten of these terms and write each one down on a slip of paper.

3. Fold the slips of paper, mix them up and place them in a hat (or other small container).

4. Divide into two teams of two, Team A and Team B.

5. One member (Student A) from Team A takes a slip of paper and draws a picture of the selected term on a sheet of blank paper. His/Her teammate can make one guess as to which term has been drawn. If the teammate guesses correctly, the team gets a point and Student A takes another slip of paper. If the teammate doesn't guess correctly, the team gets no point and the turn passes to Team B.

6. The first team to reach five points wins.

be old hat

Would You Like to Work Together?

In this section, you will work with another student on a joint two-part project: Part A is a writing project, and Part B is a speaking project.

For a trivia game activity focusing on the simple past tense in the active and the passive voices, see pages 93–94 of the companion volume *Parallels: Taking a Stand in English—English Grammar*.

Project Overview

In the warm-up section of this unit (pp. 35–36), you responded to five multiple-choice trivia questions about animal cloning. Trivia questions are factual questions about general topics such as sports, literature, history, etc. In this project, you and your partner will challenge another pair of students to a game of science trivia, focusing specifically on animal cloning.

Writing Trivia Questions

A good trivia question must be factually accurate. To write factually accurate questions (and persuasive essays!), you must first do some research using *credible* sources. To judge website credibility, ask yourself the following ten questions suggested by the School of Journalism and Library Science:

1. Who is responsible for the web content?

2. Is the person responsible qualified?

3. What are his or her academic credentials?

4. Are the creation and editing dates indicated?

5. Is the content up-to-date?

6. What is the focus of the site?

7. Is the site well-organized?

8. Is the content of the website biased?

9. Are sources listed?

10. Are sources varied and verifiable?

Required
• Computer
• Internet access

Procedure

Part A

1. Working individually, "surf the Net," looking for credible scientific websites on animal cloning. Browse through these sites, looking for factual information that could be used to write good trivia questions. For example, you could go to the David Suzuki Foundation website and learn that *clone* comes from the Greek word meaning "cutting." (Plants can be reproduced from cuttings.) A good multiple-choice trivia question would be the following:

   Clone *comes from the Greek word meaning:*
   a) "cutting"
   b) "copying"
   c) "reproduction"

   The correct answer is (a).

   Be sure to record your references using the format suggested in the chart on page 185. For the example cited above, the reference is as follows:

David Suzuki Foundation. "Cloning technology comes of age." Retrieved: 6 September 2008. http://www.davidsuzuki.org/About_us/Dr_David_Suzuki/Article_Archives/weekly09270001.asp

You may wish to have students refer to "Appendix A: Common Information Question Words" (p. 130) in the companion volume *Parallels: Taking a Stand in English—English Grammar*.

2. Working with your partner, write five multiple-choice trivia questions based on your individual research. (Don't forget to indicate the correct answer for each question!) Use a word processor. Run a spell-check and submit a printout of your questions to your teacher for correction. Save a copy of your work.

3. Correct your saved copy and print out your work.

Part B

1. Pair off with another group of two and sit facing one another.

2. Team 1 reads its first question aloud to Team 2. (Either team may start.) The members of Team 2 may not read the question: they may only hear the question. Should the members of Team 2 have difficulty understanding, they may ask for clarification using one or more of the following expressions:

Could you repeat that?
How do you spell …?
I'm sorry; I didn't understand. What does … mean?

If Team 2 answers correctly, the members are awarded a point. If not, no point is awarded.

3. Team 2 reads its first question aloud to Team 1. The members of Team 1 may not read the question: they may only hear the question. Should the members of Team 1 have difficulty understanding, they may ask for clarification using one or more of the expressions listed in step two. If Team 1 answers correctly, the members are awarded a point. If not, no points are awarded.

4. Repeat Steps 2 and 3 until all ten multiple-choice trivia questions have been asked and answered.

tie equal score

5. The winner is the team that scores the most points. In the case of a **tie**, each team creates an additional "tie-breaking" question. In the case of a disputed answer, return to the original source and re-evaluate website credibility!

UNIT 3

Have You Heard about Adam and Steve and Their Daughter Eve?

Everyone has heard the story of Adam and Eve, the mythical parents of the first human family. The whimsical title of this unit draws attention to the fact that the definition of the traditional human family is being challenged as a result of recent judicial and technological changes. Nowadays same-sex couples can marry and adopt children, and infertile couples can hire surrogate mothers to have children for them. Times, as they say, are changing.

Cultural anthropologist Mary Catherine Bateson wrote: "The family is changing, not disappearing. We have to broaden our understanding of it, look for the new metaphors." Do the new metaphors include same-sex adoption? Surrogate children? What do you think? Let's find out.

SECTION A

Gay and Lesbian Families

Examines the controversial issue of same-sex adoption.

SECTION B

Commercial Surrogacy

Examines the morality of paying a woman to have a child.

Gay and Lesbian Families

Did You Know?

There is an old poem about love, marriage and children that goes, "First comes love; then comes marriage; then comes baby in the baby carriage."

Up until recently, this description of the traditional family applied only to opposite-sex couples. This is no longer the case.

common-law living as a couple, but not married

- In May 1995, Ontario became the first province to legalize adoptions by same-sex couples.
- On April 11, 2000, the Canadian parliament redefined the term ***common-law*** to include same-sex partners.
- By December 2004, same-sex marriage was available to residents of British Columbia, Manitoba, Nova Scotia, Ontario, Quebec, Saskatchewan and the Yukon.
- On June 28, 2005, Canada's House of Commons approved same-sex marriage.

The federal government's legal recognition of same-sex couples simultaneously redefined the traditional Canadian family and reinforced the rights of Gays and Lesbians, allowing them to adopt children.

While the Canadian Supreme Court, guided by the *Canadian Charter of Rights and Freedoms*, supports equal rights for same- and opposite-sex couples, the

Canadian population remains divided on the issue. This division only deepens once the issue of same-sex adoption is considered.

Let's examine the arguments surrounding the issue of same-sex adoption.

Same-sex adoption is right because it	Same-sex adoption is wrong because it
1. affirms equal rights for same- and opposite-sex couples.	1. deprives children of either male or female role models.
2. provides caring and compassionate parents for children in need of a family.	2. results in children being harassed.
3. increases the number of parents available to adopt difficult-to-place children.	3. places children in an "undesirable" environment.

Very few issues have polarized the Canadian population as much as the issue of same-sex adoption. Everyone seems to have a strong opinion one way or the other. When public opinion is polarized, emotions run high. While working through this unit, you are encouraged to reflect upon Voltaire's famous words: "I disapprove of what you say, but I will defend to the death your right to say it."

What's the Buzz?

Below is a series of quotes.

- Work with a partner or in groups of three or four.
- For each quote, indicate with an "X" whether the speaker would likely be for or against same-sex adoption.

VOCABULARY TIP
For this exercise, it is not essential to understand every word; simply try to capture the gist of each speaker's comments.

For	Quotes	Against
☐	1. Family Research Council Director Peter S. Sprigg: "In truth, what makes a family is one man and one woman united in marriage for a lifetime, and bearing children from that union."	☒
☒	2. American Academy of Pediatrics (AAP) report: "… children are better adjusted when their parents report greater relationship satisfaction, higher levels of love and lower inter-parental conflict regardless of their parents' sexual orientation." (As cited in *Sexuality Information and Education Council of the United States*.)	☐

This exercise could be followed up with a discussion on source credibility. See the "Would You Like to Work Together?" sections in Unit 2 (p. 31 and p. 45) for a cooperative exercise on evaluating source credibility. You may also wish to ask students to return to the original sources, which you will find in the Teacher Section of the companion website under "References," and read these quotations in context.

For	Quotes	Against
X	3. Behavioural pediatrician Dr. Ellen Perrin: "There are more similarities than differences in parenting styles and attitudes among gay and non-gay parents." (As cited in *Sexuality Information and Education Council of the United States.*)	☐
☐	4. Joseph Card. Ratzinger and Angelo Amato as approved by John Paul II: "Allowing children to be adopted by persons living in such (same-sex) unions would actually mean doing violence to these children, in the sense that their condition of dependency would be used to place them in an environment that is not conducive to their full human development."	X
☐	5. Family Research Council Policy Analyst Yvette C. Schneider: "Using 'biology' as a stamp of legitimacy, activists have pushed for special rights, from sex-partner subsidies to 'gay marriage' to adoption. Without scientific evidence to support such claims, it is wrong and dangerously misleading to say that people are born homosexual and cannot change."	X
X	6. Entertainer and adoptive (lesbian) parent Rosie O'Donnell: "America has watched me parent my children on TV for six years. They know what kind of parent I am." (As cited in Dulong, 2002.)	☐

Discussion

Answers will vary. Students might need a dictionary for this exercise.

■ **Working with a partner or in a small group, discuss and respond to the questions below. Be prepared to share your responses with the class.**

1. In general terms, a family is a group of people. Clarify this definition by being more specific; in your own words, what is a family?

_____

_____

_____

2. Write down five adjectives that you associate with the word *family*. (You might wish to use a dictionary for this exercise.)

a) _____ d) _____

b) _____ e) _____

c) _____

3. In your opinion, do same-sex couples with (or without) adopted children fit your definition (question 1) and description (question 2) of a family? Explain.

_____

_____

_____

For additional reading practice, visit the companion website.

Lisa Fitterman is a well-known columnist whose article "A New Family Man" appeared in the *Montreal Gazette* on December 22, 2003. Given the context of this unit, who do you think the "new family man" is?

Before Reading

▬ Remember to skim and scan; read the defined words and comprehension questions before you read the article.

While Reading

Lisa Fitterman's article is highly entertaining because she uses an anecdote (or a short story) to capture your interest. Anecdotes activate your imagination—you imagine the story as it is told to you. Enjoy the story, but don't lose sight of the author's main point. Remember to ask yourself why the author is telling you the story.

A NEW FAMILY MAN

BY LISA FITTERMAN

toddler young child learning to walk

wreak havoc cause destruction

surrogate woman who gives birth for another

fathom comprehend

pass on share

About two years ago, during a business trip to New York City, a friend met a gay couple and their adorable **toddler**, who was **wreaking havoc** underfoot.

"The usual way, darling," they replied. "Adoption!"

5 The story came back to me during a conversation I had with Kevin Durkee, a new father who happens to be gay and also happened to be single when a **surrogate** gave birth last spring to his daughter.

Being a gay/single/new father was a triple whammy, one that I, who have chosen not to have kids because (a) I didn't want to have them alone, and 10 (b) I'm much too selfish, could barely **fathom**.

"Why?" I asked him.

"Because I really didn't have any other thought, to be honest," he said from his home in Toronto. "I wanted to **pass on** traditions. I had a great growing up and great parents, so it was a normal thing that I'd be a dad. 15 Sure, when I came to the realization that I wanted a husband rather than a wife, the process was a bit more of journey."

Durkee, 34, who spent the first six years of his life in Cowansville, was recently the first gay daddy to be featured on the Life Network's *Birth Stories*, a long-running series that follows mostly mommies-to-be to
20 **labour** and beyond. In a way, it's testament both to how our definition of the word "family" is fast-changing, and to how the very notion of gays and gay life has entered **mainstream** culture in ways that society could never have imagined even twenty years ago.

The "usual way" is usual no longer.

25 Consider *Vanity Fair* magazine's December cover story on gays and lesbians as the latest "It" people. Or *It's All Relative*, the ABC sitcom that features two gay dads and pits them against the homophobic parents of their daughter's fiancé. Or Rosie O'Donnell's in-your-face motherhood and the so-called "gayby boom." Or the fact that gays and lesbians can now legally
30 marry in Ontario and B.C., with possibly more changes to come.[1]

Of course, cultural and societal changes haven't eradicated homophobia, not by a long shot. Last month, MP Larry Spencer, the former Canadian Alliance's [political party] family issues critic, **yearned** publicly for the days when homosexuality was illegal, and only a few weeks ago, a seven-
35 year-old boy in Louisiana was punished at his school for using the word "gay" when describing his mother to a classmate.

Durkee, a former executive with the Walt Disney Co., admits that sometimes, when he walks into a store pushing Taylor's stroller, people coo and ask, "Where's Mommy today?" He says it's always a judgment call
40 whether or not to reply that she has two dads (a boyfriend recently moved in with them) or fluff it off and lie.

And his own friends were polarized by his decision to use a surrogate— still the centre of an ethical debate—over adoption or **foster care**. He tried to explain that he really wanted his first child to be biological, and
45 he thought that with surrogacy, he could better control the variables.

To a certain extent, he did—until the day Taylor was born. It was in the middle of the SARS [Severe Acute Respiratory Syndrome] epidemic in Toronto and Durkee had to film himself for *Birth Stories* in the hospital because no one else was allowed in. Friends set up camp chairs in the
50 parking lot to wait for news.

"In a way, it was the saddest moment of this entire experience," he says.

But it also marked the start of the happiest of journeys. Durkee knows that his little family might not be the norm, but he says that if a woman can decide to have a baby on her own, why can't a man play by the same rules?

55 Then, just for a moment, he **betrays** a little doubt, a symptom of the self-knowledge that, even though he speaks for himself, some will also consider him representative of what constitutes the new kind of family.

"So," he asks, "how did I do?"

676 words

---

1. In 2005, Canada became the fourth country in the world to legalize same-sex marriage.

Reading Comprehension

▬ **Respond to each of the questions below.**

1. In line 8, the author writes, "Being a gay/single/new father was a triple whammy ..." From the context, what do you think the expression "a triple whammy" means?

   three difficult (or challenging) things happening more or less at the same time

2. The author of the text has children of her own.   TRUE ☐ FALSE ✓

   The answer to question 2 is false because the author claims she didn't want to be a single mother and was too selfish to have children.

3. Kevin Durkee
   a) is in his early twenties.
   b) adopted a baby girl.
   c) originally thought he was too selfish to have children.
   (d) had a great childhood and wanted to give his own children a great childhood as well.

4. What significance does the author give to Durkee's appearance on the television show *Birth Stories*?

   She feels Durkee's appearance on TV is a good indication that the definition of "family" is changing and that

   gays and gay life are becoming part of mainstream culture.

5. In your own words, explain what the author means when she writes, "The 'usual way' is usual no longer." (line 24)

   She means that the traditional definition of the family from "one man and one woman and a child

   (or children)" has been enlarged to include alternative definitions (or that there is more than one type of

   family or way of starting a family).

6. Which of the following statements is **false**?
   a) According to a recent magazine issue, it is currently "fashionable" to be gay or lesbian.
   (b) *It's All Relative*, an American television program, encourages homophobia.
   c) Well-known adoptive mom Rosie O'Donnell publicly talks about her same-sex orientation.
   d) None of the above.

7. Explain the meaning of the term "gayby boom" in line 29.

   The term "gayby boom" is a play on the words "baby boom," meaning that many gays (and lesbians) are

   now opting to have children.

8. Which of the following is an example of homophobia?
   a) MP Larry Spencer's opinion of homosexuality
   b) A Louisiana school's reaction to a seven-year-old boy's use of the word "gay"
   c) The reaction of Kevin Durkee's friends to his use of a surrogate mom
   (d) Both a and b

9. Kevin Durkee believes that if a woman has the right to be a single mother, a man should have the right to be a single father as well.

TRUE ☑ FALSE ☐

Question 10 tests the student's ability to identify the main idea of the text.

10. What is the main idea of Lisa Fitterman's article?
   a) In spite of recent cultural and societal changes, homophobia still exists, and same-sex adoption remains a contentious issue.
   b) More gays and lesbians should adopt children.
   c) Same-sex adoption is morally unacceptable.
   d) Same-sex couples can have children through either adoption or surrogacy.

GRAMMAR TIP
A preposition shows the relationship between a noun or a pronoun and other words in a sentence. *In spite of* is a preposition; synonyms of *in spite of* include "despite," "regardless of" and "notwithstanding."

Discussion

Answers will vary. With respect to question 3, the issue of commercial surrogacy is dealt with specifically in Section B of this unit.

▬ **In small groups, discuss your answers to each of the questions below. Be prepared to share your group's ideas with the rest of the class.**

1. Do you want to be a parent? Why or why not?

2. If you had a choice between adopting a child and having one of your own, what would you prefer? Explain your preference.

3. How do you feel about people who hire surrogate mothers in general? How do you feel about Kevin Durkee's decision to hire a surrogate mother in particular?

Word Work

In the article, ten terms or collocations are defined for you:

Adjective	Collocations	Nouns	Verbs
1. mainstream	2. foster care 3. wreak havoc	4. labour 5. surrogate 6. toddler	7. betray 8. fathom 9. pass on 10. yearn

Answers will vary. Students are asked to write ten sentences, one for each of the terms defined in the "Word Work" chart. Model sentences are included in the Additional Notes in the Teacher Section of the companion website.

▬ **Working individually or in pairs, go back and reread the definitions of these terms.**
▬ **Next, reread the sentences in which the terms appear for an example of correct usage in context.**
▬ **Finally, demonstrate your understanding by writing ten sentences of your own on a separate sheet of paper, correctly using one of the terms in each of the sentences.**
▬ **Be ready to share some of your sentences with the entire class to verify vocabulary usage.**

Have You Heard?

For additional listening practice, visit the companion website.

spouse husband or wife

On May 19, 1999, the CBC news program *The National* ran a feature report entitled "Love and the Law" by award-winning reporter Michael McAuliffe. The report aired one day prior to the Canadian Supreme Court's eight-to-one decision that Ontario's previous legal definition of **spouse** (a person in a heterosexual relationship) was a violation of Section 15 of the 1982 *Canadian Charter of Rights and Freedoms*. The segment is about the historical legal battle to redefine the word *spouse* to include same-sex couples.

Pre-Watching Vocabulary

The students' inferred meanings will vary. Make sure students record the dictionary definitions in the chart on page 57, as these definitions are used in the word search vocabulary review activity on pages 61–62. Incidentally, *hodgepodge* is a Canadian variant of the British *hotchpotch*.

gonna informal spoken form of *going to*

Below you will find a series of ten quotes taken from the video. Each quote contains a word (or words) in italics.

- Working alone or with a partner, try to infer the meaning of the words from the context.
- Then verify your inferences by looking them up in a dictionary.
- Use the chart at the end of the section to record your answers. The first one has been done for you as an example.

1. It was very rare that I (Kelly Kane) was late for work, but this morning we were just *goofing off* and it was all around who was **gonna** wear which pair of shoes. And we were just kind of light and goofing off about these shoes. And I was saying that, you know, no, you wear these shoes. And that made me late for work.

2. But on the morning of October 21, 1993, Robin Black left for work—on her bicycle. Along the route, a garbage truck made a wrong turn down a one-way street and Robin was killed. Most people would have spent the last six years *grieving*, healing and trying to move on.

3. It's the case of "M" versus "H," the initials of two women who lived together for more than a decade, but who went through an acrimonious breakup in 1992. Destitute after moving out of the house, "M" *sued* "H" for spousal support.

4. Kelly Kane says that she doesn't, "… *put all of (her) eggs in one basket* … (she is) prepared for it (the court decision) to go either way."

5. The ruling will have national implications—helping to standardize the current gay rights *hodgepodge* across the country. From having no recognition of same-sex partnerships in Newfoundland or PEI, to Quebec, where the government tabled the most sweeping legislation in Canadian history to redefine the legal meaning of the word "spouse" to include gay couples.

WORD CULTURE
An older variant of the expression *to put all of one's eggs in one basket* is *to trust all one's goods to one ship*. Both expressions evoke images associated with risk: It is risky to put all your eggs in one basket because if you drop the basket, you break all your eggs; It is risky to put all your possessions on one ship because if the ship sinks, you lose everything.

6. When Jim Egan and Jack Nesbit sued Ottawa over Old Age Pensions in the mid-1990s, a deeply divided Supreme Court wasn't prepared to go that far in recognizing same-sex couples. But it did *urge* governments to begin taking the initiative.

7. Governments were slow to act. When Delwin Vriend *was fired* from his teaching job in Alberta for being gay, the provincial government refused to even consider his complaint. The Supreme Court lost its patience.

8. Bruce Ryder is a professor of constitutional law at York University, who says that in the relatively *swift* evolution of gay and lesbian rights in Canada, this week's ruling in "M" versus "H" may do for gay couples what Vriend's case did for individuals …

9. Gary Walsh and the Evangelical Fellowship of Canada, "… think that God has revealed the divine intention for the family as being the *core* of the whole social fabric. We see maleness and femaleness as givens … I get my orientation from the creation story that says: 'and God said let us make persons in our own image, male and female.'"

10. "Of course the law should support traditional families and children who live in traditional families and the spouses of traditional families," Ryder says. "But I think it's a serious error to presume that providing support to other families in some way *threatens* social support for traditional families."

VOCABULARY TIP
False friends are words from two different languages that look similar, yet differ in meaning. The English word *fabric* and the French word *fabrique* are false friends: *fabric* translates literally as "tissu" (material) and figuratively as "structure" (as in "social structure") in French while *fabrique* translates literally as "factory" in English. It is important to be aware of false friends when learning a second language.

Terms	Inferred Meanings	Dictionary Definitions
1. goof off (verb)	*playing around*	*waste time instead of working*
2. grieving (adverb)	Answers will vary.	mourning
3. sue (verb)	Answers will vary.	take someone to court for compensation
4. put all of your eggs in one basket (expression)	Answers will vary.	depend completely on one person (or thing) or on the outcome of one particular plan
5. hodgepodge (noun)	Answers will vary.	mixture of unrelated things
6. urge (verb)	Answers will vary.	strongly recommend
7. be fired (verb)	Answers will vary.	lose a job
8. swift (adj.)	Answers will vary.	fast
9. core (noun)	Answers will vary.	centre
10. threaten (verb)	Answers will vary.	express an intention to hurt

Watching Comprehension

— While you are watching the video, indicate whether each of the following statements is true or false.

— If the statement is false, explain why it is false.

1. Kelly Kane and Robin Black had been together for six years before Robin was killed in an accident on her way to work.

   TRUE ☑ FALSE ☐

   _____

   _____

2. Kelly Kane took her fight to have her relationship with Robin legally recognized to the Supreme Court of Canada.

   TRUE ☐ FALSE ☑

   A legal case referred to as "M" vs "H" went to the Supreme Court to determine whether Gays and Lesbians had the right to spousal support.

3. The Ontario government forced Kelly Kane's insurance company to pay her a death benefit.

   TRUE ☐ FALSE ☑

   An Ontario court ruled that Kelly Kane was a spouse for the purpose of The Insurance Act, forcing the insurance company to honour her death benefit claim. However, the Ontario government opposed the court decision and filed an appeal.

4. Pierre Trudeau claimed that, "There is no place for the state in the bedrooms of the nation."

   TRUE ☑ FALSE ☐

   _____

   _____

5. Gary Walsh of the Evangelical Fellowship of Canada defines a spousal relationship as "... a man and a woman with the capacity to procreate ..."

   TRUE ☑ FALSE ☐

   _____

   _____

6. Gary Walsh is completely against the recognition of same-sex arrangements.

   TRUE ☐ FALSE ☑

   He is willing to have other types of relationships recognized; however, he is unwilling to redefine the terms "family" or "marriage" to include same-sex couples.

7. Law Professor Bruce Ryder claims that Canadian society no longer condemns non-procreative sexual behaviour and therefore can no longer deny legal recognition to same-sex couples.

   TRUE ☑ FALSE ☐

   _____

   _____

8. Gary Walsh believes that some things, such as the traditional definition of the family, are absolutely true and shouldn't be changed.

TRUE ☑   FALSE ☐

_____

_____

For more information on the fight for gay and lesbian rights in Canada, visit the CBC digital archive at http://archives.cbc.ca/.

Question 10 tests the student's ability to identify the main idea of the segment.

9. Kelly Kane is ready to give up the fight for the legal recognition of her relationship to Robin Black.

TRUE ☐   FALSE ☑

She is willing to continue the fight to honour Robin's memory; in addition, she wants to participate in the

fight for gay and lesbian rights.

10. In general, this video presents the debate surrounding the recognition of same-sex couples and the legal and societal consequences of this recognition.

TRUE ☑   FALSE ☐

_____

_____

Would You Write That Down?

For additional writing practice, visit the companion website.

Answers will vary. In free-form writing, no specific structure is required; however, the student is asked to write 75 to 100 words. You may wish to increase or decrease the number of words required. The free-form writing assignments are great for "sampling" student writing ability.

WRITING SUGGESTION
When writing an essay, avoid structures like "I think that …" and "I feel that …" As it is *your* essay, the readers already understand that they are reading about *your* thoughts and *your* feelings.

Your teacher may ask you to complete one or more of the writing assignments below. If asked to write an essay, be sure to structure your writing clearly.

Free-form Writing

■ **Write 75 to 100 words in response to one of the following questions:**

1. Would you be any different if a same-sex couple had raised you? If so, how would you be different?

2. Can a single parent raise a child as well as a couple? Why or why not?

3. In general, do you think that Canadians are homophobic? Explain.

Essay Writing

■ **Write a 300- to 400-word essay using one of the thesis statements on page 60.**

■ **Do some research on the Internet to find evidence that supports your chosen thesis statement. (See Appendix A to review the structure of a persuasive essay.)**

Answers will vary. The recommended essay format for *Parallels: Taking a Stand in English* is the persuasive essay (see "Appendix A: The Persuasive Essay" on page 182), but you may opt for another essay structure. The student is asked to write 300 to 400 words. You may also wish to increase or decrease the number of words required.

1. Women make (or do not make) better parents than men.

2. Same-sex marriage is (or is not) wrong.

3. Same-sex couples make (or do not make) suitable parents.

4. Homophobia is (or is not) a pressing problem in Canada.

5. Sexual orientation is (or is not) a choice.

Would You Speak Up?

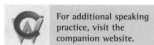
For additional speaking practice, visit the companion website.

Your teacher may ask you to participate in one or more of the following speaking activities.

Discussion

SPEAKING SUGGESTION
When possible, use an anecdote to illustrate a point. An anecdote grabs the listeners' attention because it involves their imaginations.

- In small groups, consider one (or more) of the following questions.
- Be prepared to share your thoughts with other groups in the class.

1. Is family important? Why or why not?

2. Why do most Canadians under the age of thirty-five support same-sex marriage while most Canadians over the age of sixty-five do not?

3. Do young children need a mother more than they need a father?

4. *Equal rights* doesn't imply *identical rights*; same-sex couples aren't the same as opposite-sex couples and therefore shouldn't have the same rights. Comment.

5. In Lisa Fitterman's article "A New Family Man," Kevin Durkee implies that society accepts single mothers, so it should also accept single fathers. Is being a single mom the same as being a single dad?

Answers will vary. As indicated in the Speaking Suggestion above, encourage students to use anecdotes to capture the listener's attention. Remind them that an anecdote must illustrate a point. The video segment, "Love and the Law" (p. 56) used the story of Kelly Kane and Robin Black to capture the viewer's attention.

Discourse

Answers will vary. Discourse structure is outlined in "Appendix B: Discourse and Debate" (p. 192). Given the polemic nature of *Parallels: Taking a Stand in English*, a persuasive discourse structure is recommended. The suggested speaking time is five minutes; you may wish to increase or decrease the required speaking time.

- Prepare a structured, five-minute speech on one of the following thesis statements. (See Appendix B for a suggested speech structure.)
- Do some research to find evidence that supports your chosen thesis statement. Make sure your speech has an introduction, a development and a conclusion.

1. Same-sex couples should (or should not) have identical rights to opposite-sex couples.

2. Same-sex marriage is (or is not) a threat to the traditional Canadian family.

3. Older Canadians are (or are not) more homophobic than younger Canadians.

4. Homophobia can (or cannot) be eliminated.

5. Family is (or is not) important.

Debate

▬ **Debate the following proposal: Same-sex adoption is wrong. (See Appendix B for the rules of debate.)**

What's That Word Mean Again?

Twenty terms were presented in this part of Unit 3—ten from the reading section and ten from the listening section. Go back and review these words and then test your vocabulary by completing the activity below.

Word Search

In the following activity, you are asked to find, *from their definitions alone*, vocabulary terms defined in the reading and listening activities in this section of Unit 3. Without referring back to the activities, do you think you can find the terms? Let's find out.

Required
• A pen or pencil
• A great deal of patience!

Instructions
1. Decide which words the definitions represent.

2. Find the words in the grid. (Words can appear horizontally, vertically and diagonally.)

3. When you are finished, the first thirty-two unused letters in the grid will spell out an English proverb. To uncover the proverb, pick out the letters from left to right, moving from the top line down to the bottom line.

D	O	N	O	T	N	O	S	S	A	P	F	P	U	T
E	S	U	R	R	O	G	A	T	E	G	F	A	L	L
O	R	F	Y	O	U	R	E	G	N	G	O	S	I	N
O	E	O	H	N	E	Y	B	I	A	T	F	I	W	S
S	K	R	C	O	E	E	V	T	M	H	O	G	W	R
Y	L	H	A	A	D	E	T	A	Q	N	O	J	L	N
L	L	D	R	C	I	G	E	F	G	Z	G	R	F	E
Z	A	N	H	R	R	R	E	R	N	B	H	Q	A	T
Q	B	B	G	Y	T	E	E	P	E	X	L	J	T	A
Y	B	T	O	S	A	L	T	F	O	L	Z	U	H	E
T	Y	M	N	U	D	R	I	S	M	D	P	R	O	R
H	H	I	J	D	R	R	T	W	O	M	G	G	M	H
W	A	G	O	M	E	Y	W	E	K	F	H	E	L	T
M	J	T	L	D	D	M	C	Z	B	C	F	P	T	G
S	U	E	C	O	V	A	H	K	A	E	R	W	J	Y

Proverb: Do not put all of your eggs in one basket.
__ __ ___ ___ __ ____ ____ __ ___ _____ .

Definitions

1. lose a job (two words)

2. show something unintentionally

3. centre

4. comprehend

5. providing parental care for an unrelated child (two words)

6. waste time instead of working (two words)

7. mourning

8. mixture of unrelated things

9. process of childbirth

10. reflecting the norm

11. share (two words)

12. take someone to court for compensation

13. woman who gives birth for another

14. fast

15. express an intention to hurt

16. young child learning to walk

17. strongly recommend

18. cause destruction (two words)

19. want something difficult to have

Would You Like to Work Together?

sample test group

In this section, you will work with another student on a joint writing and speaking project.

Project Overview

An opinion poll is an investigation of public opinion. A **sample** of a given population is questioned and, if the sample is representative, the results are applied to the population as a whole. For this project, you will prepare and conduct an opinion poll on same-sex adoption and compile the results in a brief report.

Types of Questions

Questions can be divided into two types: open- and close-ended. Open-ended questions are questions to which there is more than one answer: How do you feel about same-sex adoption? Open-ended questions are good for breaking the ice and the respondents' answers provide a good source of quotable material. Close-ended questions are questions to which there are a finite number of answers: Should gay and lesbian couples be allowed to adopt? (The answer is either "yes" or "no.") The following are examples of close-ended questions frequently found in opinion polls:

Categorical

Circle one: male / female

Multiple Choice

How many children do you have?
Circle one answer.

a) none   **b)** one   **c)** two   **d)** three or more

Likert Scale

How important is it for a child to grow up in a home with both a mother and a father?
Circle one answer.

1	**2**	**3**	**4**	**5**
not important at all	somewhat important	unsure	very important	extremely important

extended family
family unit comprised of parents, children, grandparents, aunts and uncles, cousins, etc.

Ordinal

Write a number between 1 and 5 beside each of the items below. Put a "1" next to the item that is **most** important to you personally, and a "5" next to the item that is **least** important to you personally.

_____ **a)** growing up in a loving family   _____ **d)** growing up in a family with opposite-sex parents

_____ **b)** growing up in a two-parent family   _____ **e)** growing up in an **extended family**

_____ **c)** growing up in a wealthy family

In this project, you will use both open- and close-ended questions.

Required
- A partner and ten opinion poll participants
- A computer
- Internet access
- Printouts

Procedure: Preparing the Opinion Poll

Working with your assigned (or chosen) partner, prepare a two-part opinion poll as outlined below:

Part A: List of Interview Questions

1. Prepare ten open-ended icebreaking questions to ask participants. The purpose of icebreaking questions is to put participants at ease and elicit quotable material; as such, questions must be non-threatening yet pertinent to the topic at hand.

   Example questions include:
   a) What is same-sex adoption?
   b) What do you know about same-sex adoption in Canada?
   c) Do you know any same-sex couples who have adopted children?
   d) Do you know any opposite-sex couples who have adopted children?
   e) How do you feel about adoption in general?

2. Submit your questions to your teacher for correction.

3. Type your corrected list of interview questions, leaving enough blank space under each question for you to write down the participants' answers.

4. Print ten copies of your list of interview questions, one for each participant.

Part B: Questionnaire

by hand in writing (not using a machine)

5. Prepare ten close-ended questions to be included in a questionnaire that participants will fill out **by hand**. Your first two questions should determine the gender and age of the participants. The ten questions should be of various types (categorical, multiple choice, Likert Scale and ordinal) and must be pertinent to the topic at hand.

6. Submit your questions to your teacher for correction.

7. Type your corrected list of questions, adding the following:
   a) A title: Opinion Poll on Same-Sex Adoption
   b) Introductory instructions: Please respond to each of the ten questions below. Answering the questions will only take a few minutes. Your participation is voluntary. The results of the poll will be presented to my English teacher as part of a class project; the results may be discussed in class. Your confidentiality will be respected. Do not write down your name.

8. Print ten copies of your opinion poll, one for each participant.

Procedure: Conducting the Opinion Poll

1. Find ten people (both males and females) willing to respond to your opinion poll. Select participants from each of the following age groups: teenagers (13 to 19 years of age); young adults (20 to 29 years of age); middle-aged adults (30 to 49 years of age); older adults (50 to 69 years of age); and the elderly (70+ years of age).

2. Each partner interviews five participants. For each participant, begin with the ten interview questions. Before conducting the interview:
   a) inform the participant that his or her anonymity will be respected;
   b) inform the participant of the context in which the poll is being conducted (a class project);
   c) ask the participant for permission to record his or her answers;
   d) inform the participant that he or she may be anonymously quoted when you compile the results and type your findings in a brief report.

3. While interviewing, record your participants' answers.

4. Once the interview has been completed, ask each participant to fill out the questionnaire.

5. Thank each participant for participating in your opinion poll.

Procedure: Compiling the Results in a Brief Report

When compiling the results:

Remind students to put a comma before a direct quotation. For more information on commas and quotation marks, refer to Appendix D of the companion volume *Parallels: Taking a Stand in English— English Grammar*.

1. Describe the sample.
   Example: *Ten participants ranging in age from 17 to 74 responded to the poll. Equal numbers of males and females participated.*

2. For each of the twenty questions (ten from the interview part of the opinion poll and ten from the questionnaire part of the opinion poll), indicate the breakdown of the responses.
   Examples: *One participant was unable to give a clear definition of same-sex adoption. He said, "Is that when a woman adopts a girl and a man adopts a boy?"*

   Three participants indicated that they had no children.

   Include a minimum of two quotes from the interview part of the opinion poll.

3. Draw conclusions.
   Example: *In general, age does not seem to be a factor as to whether one supports or opposes same-sex adoption.*
   Note: Due to the sample size (and non-randomized nature of the sampling), findings cannot be generalized to a given population.

4. Include an example of the opinion poll distributed. Do not include the actual polls completed: dispose of these polls in a manner that respects the participants' confidentiality (shredding, etc.).

5. Submit your assignment to your teacher for evaluation.

Commercial Surrogacy

Did You Know?

"I don't have any children—that I know of!"

Up until recently, this old joke belonged exclusively to men; however, thanks to rapid progress in the field of Assisted Human Reproduction (AHR), women can now lay claim to this tired gag as well.

More seriously, advances in AHR techniques—particularly those related to human surrogacy—have shaken society at its base, challenging the very definition of motherhood itself.

Imagine for a moment that Mr. and Mrs. Smith want—but cannot have—a child because Mrs. Smith has had a hysterectomy. Mrs. Smith's sister donates an egg, which is fertilized with Mr. Smith's sperm in vitro, and the resulting embryo is transferred to a surrogate mother who gives birth to a healthy "test-tube" baby nine months later. Who is the baby's mother? Is it Mrs. Smith because she will raise the baby? Is it Mrs. Smith's sister because she is genetically related to the baby? Or is it the surrogate mother because she carried the baby for nine months?

Indeed, motherhood must now be considered in social, genetic *and* gestational terms (William-Jones).

Now let's examine surrogacy itself. Basically, there are two types of surrogacy: altruistic and commercial.

In altruistic surrogacy, the surrogate mother receives no payment for her services, but in commercial surrogacy, the surrogate mother is compensated for her labour—pun intended! (The word *labour* means both *work* and *childbirth*.)

In Canada, the *Assisted Human Reproduction Act*, adopted by the Canadian Parliament on October 28, 2003, prohibits commercial surrogacy.

Needless to say, commercial surrogacy has both its supporters and its detractors. Let's examine the arguments for both sides.

Commercial surrogacy is right because it	Commercial surrogacy is wrong because it
1. provides infertile and gay couples with the opportunity to have children.	1. does psychological harm to surrogate mothers and children.
2. liberates women who want to have children without giving birth to them.	2. represents "baby selling."
3. helps surrogate mothers make money.	3. threatens the institutions of marriage and family.

It is illogical to bring a child "artificially" into an overpopulated world that has a multitude of children waiting to be adopted. However, the decision to have a child is an emotional—not a logical—one. In this debate, you will have to think with your heart *as well as* your head.

What's the Buzz?

Below is a series of quotes.

- Work with a partner or in groups of three or four.
- For each quote, indicate with an "X" whether the speaker would likely be for or against commercial surrogacy.

VOCABULARY TIP
For this exercise, it isn't essential to understand every word; simply try to capture the gist of each speaker's comments.

For	Quotes	Against
☐	1. Feminist and lawyer Maureen McTeer: "… I am appalled that my profession plays the angles, treating commercial surrogacy as just another commercial contract—just another way to make money."	☒

→

For	Quotes	Against
☒	2. New Zealand surrogate mother Maewa Kaihau: "Legislation to prohibit surrogates from receiving payments or benefits for the act of carrying a child for the commissioning parents should not be approved." (As cited in *The New Zealand Herald*)	☐
☒	3. British Columbia Civil Liberties Association: "It is undoubtedly the case that the idea of commercial surrogacy offends some people's sensibilities. But the mere causing of offence is not grounds for legal sanctions in a free and democratic society."	☐
☐	4. Lawyer and activist Andrew Kimbrell: "It is the attempt to commodify the act of child-bearing and to commodify children … It is baby selling, pure and simple, which we have forbidden in all fifty states but under the guise of a surrogacy contract tried to legalize." (As cited on Minnesota Public Radio)	☒
☐	5. Focus on the Family Canada: "The ethical, moral and practical difficulties with surrogate motherhood are grave enough to bring its value to society into question."	☒
☒	6. George Dvorsky, Vice-President of the Toronto Transhumanist Association: "People should be wary of any attempt by the Canadian government to control the reproductive processes of their bodies …"	☐

Discussion

- **Working with a partner or in a small group, discuss and respond to the questions below. Be prepared to share your responses with the class.**

1. In the simplest of terms, a mother is a female parent. Expand upon this definition; in your own words, what is a mother?

   _____

   _____

2. Write down five adjectives that you associate with the word *mother*. (You might wish to use a dictionary for this exercise.)

   a) _____   d) _____

   b) _____   e) _____

   c) _____

3. In the previous section, you were asked to identify the "real" mother of a test-tube baby—Mrs. Smith, Mrs. Smith's sister or the surrogate. According to your definition (question 1) and description (question 2) of *mother*, which of the three women has the strongest claim to being the baby's mom? Explain your answer.

_____

_____

_____

Have You Read?

For additional reading practice, visit the companion website.

Susan Ruttan is a columnist for *The Edmonton Journal*. Her article "They Aren't Just Babies Anymore, They're Products" appeared in *The Times Colonist* in Victoria on Sunday August 19, 2001. From the context of this unit, what babies do you think she is writing about?

Before Reading

▬ Remember to skim and scan; read the defined words and comprehension questions before you read the article.

While Reading

Susan Ruttan uses an anecdote (or a short story) to illustrate her main point *and* capture your interest. Anecdotes activate your imagination—you imagine the story as it is told to you. Enjoy the story, but don't lose sight of the author's main point. Ask yourself why the author is telling you the story.

READING STRATEGY
When doing an assigned reading, think about *why* the teacher has assigned the reading. Doing so will help you focus your attention on the task at hand. Remember—a focused reader is an effective reader.

THEY AREN'T JUST BABIES ANYMORE, THEY'RE PRODUCTS

BY SUSAN RUTTAN

"Family building," said California lawyer Diane Michelsen this week, "is a very private matter."

No it isn't, not any more. Not when baby-making is turned into an industry. Not when Michelsen's clients, two well-off Berkeley lawyers, hire a British
5 single mom to produce a baby for them, and then **balk** when the "product" isn't quite what they ordered. When babies become a consumer product, public contract fights and lawsuits are an inevitable by-product.

balk object

Charles Wheeler, 50, and Martha Berman, 47, are probably decent people—smart, busy, accomplished. They wanted a family, so they hired single mom Helen Beasley to produce it, using Wheeler's sperm and an egg donor's egg.

However, they didn't want a family to the extent of caring for **twins**. Their order was for one baby, not two. So, when Beasley was found to be carrying twins, and refused to **abort** one, they **bowed out** of the deal. Some other couple will take the twins.

If this were a car the lawyers had ordered, or even a new puppy, the scenario wouldn't be repugnant. But a baby is not a puppy. It cannot be traded from one set of parents to another, as if it had no genetic inheritance from the two parents whose egg and sperm created it. It should not be the subject of business deals between couples with the money to pay and young women with the time to **breed**. Thank heaven that Canada is planning to outlaw surrogacy for money.[2]

Some will argue that there's always been a lot of irresponsible baby-making, that high-tech baby-making is no worse.

It's worse. For one thing, the irresponsible people aren't sixteen-year-olds having sex in the back seat of a car; they are for the most part middle-aged professional people—including an increasing number of gay men—who have the money to pay for the services of a surrogate mother. We expect mature adults to act more responsibly than horny teenagers.

We expect their commitment to parenting to be deep enough to accept twins.

Parenting cannot be reduced to some new lifestyle choice which can be tried out for a while, or tailored to one's exact specifications. Bringing a child into the world is a holy act; raising it is a life-altering experience.

New reproductive technologies allow anyone of any age to become a parent—a sixty-two-year-old French woman just had a baby using her brother's sperm, for crying out loud.

The technologies have been a blessing to **infertile** couples, but they are pushing the bounds of parenthood in ways which will not always be good for kids.

Some of the surrogate mother websites make chilling reading. One site breaks motherhood down into three components:

- The genetic mother, a.k.a. the egg donor
- The gestational mother, who carries the fetus for nine months
- The social mother, who helps raise the child

The Berkeley lawyers, and many others, followed this pattern, with three different women taking on the three roles.

Such a division of labour diminishes the experience of motherhood and diminishes the connections between mother and child. It serves the

---

2. The Canadian parliament outlawed commercial surrogacy on Oct. 28, 2003.

twins two children born together

abort end a pregnancy

bow out renounce

breed reproduce

infertile sterile

WORD CULTURE
The expression *for crying out loud* is a euphemism (less offensive synonym) for "for Christ's sake." The expression dates back to around 1900, and many sources credit the American cartoonist Thomas Aloysius Dorgan with creating the expression.

GRAMMAR TIP
The abbreviation *a.k.a.* stands for "also known as." Abbreviations that appear in lowercase letters generally require periods while abbreviations that appear in uppercase letters generally do not: e.g. (for *exempli gratia* meaning "for example") and CEO (for Chief Executive Officer). For more information on abbreviations, see "Appendix D" of the companion volume *Parallels: Taking a Stand in English— English Grammar*.

adults' interest, not the child's. It takes us into unknown territory, into the old sci-fi world where breeders are a special sub-category.

I appreciate that families take many forms. Children can get loving and consistent parenting from gay parents, grandparents, single parents, even
55 teenage parents.

But the desire of people to be parents, despite the handicaps of age, infertility or sexual preference, should not blind us to the fact that genetic inheritance matters.

A good chunk of what a child is—personality, **IQ**, health problems, looks—
60 is what he inherits from his parents. Deliberately separating babies from the two people in the world who share that genetic inheritance, the biological parents, deprives those babies of a fundamental link with the people who are more like them than any others. It should not be done lightly.

People who raise adoptive and **foster children** are heroes. In many
65 ways, that's the ultimate parenting, caring for a child not your own.

Yet, I have talked to enough people who yearn to find their birth mothers to know that reducing the role of biological parent to a commercial egg or sperm donor will leave many people, at some point in their lives, wondering who they really are.

70 The global march of ever-more-exotic forms of reproductive technology is unlikely to be halted. Internet sites offer an array of services—egg **donors**, sperm donors, embryos, surrogates.

And there are enough people **eager** to be parents that they'll make the kind of Internet deal that the two Berkeley lawyers made. As long as people are
75 willing to pay, the industry will grow.

The ban on commercial surrogacy proposed by the Chrétien [former Canadian Prime Minister] government will drive Canadian customers to seek surrogate mothers south of the border.

Fine; let them go. At least in this country we'll be able to say that we put
80 the long-term rights of the child ahead of adults' right to buy themselves a family.

841 words

Reading Comprehension

▬ **Respond to each of the questions below.**

The answer to question 1 is false because the author states that family building is no longer a private matter when family building becomes an "industry."

1. The author agrees that family building is a private matter. TRUE ☐ FALSE ☑

2. Explain the following sentence in your own words: "When babies become a consumer product, public contract fights and lawsuits are an inevitable by-product." (lines 6–7)

   When babies are treated as objects to be bought and sold, society can expect legal battles to arise, as occurs in all other "matters of trade."

For question 3, option d) is false because the egg was donated.

3. Which of the following statements is false?
   a) Charles Wheeler and Martha Berman wanted only one child.
   b) The surrogate mother refused to abort one of the twins.
   c) Charles Wheeler was the genetic father of the twins.
   d) The British surrogate was the genetic mother of the twins.

4. The author is in favour of the criminalization of commercial surrogacy. TRUE ☑ FALSE ☐

5. Explain why the author thinks that new technologies are worsening the problem of "irresponsible baby-making."

   "Irresponsible baby-making" was associated in the past with young people; however, now it is

   middle-aged professional people who are acting irresponsibly; the author implies that such people

   should "behave better," but they don't. That is why the problem is worse.

6. Explain the meaning of the expression "for crying out loud" in line 39.

   This expression communicates exasperation (or annoyance).

The answer to question 7 is false because in line 42, the author writes that the three categories of motherhood make for "chilling" reading on surrogate mother websites.

7. The author supports the division of motherhood into three categories: genetic, gestational and social. TRUE ☐ FALSE ☑

8. Explain the following sentence in your own words: "A good chunk of what a child is—personality, IQ, health problems, looks—is what he inherits from his parents." (line 59)

   This sentence indicates that the author believes that "nature" (or genetics) has a strong impact on the

   physical and mental characteristics of a child.

9. The author thinks that
   a) a child separated from his or her biological parents is likely to question his or her identity.
   b) commercial surrogacy can be banned worldwide.
   c) the number of people wanting to hire surrogate mothers is decreasing.
   d) Canadians can be stopped from hiring surrogate mothers in the U.S.

Question 10 tests the student's ability to identify the main idea of the text.

10. The main idea of Ms. Ruttan's column is
    a) commercial surrogacy results in lawsuits.
    b) commercial surrogacy offers hope to many infertile couples.
    c) parenting is a private matter.
    d) commercial surrogacy is wrong because it puts the adult's interests ahead of the child's.

Discussion

Answers will vary.

- In small groups, discuss your answers to each of the following questions. Try to arrive at a group consensus.
- Be prepared to share your group's ideas with the rest of the class.

1. What do you think of the Wheelers' decision not to accept the twins?

2. Should reproductive technologies be used to help senior citizens give birth? Justify your response.

3. Should children have the legal right to know the identities of their biological parents? Explain.

Word Work

In the article, ten new terms or collocations are defined for you:

Adjectives	Collocation	Nouns	Verbs
1. eager 2. infertile	3. foster child	4. donor 5. IQ 6. twins	7. abort 8. balk 9. bow out 10. breed

- Working individually or in pairs, go back and reread the definitions of these terms.
- Next, reread the sentences in which the terms appear for an example of correct usage in context.
- Finally, demonstrate your understanding by writing ten sentences of your own, correctly using one of the terms in each of the sentences.
- Be ready to share some of your sentences with the entire class to verify vocabulary usage.

Have You Heard?

For additional listening practice, visit the companion website.

On May 9, 2002, the CBC news program *The National* ran a feature entitled "Policing Reproduction" by reporter Alison Smith, with guests Patricia Baird, Murray Croach and Jeff Nisker. The segment is about the debate surrounding the regulation of reproductive technologies in Canada.

Pre-Watching Vocabulary

On page 74, you will find a series of ten quotes taken from the video. Each quote contains a word (or words) in italics.

- Working alone or with a partner, try to infer the meaning of the words from the context.
- Then verify your inferences by looking them up in a dictionary.
- Use the chart at the end of the section (page 74) to record your answers. The first one has been done for you as an example.

1. "Earlier we told you about the proposed new reproductive technology legislation. But just how it would work is still *murky* territory."

2. "It used to be that there was just one simple answer. One way to have a child. Of course, the basic principle is still the same, but the answer now can be a lot more complicated. Reproductive science has opened up a *realm* of possibilities for those who could once only dream of having a child."

3. "Today's legislation is an attempt to *set out* the rules and impose criminal penalties for breaking them."

4. "Well, I think this legislation is long *overdue*. I think we've actually let families in this country not have the best protections that they could and the best information that they could in this field."

5. "It is ... the industry that has hired the woman, that has bought her eggs and sold her eggs to which the legislation is *aimed*."

6. "... at long last we have the *will* to act on this."

7. "She (the patient) has to have an invasive procedure where a *needle* is put through into the pelvic cavity to retrieve the eggs, usually under ultrasound."

8. "I think the patient/client is not somehow being *accountable* for any of this ... the way they're trying to control this (reproductive technology) is by the physician."

9. "If ... physicians or businessmen who *own* reproductive companies or services do not follow the regulations ... physicians would lose their professional status ..."

10. "So a woman who is *pregnant* of a commercial surrogacy arrangement (outside of Canada) ... when she comes back to Canada, we will care for her."

VOCABULARY TIP
False friends are words from two different languages that look similar, yet differ in meaning. The English word *actually* and the French word *actuellement* are false friends: *actually* translates as "en fait" (in fact) in French while *actuellement* translates as "at present" in English. It is important to be aware of false friends when learning a second language.

Words	Inferred Meanings	Dictionary Definitions
1. murky (adj.)	*confusing*	*unclear*
2. realm (noun)	Answers will vary.	range
3. set out (verb)	Answers will vary.	establish
4. overdue (adj.)	Answers will vary.	late
5. aim (verb)	Answers will vary.	target
6. will (noun)	Answers will vary.	determination
7. needle (noun)	Answers will vary.	syringe
8. accountable (adj.)	Answers will vary.	responsible
9. own (verb)	Answers will vary.	possess
10. pregnant (adj.)	Answers will vary.	expecting a child

Watching Comprehension

■ **While you are watching the video, indicate whether each of the following statements is true or false.**

■ **If the statement is false, indicate why it is false.**

1. Reproductive science has complicated the "business" of baby making.

   TRUE ✓ FALSE ☐

   _____

   _____

2. The legislation is aimed at preventing the (continued) commercialization of reproductive procedures in Canada.

   TRUE ✓ FALSE ☐

   _____

   _____

3. The report presented by the Royal Commission chaired by Patricia Baird was immediately acted upon.

   TRUE ☐ FALSE ✓

   At the time of the broadcast, the journalist indicates that the government first attempted to regulate

   reproductive technology a decade ago and that the resulting report "never went anywhere."

4. The Assisted Human Reproduction Agency of Canada will maintain a health information registry of donors, patients and the resulting children.

   TRUE ✓ FALSE ☐

   _____

   _____

5. Hormonal treatment is required in the egg retrieval process.

   TRUE ✓ FALSE ☐

   _____

   _____

6. The legislation imposes only legal—not moral—limits.

   TRUE ☐ FALSE ✓

   The reporter indicates that by banning commercial surrogacy, the act imposes moral limits.

   _____

7. Dr. Murray Croach believes the legislation is fair to both doctors and patients.

   TRUE ☐ FALSE ✓

   He believes that patients are not accountable enough and that the legislation places too much legal

   responsibility on physicians.

8. Commercial surrogacy is legal in parts of the United States.

   TRUE ✓ FALSE ☐

   _____

   _____

For more information on reproductive technologies in Canada, go to the CBC digital archive at http://archives.cbc.ca/.

9. Patricia Baird is unconcerned about what nations other than Canada do with their reproductive technologies.

TRUE ☐ FALSE ☑

She believes that Canada "has to get its own house in order" and then work in the international community to make sure that other countries participate in some global agreement on reproductive technologies.

Question 10 tests the student's ability to identify the main idea of the segment.

10. The reporter, Alison Smith, takes a clear personal position on the debate over the proposed legislation to regulate reproductive technologies in Canada.

TRUE ☐ FALSE ☑

As a journalist, she presents "both sides" of the issue.

Would You Write That Down?

Your teacher may ask you to complete one or both of the writing activities below. If asked to write an essay, be sure to structure your writing clearly.

For additional writing practice, visit the companion website.

Answers will vary. In free-form writing, no specific structure is required; however, the student is asked to write 75 to 100 words. You may wish to increase or decrease the number of words required. The free-form writing assignments are great for "sampling" student writing ability.

WRITING SUGGESTION
When writing an essay, avoid structures like "I think that ..." and "I feel that ..." As it is *your* essay, the readers already understand that they are reading about *your* thoughts and *your* feelings.

Answers will vary. The recommended essay format for *Parallels: Taking a Stand in English* is the persuasive essay (see "Appendix A: The Persuasive Essay" on page 182), but you may opt for another essay structure. The student is asked to write 300 to 400 words. You may also wish to increase or decrease the number of words required.

Free-form Writing

- Write 75 to 100 words in response to one of the following questions:

1. Which mother is most important for the child—the genetic mother, the gestational mother or the social mother? Justify your response.

2. Should a surrogate child know the identity of his or her gestational mother? Explain.

3. Should a surrogate child know the identity of his or her genetic mother? Explain.

Essay Writing

- Write a 300- to 400-word essay using one of the thesis statements below.
- Do some research on the Internet to find evidence that supports your chosen thesis statement. (See Appendix A to review the structure of a persuasive essay.)

1. Commercial surrogacy should (or should not) be allowed in Canada.

2. Surrogate motherhood should (or should not) be treated as a legitimate profession.

3. Commercial surrogacy is (or is not) baby selling.

4. Surrogacy is (or is not) an important social issue.

5. Canadians should (or should not) allow the government to control reproduction.

Would You Speak Up?

For additional speaking practice, visit the companion website.

Your teacher may ask you to participate in one or more of the following speaking activities.

Discussion

Answers will vary. As indicated in the Speaking Suggestion above, encourage students to use anecdotes to capture the listener's attention. Remind them that an anecdote must illustrate a point. In her article, "They Aren't Just Babies Anymore, They're Products," Susan Ruttan captures the reader's attention (while making her point against commercial surrogacy) by using an anecdote of a Berkeley couple who bowed out of a surrogacy agreement.

Answers will vary. Discourse structure is outlined in "Appendix B: Discourse and Debate" (p. 192). Given the polemic nature of *Parallels: Taking a Stand in English*, a persuasive discourse structure is recommended. The suggested speaking time is five minutes; you may wish to increase or decrease the required speaking time.

Answers will vary. Debate structure is outlined in "Appendix B: Discourse and Debate" (pp. 194–198). Arguments "for" and "against" the proposal are listed on page 67. For more information on running small group or whole class debates, refer to the Additional Notes in the Teacher Section of the companion website.

- In small groups, consider one (or more) of the following questions.
- Be prepared to share your thoughts with other groups in the class.

1. Why do you think that the Canadian government supports altruistic—but not commercial—surrogacy?

2. Should infertile couples simply accept their infertility and adopt children if they really want to start a family? Justify your response.

3. If you were a child born by a surrogate mother, would you want to know? Why or why not?

4. What are the dangers of treating babies like products?

5. Susan Ruttan fears that children who result from commercial egg or sperm donation will end up wondering "who they are." Is this a serious concern?

Discourse

- Prepare a structured, five-minute speech on one of the thesis statements below. (See Appendix B for a suggested speech structure.)
- Do some research to find evidence that supports your chosen thesis statement. Make sure your speech has an introduction, a development and a conclusion.

1. Children have (or do not have) the right to know the identities of their genetic parents.

2. The Canadian government should (or should not) allow trade in human sperm and eggs.

3. Surrogacy exploits (or does not exploit) women.

4. Parenting is (or is not) a difficult job.

5. Genetics determine (or do not determine) a child's identity.

Debate

- Debate the following proposal: Commercial surrogacy is wrong. (See Appendix B for the rules of debate.)

What's That Word Mean Again?

Twenty terms were presented in this part of Unit 3—ten from the reading section and ten from the listening section. Go back and review these words and then test your vocabulary by completing the activity below.

Word Search

In the following activity, you are asked to find, *from their definitions alone*, vocabulary terms defined in the reading and listening activities in this section of Unit 3. Without referring back to the activities, do you think you can find the terms? Let's find out.

Required
- A pen or pencil
- A great deal of patience!

Instructions
1. Decide which words the definitions below represent.

2. Find the words in the grid. (Words can appear horizontally, vertically and diagonally.)

3. When you are finished, the first thirty-six unused letters in the grid will spell out an amusing saying. To uncover the saying, pick out the letters from left to right, moving from the top line down to the bottom line.

Definitions

1. end a pregnancy
2. responsible
3. target
4. object
5. renounce (two words)
6. reproduce
7. someone who donates body parts or tissue
8. enthusiastic
9. child cared for by parents unrelated by blood or adoption (two words)
10. sterile
11. acronym for "intelligence quotient"
12. unclear
13. syringe
14. late
15. possess
16. expecting a child
17. range
18. establish (two words)
19. two children born together
20. determination

F	A	M	M	U	R	K	Y	I	L	I	A	R	I
E	I	T	Y	R	B	E	S	R	E	E	D	S	C
L	N	O	N	E	T	L	N	R	E	M	P	I	T
B	F	A	N	G	D	D	I	C	O	H	Q	I	L
A	E	D	R	A	E	E	W	N	T	N	T	X	P
T	R	L	S	E	V	E	T	R	O	K	O	N	F
N	T	D	E	D	W	N	O	V	R	K	M	D	B
U	I	K	T	K	J	B	E	J	N	E	K	J	C
O	L	F	O	T	A	R	R	W	L	L	A	Z	G
C	E	C	U	J	D	Z	O	E	A	L	N	L	D
C	T	W	T	U	Z	K	H	B	E	W	I	M	M
A	P	R	E	G	N	A	N	T	Y	D	Q	W	B
M	I	A	B	O	W	O	U	T	F	X	Q	R	L
T	D	L	I	H	C	R	E	T	S	O	F	M	L

Saying: Familiarity breeds contempt and children.
_ _ _ _ _ _ _ _ _ _ _   _ _ _ _ _ _   _ _ _ _ _ _ _ _ _
_ _ _   _ _ _ _ _ _ _ _ _.

Would You Like to Work Together?

sample test group

In this section, you will work with another student on a joint writing and speaking project.

Project Overview

An opinion poll is an investigation of public opinion. A **sample** of a given population is questioned and, if the sample is representative, the results are applied to the population as a whole. For this project, you will prepare and conduct an opinion poll on commercial surrogacy and compile the results in a brief report.

Types of Questions

Questions can be divided into two types: open- and close-ended. Open-ended questions are questions to which there is more than one answer: How do you feel about commercial surrogacy? Open-ended questions are good for breaking the ice and the respondents' answers provide a good source of quotable material. Close-ended questions are questions to which there are a finite number of answers: Should commercial surrogacy be legal in Canada? (The answer is either "yes" or "no.") The following are examples of close-ended questions frequently found in opinion polls:

WORD CULTURE

The expression *break the ice* means to "conquer social reserve." Not surprisingly, the expression comes from "icebreakers," vessels used to clear sea ice to allow ships to pass.

Categorical

Circle one: male / female

Multiple Choice

How many children do you have?
Circle one answer.

a) none   **b)** one   **c)** two   **d)** three or more

Likert Scale

How important is it for a child to grow up in a home with his or her biological parents?
Circle one answer.

1	**2**	**3**	**4**	**5**
not important at all	somewhat important	unsure	very important	extremely important

Ordinal

Write a number between 1 and 5 beside each of the items below. Put a "1" next to the item that is **most** important to you personally, and a "5" next to the item that is **least** important to you personally.

_____ **a)** growing up with one's genetic mother

_____ **b)** growing up with one's genetic father

_____ **c)** growing up with one's genetic mother and father

_____ **d)** growing up with one's gestational mother

_____ **e)** growing up with loving parents who may or may not be your genetic parents

In this project, you will use both open- and close-ended questions.

Required
• A partner and ten opinion poll participants
• A computer
• Internet access
• Printouts

Procedure: Preparing the Opinion Poll
Working with your assigned (or chosen) partner, prepare a two-part opinion poll as outlined below:

Part A: List of Interview Questions
1. Prepare ten open-ended icebreaking questions to ask participants. The purpose of icebreaking questions is to put participants at ease and elicit quotable material; as such, questions must be non-threatening yet pertinent to the topic at hand.

   Example questions include:
   a) What is commercial surrogacy?
   b) What do you know about commercial surrogacy in Canada?
   c) Do you know anyone who has hired a surrogate mother?
   d) Do you know anyone who has had a child resulting from an AHR technique?
   e) How do you feel about human surrogacy in general?

2. Submit your questions to your teacher for correction.

3. Type your corrected list of interview questions, leaving enough blank space under each question for you to write down the participants' answers.

4. Print ten copies of your list of interview questions, one for each participant.

Part B: Questionnaire

5. Prepare ten close-ended questions to be included in a questionnaire that participants will fill out **by hand**. Your first two questions should determine the gender and age of the participants. The ten questions should be of various types (categorical, multiple choice, Likert Scale and ordinal) and must be pertinent to the topic at hand.

by hand in writing (not using a machine)

6. Submit your questions to your teacher for correction.

7. Type your corrected list of questions, adding the following:
   a) A title: Opinion Poll on Commercial Surrogacy
   b) Introductory instructions: Please respond to each of the ten questions below. Answering the questions will only take a few minutes. Your participation is voluntary. The results of the poll will be presented to my English teacher as part of a class project; the results may be discussed in class. Your confidentiality will be respected. Do not write down your name.

8. Print ten copies of your opinion poll, one for each participant.

Procedure: Conducting the Opinion Poll

1. Find ten people (both males and females) willing to respond to your opinion poll. Select participants from each of the following age groups: teenagers (13 to 19 years of age); young adults (20 to 29 years of age); middle-aged adults (30 to 49 years of age); older adults (50 to 69 years of age); and the elderly (70+ years of age).

2. Each partner interviews five participants. For each participant, begin with the ten interview questions. Before conducting the interview:
   a) inform the participant that his or her anonymity will be respected
   b) inform the participant of the context in which the poll is being conducted (a class project)
   c) ask the participant for permission to record his or her answers
   d) inform the participant that he or she may be anonymously quoted when you compile the results and type up your findings in a brief report

3. While interviewing, record your participants' answers.

4. Once the interview has been completed, ask each participant to fill out the questionnaire.

5. Thank each participant for participating in your opinion poll.

Procedure: Compiling the Results in a Brief Report

When compiling the results:

1. Describe the sample.

   Example: *Ten participants ranging in age from 17 to 74 responded to the poll. Equal numbers of males and females participated.*

2. For each of the twenty questions (ten from the interview part of the opinion poll and ten from the questionnaire part of the opinion poll), indicate the breakdown of the responses.

   Examples: *One participant was unable to give a complete definition of commercial surrogacy. He said, "It's the same thing as buying a kid."*

   Three participants indicated that they had no children.

   Include a minimum of two quotes from the interview part of the opinion poll.

3. Draw conclusions.

   Example: *In general, age does not seem to be a factor as to whether one supports or opposes commercial surrogacy.*
   Note: Due to the sample size (and non-randomized nature of the sampling), findings cannot be generalized to a given population.

4. Include an example of the opinion poll distributed. Do not include the actual polls completed: dispose of these polls in a manner that respects the participants' confidentiality (shredding, etc.).

5. Submit your assignment to your teacher for evaluation.

UNIT 4

Do You Have a Heart?

The title of this unit has both figurative and literal meanings. The question, "Do you have a heart?" means "Do you care?" However, it also means "Do you have an actual heart—the organ responsible for pumping blood through your body?"

You, the reader, are being asked whether or not you care about the issue of human organ donation. Knowing that thousands of people die every year due to a shortage of human organs, you are likely to care a great deal—especially if those dying include your friends and family members.

The shortage of human organs must end. In this unit, we will take a look at two controversial methods of achieving this worthy objective.

SECTION A

The Human Organ Trade

Examines the buying and selling of human kidneys.

SECTION B

Xenotransplantation

Examines the transplantation of animal organs into humans.

The Human Organ Trade

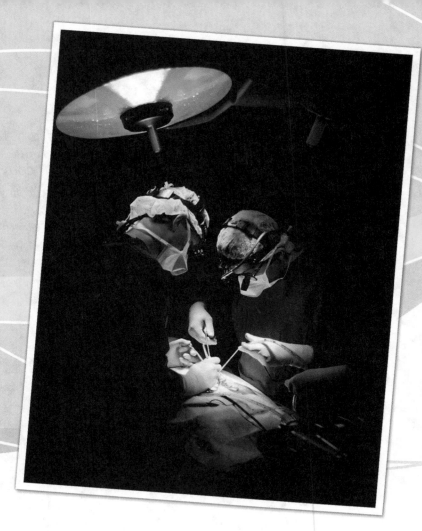

Did You Know?

kidney organ that filters waste liquid

GRAMMAR TIP
Whom is used as an object in formal written English: Whom did he tell? In informal spoken English, *who* is preferred: Who did he tell? For more information on *whom*, see Unit 10 in the companion volume *Parallels: Taking a Stand in English—English Grammar*.

The waiting list for an organ transplant in Canada is long; in fact, more than 3,500 Canadians are presently waiting for an organ (80 percent of whom need a **kidney**). Unfortunately, not every patient survives the wait. Almost one third of patients die before a transplant can be performed. To prevent these deaths, the human organ supply must be increased.

There are several ways to do this:
- Governments could run more publicity campaigns, encouraging citizens to donate organs.
- Parliament could pass a "presumed consent" law, meaning that all Canadians would be considered potential organ donors unless they specify otherwise.
- Animal organs could be genetically modified for human implantation. (See Section B of this unit.)

One controversial solution to the shortage of human kidneys is the legalization of trade in human organs.

The human body has two kidneys, only one of which is necessary for survival. We live in a world of "haves" and "have-nots," meaning that some people are rich and some people are poor. Those in favour of legalizing trade in human kidneys argue that those who can afford to buy a kidney should be allowed to do so. Those against legalization counter that people who are poor should not serve as "organ factories" for people who are rich.

What do *you* think? Is trade in human organs right or wrong? Let's examine the arguments.

Trade in human organs is right because it	Trade in human organs is wrong because it
1. allows the seller to make money.	1. endangers the seller's life.
2. saves the buyer's life.	2. exploits the seller.
3. reduces health care costs.	3. treats the human body like an object.

pit (somebody or something) against (somebody or something) make (somebody or something) an opponent of (somebody or something else)

The debate surrounding the human organ trade is of global significance, **pitting industrialized countries against developing countries**. People willing to sell an organ typically live in great poverty, and the world's poorest people live in "Third World" nations in Africa, Asia and Latin America. Should we, as citizens of a global village, permit such a trade? This is the question that you will be asked to answer.

What's the Buzz?

Answers will vary. For a comment on statement 5, see the Additional Notes in the Teacher Section of the companion website.

Let's personalize the issue of trade in human organs.

- **For each of the statements below, indicate whether you agree, disagree or are unsure.**
- **Be prepared to discuss your answers with the class.**

Statements	Agree	Disagree	Unsure
1. If I had no other choice, I would buy a kidney to survive.	☐	☐	☐
2. I would rather buy a kidney for a family member than donate one of my own.	☐	☐	☐
3. If I were extremely poor, I would sell a kidney.	☐	☐	☐
4. I would be willing to donate a kidney to a stranger.	☐	☐	☐
5. My body belongs to me.	☐	☐	☐

Discussion

■ **Get into groups of three or four and consider the questions below.**

■ **Present your findings to the rest of the class.**

Note: As one group is presenting, be prepared for your teacher to intervene and ask you for *your* opinion.

1. How do people in Canada become organ donors?

2. How many people in the group are organ donors?

3. Why do most people choose not to be organ donors?

Have You Read?

Ronald Bailey is an environmental journalist, lecturer and science correspondent for *Reason* magazine. His article "I Am, Therefore I Sell" appeared in the *Ottawa Citizen* on January 7, 2004. The title of Mr. Bailey's article is a play on René Descartes's famous words, "I think; therefore, I am." From the title of Mr. Bailey's article, can you make an educated guess as to how he feels about trade in human organs? Is he for or against it?

READING STRATEGY
Many people find it helpful to "read with their hands," meaning they underline, highlight and annotate text as they read.

Students are asked to determine the meaning of the word *schlub* from the context (line 8). This word, a variant of the Yiddish *zhlub*, (insultingly) refers to a person lacking in social skills or refinement. For the purpose of this exercise, accept *guy* (or equivalent) as a possible meaning.

Before Reading

■ **Read the defined words and comprehension questions before reading the article. Skim for the main ideas and scan for the answers to the questions.**

While Reading

When reading articles in your first language, do you ever come across words you don't know? The answer is probably *yes*. Do you immediately look up the word in a dictionary, or do you first try to guess the meaning of the word from the context in which it is used? Most effective readers try to "guess from context" before turning to a dictionary.

■ **In the following article, if you come across a word that you don't know, try to figure out what it means from the context. For example, try to figure out what the word *schlub* (line 8) means from the context alone.**

I Am, Therefore I Sell

bootlegger dealer in illegal merchandise

An international ring of human organ **bootleggers** involving people in South Africa and Brazil was broken up in early December. Almost everyone thought that these transactions—even though they saved some people's lives, increased some people's options and involved no

evil immoral

5 force or coercion—were **evil**.

Opposition to selling organs is visceral, so to speak, in most people, and is reflected in the laws of nearly every nation.

groggily sleepily
pain agony

We've all heard the urban legend about some poor schlub who **groggily** comes to in a hotel room writhing in **pain** with a huge set of stitches
10 down his back, usually in a bathtub full of ice. The last thing he remembers was sitting at the bar drinking with a leggy blonde. It turns out that he's missing one of his kidneys.

tale story

Poor countries are frequently swept with gruesome scare **tales** of hapless children being kidnapped and shipped off to Europe or the United States
15 where their organs are taken for the benefit of rich kids. When I was working in Costa Rica in the early 1990s, a member of the National Assembly held a press conference where she declared that she knew the identity of a local kid who had been kidnapped and whose kidney had been taken. She promised to bring him forward in the next few days. She never did.

ghoulish morbid

20 So far, there's no evidence these **ghoulish** scenarios have ever really happened. But they might happen one day. Circumstances are emerging that could make a black market in involuntarily obtained human organs easier and more attractive.

randomly arbitrarily

With transplants today, organs have to be genetically matched to the
25 patient's immune system so that they won't be rejected. That means that **randomly** acquiring organs by knocking people over the head won't do. However, scientists might soon create new drugs that are better at handling immune rejection. That would widen the range of organs that could be useful to any given patient. Such medical advances could tempt
30 unscrupulous people to supply desperate patients with transplantable organs from anyone they can get their hands on, willing or not.

And more and more doctors around the world have received the specialized training needed to successfully transplant organs. Such doctors in poor countries might well succumb to the temptation to make a bit more
35 money for themselves.

worldwide internationally

Not only the means, but also the motives exist to jumpstart an involuntary organ market: The shortage of transplantable organs continues to worsen **worldwide**. In the United States alone, the list of patients waiting for an organ continues to lengthen. There are, for example, some 83,000 people
40 waiting for a kidney.

despite in spite of

Despite all the above, involuntary black markets in human organs are not inevitable. Aboveground markets and science can keep those urban legends legendary.

© Pearson Longman – Reproduction prohibited   The Human Organ Trade **Section A** | 87 |

Medical progress offers the prospect of several different ways to end the
45 shortage of good transplant organs. Embryonic and adult stem cells
might be used to repair or replace damaged organs and tissues. Other
research underway now uses genetic techniques to "humanize" animal
organs so that they would be compatible with human immune systems. And
researchers are also trying to create artificial organs for transplanting.

50 But until the march of science makes these or other means of supplying
needed organs a reality, changes in the law can allow markets to help in
the here and now.

The recently busted network of organ sellers operating in South Africa
and Brazil was purchasing kidneys from **healthy** but poor Brazilians who
55 were flown to a private hospital in Durban, South Africa. Each of the
Brazilians sold one of their kidneys, which were removed and installed in
foreign transplant patients. The sellers received between $10,000 and
$13,000 U.S., with all their expenses paid.

"They're mostly poor people just trying to make a better life for them-
60 selves," said Manoel Caetano Cysneiros, a police spokesman in Recife,
Brazil. "They'll probably buy a house or a small business with that
money." In fact, it has been reported that several people who sold one of
their kidneys were sufficiently satisfied with the deal that they returned
home and urged others to do the same.

65 The transplant patients apparently paid about $120,000 U.S. each for the
operations. The patients—now freed of onerous and expensive dialysis
treatments—can live relatively normal lives. On the face of it, this voluntary
transaction appears to be another classic win-win market phenomenon. So
what is so wrong with the voluntary sale of human organs?

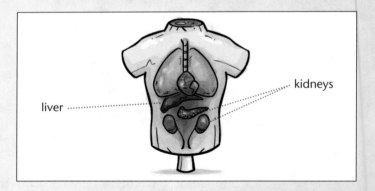

liver .... kidneys

70 In recent years many doctors and bioethicists have warmed to the idea that
at least in certain circumstances it's all right to buy and sell human organs.
Last April, a South African legal expert endorsed the idea that a person
"should have the right" to decide to sell a kidney. Just the day before the
South African story broke, the BBC reported on a doctors' conference in
75 Britain that considered the ethics of buying and selling organs. Professor
John Harris from Manchester University opined that people should have
the right to sell a kidney, part of their liver, or bone marrow.

Jailing people for the voluntary sale of human organs helps neither those
who need the organs nor those willing to sell them. Until medical science
80 comes up with new ways to ease the growing shortage of transplantable

healthy in good
condition

VOCABULARY TIP
The expression *on the face
of it* means "judging by
appearances only." The
expression is used when
one describes the way a
situation seems to be in
order to show that one
thinks the situation is
completely different: On
the face of it, they are
happily married; however,
I strongly suspect their
marriage is in trouble.

organs, making the current voluntary black market into a white market with legally enforceable contracts could well forestall the development of an involuntary black market in organs. That would be win-win for us all.

940 words

Reading Comprehension

■ **Respond to each of the questions below.**

1. A *pun* is a play on words. In line 6, the author writes, "Opposition to selling organs is visceral …" Explain how the word *visceral* is a pun.

   The word visceral has two meanings: 1) emotional and 2) relating to internal body organs. The pun involves using the word in both its figurative and literal senses.

2. The author doesn't believe the story of the "poor schlub" who loses a kidney (lines 8–10).   TRUE ✓ FALSE ☐

3. According to the author, stories of kidnapping and organ theft
   a) are unheard of.
   b) have been proven true.
   c) could never happen.
   (d)) might one day be proven true.

4. In your own words, explain how improved anti-immune rejection drugs might actually encourage the involuntary black market?

   Organ donors and recipients must be genetically matched; if the match is not close enough, the recipient's body will reject the organ. If anti-rejection drugs are improved, it is conceivable that "any organ will do" and this situation will encourage the growth of the involuntary black market.

See Section B in this unit for more information on the humanizing of animal organs.

5. List three ways that medical science might one day be able to end the human organ shortage.
   a) by using embryonic and adult stem cells to repair or replace damaged organs and tissues;

   b) by humanizing animal organs (see Section B in this unit);

   c) by creating artificial organs.

The answer to question 6 is false because poor Brazilians who were paid to donate organs encouraged others to do the same.

The answer to question 7 is false because the author indicates that support is growing slowly, stating that many (but not all) doctors and bioethicists have "warmed to the idea" in recent years. Nowhere does the author state that support is "wholehearted."

6. Poor Brazilians who sold one of their kidneys warned other Brazilians not to do the same.   TRUE ☐ FALSE ✓

7. Bioethicists wholeheartedly support trade in human organs.   TRUE ☐ FALSE ✓

8. In addition to kidneys, what other human tissues could be part of the proposed human organ trade?

part of the liver or bone marrow
_____

_____

The answer to question 9 is false because the author claims that jailing people helps neither the donor nor the recipient.

Question 10 tests the student's ability to identify the main idea of the text.

9. The author believes that those involved in the voluntary sale of human organs should be jailed.   **TRUE** ☐ **FALSE** ☑

10. In general, the author believes that
    a) individuals should have the right to buy and sell human organs.
    b) the involuntary black market in human organs must be stopped.
    c) the voluntary trade of human organs is a long-term solution to the current human organ shortage.
    d) trade in human organs should be allowed and regulated until science can come up with better solutions to the current organ shortage.

Discussion

Answers will vary. Go to http://snopes.com/ for examples of urban legends you can share with your students.

- **In small groups, discuss your answers to each of the questions below.**
- **Be prepared to share your group's ideas with the rest of the class.**

1. Why do people tell urban legends? Do you know any urban legends? If so, what are they?

2. According to the article, organ recipients paid $120,000 U.S. and organ sellers received between $10,000 and $13,000 U.S. Who do you think got the difference?

3. Are poor Brazilians who sell their kidneys being exploited? Why or why not?

Word Work

In the article, ten terms are defined for you:

Adjectives	Adverbs	Nouns	Preposition
1. evil	4. groggily	7. bootlegger	10. despite
2. ghoulish	5. randomly	8. pain	
3. healthy	6. worldwide	9. ~~tale~~	

- **In the text below, there are ten terms in italics. Replace each of the terms with one of the words from the list above. Pluralize nouns as required. The first one has been done for you as an example.**

WORD CULTURE
The term *bootlegging* originates from the hiding of a small bottle of alcohol in the leg of a boot at a time in the American past when men wore high boots and alcohol consumption was illegal. A person who participates in bootlegging is, of course, a bootlegger.

Have I ever told you the *story* (1._____tale_____) of the day my grandfather almost got killed? My grandfather was a Canadian police officer during the American Prohibition in the 1920s. During that time, alcohol was illegal in the U.S.—but not in Canada. Many Americans became *dealers in illegal alcohol* (2._____bootleggers_____), getting their supply in Canada and selling it in the States. Supporters of Prohibition believed that many *immoral* (**3.** _____evil_____) acts could be directly linked to alcohol consumption. At any rate, my grandfather was responsible for patrolling the U.S./Canadian border. Every day he would try to catch the smugglers, never going twice to the same place at the same time. He would *arbitrarily* (**4.** _____randomly_____) choose his checkpoints to make sure the criminals wouldn't discover his routine. One morning, he decided to go out early. He'd only had a couple of hours rest. He *sleepily* (**5.** _____groggily_____) got into his truck and started toward his destination. *In spite of* (**6.** _____Despite_____) two or three cups of coffee in his body, he still wasn't fully awake and he crashed his vehicle into a lamppost. As he got out of his truck, the upper part of the post came crashing down, hitting him on the right shoulder, dislocating his arm. My grandfather was in *agony* (**7.** _____pain_____). Unfortunately, my grandfather was not *in very good physical condition* (**8.** _____healthy_____). He smoked and drank more than he should. As he lay on the side of the road, he began to have *morbid* (**9.** _____ghoulish_____) thoughts. He was certain he was going to die—and he began hallucinating that the smugglers were going to get him. He passed out and woke up several hours later, back at the border patrol office. He didn't know how he'd gotten there, but beside him was a bottle of Canadian whiskey and a note that read, "Caught you lying down on the job— thought you could use a lift!" After that, when anyone would suggest banning alcohol *internationally* (**10.** _____worldwide_____), my grandfather would laugh and say, "I'll drink to that!"

H ave You Heard?

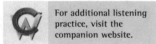

For additional listening practice, visit the companion website.

Shelagh Rogers, journalist and broadcaster for the CBC radio program *This Morning*, interviewed University College of London professor Janet Radcliffe and *Globe and Mail* investigative reporter Lisa Priest about the human organ trade in a segment entitled "The Organ Trade: Should the Sale of Kidneys Be Legalized?" You will hear an excerpt from the interview, which was originally broadcast on June 8, 2001.

Pre-Listening Vocabulary

■ **Match each term with its definition. The first one has been done for you as an example.**

Terms		Definitions
1. abhorrent	_h_	a) permanent mark on the skin left by a cut
2. expensive	c	b) condemn
3. get rid of	f	c) costly
4. medic	i	d) intermediary
5. middleman	d	e) strange
6. odd	e	f) dispose of
7. overseas	g	g) out of the country
8. purchase	j	h) ~~repugnant~~
9. revile	b	i) someone trained to give medical treatment
10. scar	a	j) buy

■ **After verifying your answers with your teacher, find a partner and correctly use the above terms in ten sentences of your own. Each partner is responsible for writing five sentences that demonstrate the correct usage of the terms.**

While Listening

You will hear the interview twice.

■ **The first time you listen, try to determine the speakers' positions on trade in human organs.**

■ **The second time you listen, pay attention to the details of what each speaker has to say, taking point-form notes to help you remember the information.**

LISTENING STRATEGY
Where are the best seats in a classroom? In the front, of course! Why? Because there are fewer distractions. Effective listeners are focused listeners. When speakers say something with which you disagree, don't lose your focus and start thinking about why they are wrong—think about what they are saying. Not everybody can sit in the front of the class, but with a little self-discipline, everybody can be a focused listener.

Listening Comprehension

▬ **Referring to your notes, respond to each of the questions below.**

The answer to question 1 is false because Ms. Richards says that feeling that something is abhorrent is not a good reason for stopping it.

1. Janet Radcliffe Richards believes that trade in human organs should be banned because it is abhorrent.   TRUE ☐ FALSE ☑

2. According to Lisa Priest, how many years can a Torontonian wait for a kidney transplant?
   up to six years

3. Fill in the blank. "_____Dialysis_____" isn't a cure.

4. Lisa gives two reasons why transplantation is better than dialysis. What are they?
   a) A transplantation removes the need for the patient to have dialysis several times a week for the rest of his or her life.
   b) A transplantation is cheaper than dialysis (by about $176,000 over a five-year period).

The topic of trade in executed Chinese prisoners' organs would make a great research topic, involving human rights in general and the topics of human organ trade and capital punishment in particular.

5. In Canada, there is a black market for kidneys from China. One source of the kidneys is from accident victims. What is the other source?
   executed Chinese prisoners

6. According to Janet, the medical community objects to trade in human organs more than the general public.   TRUE ☑ FALSE ☐

7. Janet
   a) finds the arguments against trade in human organs weak.
   b) believes there is a danger that poor people will be exploited.
   c) believes that exploitation of the poor should be stopped.
   d) All of the above

8. At the end of the interview, Lisa criticizes Canadians. What is her criticism?
   She criticizes Canadians for being against trade in human kidneys all the while not offering other solutions to those dying from lack of donor organs.

Questions 9 and 10 test the student's ability to identify the two main ideas presented in the segment.

9. Is Lisa for or against legalizing the sale of human kidneys?
   Lisa is for legalizing the sale of human kidneys.

10. Is Janet for or against legalizing the sale of human kidneys?
    Janet is for legalizing the sale of human kidneys.

Would You Write That Down?

For additional writing practice, visit the companion website.

Your teacher may ask you to complete one or more of the writing assignments below.

> **WRITING SUGGESTION**
> First impressions count. When submitting a written assignment, make sure that it is easy to read. For in-class assignments, if your handwriting isn't legible, print. Use a word processor for assignments that you can prepare at home. Leave enough room for your teacher to correct and comment; double space and leave a 2.5 cm margin. Before handing in a written assignment, ask yourself what kind of first impression it makes. The first impression will surely count when you get your grade!

Free-form Writing

Answers will vary. In free-form writing, no specific structure is required; however, the student is asked to write 75 to 100 words. You may wish to increase or decrease the number of words required. The free-form writing assignments are great for "sampling" student writing ability.

- **Write 75 to 100 words in response to one of the following questions:**

1. Are you an organ donor? Why or why not?

2. Do you think you should have the right to sell any body part that you wish? Explain.

3. Would you buy a kidney from a poor person in the Third World in order to save your own life or that of a loved one? Explain.

Essay Writing

Answers will vary. The recommended essay format for *Parallels: Taking a Stand in English* is the persuasive essay (see "Appendix A: The Persuasive Essay" on page 182), but you may opt for another essay structure. The student is asked to write 300 to 400 words. You may also wish to increase or decrease the number of words required.

- **Write a 300- to 400-word essay using one of the thesis statements below.**
- **Do some research on the Internet to find evidence that supports your chosen thesis statement. (See Appendix A to review the structure of a persuasive essay.)**

1. Canadian doctors should (or should not) provide post-operative care for patients who have bought a kidney overseas.

2. Young people waiting for an organ transplant should (or should not) be given priority over old people.

3. Treating the human body as a commodity is (or is not) wrong.

4. Canada should (or should not) boycott countries that permit trade in human organs.

5. The involuntary black market in human organs is (or is not) a serious global issue.

Would You Speak Up?

For additional speaking practice, visit the companion website.

Answers will vary.

SPEAKING SUGGESTION
Before speaking in public, ask yourself the following question: Why is what I have to say important? Once you know the answer, be sure to tell the audience; this will encourage them to listen more attentively.

Your teacher may ask you to participate in one or more of the speaking activities below.

Discussion

- In small groups, consider one (or more) of the following questions.
- Be prepared to share your thoughts with other groups in the class.

1. How do you feel about signing an organ donation card?

2. Why do you think most people oppose trade in human organs?

3. Can the voluntary black market in human organs be stopped? Why or why not?

4. How is selling your labour different from selling a body part?

5. How do you *feel* about trade in human organs? What do you *think* about trade in human organs? Are your feelings and thoughts the same or different? Explain.

Answers will vary. Discourse structure is outlined in "Appendix B: Discourse and Debate" (p. 182). Given the polemic nature of *Parallels: Taking a Stand in English*, a persuasive discourse structure is recommended. The suggested speaking time is five minutes; you may wish to increase or decrease the required speaking time. As indicated in the Speaking Suggestion above, encourage students to tell the audience why what they have to say is important!

Discourse

- Prepare a structured, five-minute speech on one of the thesis statements below. (See Appendix B for suggested speaking structure.)
- Do some research to find evidence that supports your chosen thesis statement. Make sure your speech has an introduction, a development and a conclusion.

1. Trade in human organs should (or should not) be legalized in Canada.

2. The Canadian government should (or should not) make organ donation obligatory.

3. Trade in human organs is (or is not) necessary.

4. Urban legends are (or are not) based on truth.

5. Science can (or cannot) eliminate the shortage of human organs.

Answers will vary. Debate structure is outlined in "Appendix B: Discourse and Debate" (pp. 194–198). Arguments "for" and "against" the proposal are listed on page 85. For more information on running small group or whole class debates, refer to the Additional Notes in the Teacher Section of the companion website.

Debate

- Debate the following proposal: The human organ trade is wrong. (See Appendix B for the rules of debate.)

What's That Word Mean Again?

In the reading and listening sections, we focused on twenty terms—ten from each section. The activity below is designed to help you review some of this vocabulary.

Hangman

Do you remember playing the language game Hangman in primary school? Play a few games with a partner to review key vocabulary.

Required
- A pen or pencil
- Five sheets of blank paper
- A bit of luck!

Instructions

1. With a partner, review the twenty terms presented in the reading and listening sections of this part of Unit 4.

2. Set up a Hangman game as indicated in the illustration.

3. Student A secretly chooses a word from the list and draws a blank for each letter in the word.

4. Student B guesses a letter. If Student B guesses correctly, Student A writes the letter on the appropriate blank. If Student B guesses incorrectly, Student A draws part of the hangman.

5. A point is awarded when Student B guesses the word **or** when Student A completes the hangman before the word is guessed.

6. Change roles and start a new game.

7. Play the best three out of five.

Remember: Don't look at the word list while you are actually playing the game.

Would You Like to Work Together?

In this section, you will work with another student on a joint writing and speaking project.

Answers will vary. This paired project encourages cooperative learning.

Project Overview

In the "Did You Know?" section of this part of the unit, you read an overview article about organ transplants in Canada (pp. 84–85). One way to summarize an article and assimilate information is to write information questions, the answers to which are found in the article you are reading. Take for example the first sentence of the "Did You Know?" article, "The waiting list for an organ transplant in Canada is long; in fact, more than 3,500 Canadians are presently waiting for an organ (80 percent of whom need a kidney)." A question you could write based on the information contained in this sentence would be, "How many Canadians are presently waiting for an organ?" Working with a partner, you will create five information questions based on the "Did You Know?" article and five information questions based on an Internet article about the human organ trade. You and your partner will then ask these ten questions to another team of two in the class.

Required

- A computer with Internet access
- A grammar textbook

Procedure

This activity is carried out in two parts.

Part A

1. Working with your chosen (or assigned) partner, create five information questions based on the "Did You Know?" article. Then go to the English version of the Wikipedia website and type "organ trade" into the search engine located in the left-hand menu; create five information questions based on this online article.

   (Base your questions only on the information contained in this article and not on the information contained in the links included in this article.) Use at least four different tenses when writing your questions. To review question formation, see *Parallels: Taking a Stand in English—English Grammar*, Units 2 to 6. After each question, name the tense used (simple present, present continuous, simple past, past continuous, present perfect, etc.).

2. Double-check your question formation and submit your list of information questions to your teacher for verification.

Part B

3. With your partner, challenge another team of two to respond correctly to your teacher-verified list of information questions. Note: You must read (not show) your questions to the opposing team and neither team may look back at the original articles.

4. Give one point for each correct answer and no points for each incorrect answer.

5. If you're unsure about the answer, ask your teacher to act as "referee."

6. Alternate asking and answering questions with the other team.

7. The team with the highest score wins!

Variation: Your teacher may increase the difficulty of this project by selecting two new (and longer) articles on organ transplants and/or the human organ trade and giving copies of the articles to all teams of two. All teams read both articles. Half the teams write questions based on Article A and half the teams write questions based on Article B. The "challenge" is then carried out as described in Part B above, pairing Article A teams with Article B teams.

Xenotransplantation

Did You Know?

diabetes disease in which there is too much sugar in your blood

According to Health Canada, xenotransplantation (or cross-species transplantation) is the transfer of living cells, tissues or organs from one species to another. Typically, the transfer is from non-human animals to human animals with the objective of improving human health. Xenotransplanted cells can treat people with **diabetes**, Alzheimer's and/or Parkinson's disease. Xenotransplanted tissues

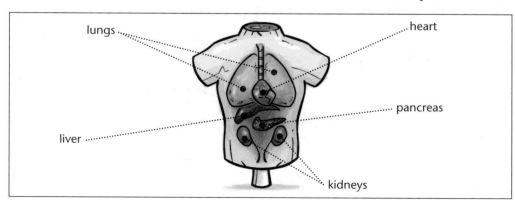

can treat burn patients and provide corneal transplants for the visually impaired and bone transplants for limb reconstruction. Xenotransplanted organs can be used for heart, lung, liver, kidney and/or pancreas transplants. Despite these uses, however, xenotransplantation has yet to become a recognized medical practice in Canada. It is still a supervised experimental practice designed to compensate one day for the shortage of human cell, tissue and organ donors in Canada.

The arguments are strong on both sides of the issue.

Xenotransplantation is right because it	Xenotransplantation is wrong because it
1. saves human lives.	1. could cause a pandemic.
2. will eventually eliminate the need for human organ donation.	2. harms the human recipient.
3. advances scientific knowledge.	3. exploits animals.

Xenotransplantation is an unknown entity. Scientists really don't know what its long-term consequences will be. For some people, this lack of knowledge is the reason why we *should not* proceed with xenotransplantation. For others, this lack of knowledge is the reason why we *should* proceed with xenotransplantation. In all scientific experimentation, potential risks have to be calculated. In this unit, you will be asked to calculate the potential risks of xenotransplantation and then determine whether or not they outnumber the potential benefits.

What's the Buzz?

Answers will vary. For a comment on question 2, see the Additional Notes in the Teacher Section of the companion website.

Let's personalize the issue of xenotransplantation.

- **For each of the statements below, indicate whether you agree, disagree or are unsure.**
- **Be prepared to discuss your answers with the class.**

Statements	Agree	Disagree	Unsure
1. Using animals for food is no different from using animals for organs.	☐	☐	☐
2. An animal life is of equal value to a human life.	☐	☐	☐
3. I would feel "weird" having an animal organ transplanted into my body.	☐	☐	☐
4. Sometimes scientists go too far.	☐	☐	☐
5. Xenotransplantation exploits animals.	☐	☐	☐

Discussion

- Get into groups of three or four and consider the questions below. Try to arrive at a consensus.
- Present your findings to the rest of the class.

Note: As one group is presenting, be prepared for your teacher to intervene and ask you for *your* opinion.

1. Some animal rights activists assert that humans and animals are of equal value and have equal rights. Do you agree or disagree with this assertion?

2. In transgenics, an organism's genome is modified with genes from another organism. It is theoretically possible to genetically modify animal organs to resemble human organs. One day, human hearts, livers and kidneys could be grown in animals and then transplanted into humans. How do you feel about using animals as "human organ factories"?

3. Scientists have theorized that the Human Immunodeficiency Virus (HIV) spread from chimpanzees to humans. With cross-species transplantation comes the risk of cross-species viral transmission. In your opinion, what percentage of risk is acceptable—a 10 percent risk, a 5 percent risk, a 0.1 percent risk? How much risk is too much risk? Explain.

> **GRAMMAR TIP**
> In general, use "'s" to indicate possession for singular nouns and "s'" to indicate possession for regular plural nouns: one organism's genome but two organisms' genomes. For more information on possessive nouns, see Unit 9 in the companion volume *Parallels: Taking a Stand in English—English Grammar*.

Have You Read?

For additional reading practice, visit the companion website.

> Michael Fumento is an attorney whose article "Pigs May Become Man's Best Friend" appeared in the *National Post* on December 19, 2003. The title of Mr. Fumento's article is a play on the saying, "A dog is a man's best friend." From the title of Mr. Fumento's article, can you make an educated guess as to how he feels about xenotransplantation? Is he for or against it?

> **READING STRATEGY**
> Many people find it helpful to "read with their hands," meaning they underline, highlight and annotate text as they read.

Before Reading

- Read the defined words and comprehension questions before reading the article. Skim for the main ideas and scan for the answers to the questions.

While Reading

When reading articles in your first language, do you ever come across words you don't know? The answer is probably *yes*. Do you immediately look up the word in a dictionary, or do you first try to guess the meaning of the word from the context in which it is used? Most effective readers try to "guess from context" before turning to a dictionary.

■ In the article below, if you come across a word that you don't know, try to figure out what it means from the context. For example, try to figure out what the word *alas* (line 38) means from the context alone.

PIGS MAY BECOME MAN'S BEST FRIEND

BY MICHAEL FUMENTO

Even the hardened Russian police were horrified. **In the nick of time**, they had rescued five-year-old Andrei in a small city near Moscow. He had no idea he was about to be sold for the equivalent of US $90,000, nor that his sellers were his own grandmother and uncle. Nor could he imag-
5 ine that the buyer wasn't interested in the whole "package"—just the kidneys, eyes and possibly heart and lungs.

Ironically, it's precisely because techniques in organ transplantation have **tremendously** improved that **grisly** trafficking in human organs has increased tremendously and the waiting list for organ transplants keeps
10 growing. In the United States, about 83,000 people are waiting (4,000 in Canada as of the end of 2002). In 2001, more than 6,100 Americans died waiting—including a friend of mine. He was 44.

Someday, researchers will be able to grow new organs for us before we need them. But until then, our best hope lies in xenotransplantation. This
15 means transferring organs such as hearts, kidneys, lungs, and livers from pigs or other animals to humans.

Pig heart valves have routinely been used in humans since 1964, but they contain no live cells. Cook Biotech, Inc. of West Layette, Indiana, is already using freeze-dried pig intestinal lining as pig patches, for everything from
20 closing up large **sores**, to regrowing cartilage in knees, to reinforcing the abdominal wall during hernia operations. The pig patch initially seals the area, and then acts as a scaffolding to allow the body to build new tissue while the porcine cells are absorbed. Rejection is never a problem.

The problem arises with the transplantation of **whole** organs. Whether
25 porcine or primate, rejection is quick and untreatable. The most promising method for overcoming rejection is biotechnology. By inserting human genetic material—preferably the recipient's own—into pigs or other donor animals, the human body should recognize the new organ as its own.

30 Since pig organs are the right size for humans, and since **swine** are cheap and easy to breed, scientists have long considered them potentially the best donors. But "when you transplant a pig organ into a nonhuman primate, it is rejected immediately," John Logan of Nextran, Inc. in Princeton, New Jersey, told *The New York Times*. "It just turns black
35 before your eyes, within thirty minutes."

The reason is a pig gene called GGTA1, which directs the production of an enzyme that attaches sugar molecules to cells in their bodies. These are instantly recognized as **foreign** in primates and attacked. (Alas, there's no **breed** of pig with NutraSweet genes.)

---

in the nick of time just in time

tremendously enormously

grisly horrible

sore skin infection

whole complete

swine pig

foreign unknown
breed type of plant or animal

40 The best way to make sugar-free pigs would be to create cloned pigs with the genes "knocked out" (rendered inactive) that are responsible for producing GGTA1 and to breed them.

PPL Therapeutics of Scotland, the makers of Dolly the sheep, did just this. It became the first company to clone pigs; then later it made cloned pigs
45 that lacked the sugar gene. Shortly thereafter, Immerge BioTherapeutics of Boston announced it too had developed swine worthy of having pearls cast before them, with miniature GGTA1-less pigs whose organs would better fit humans.

Now companies are working to defeat the rejection problem that
50 plagues all transplants, whether from pigs or people. PPL's spin-off company, Revivicor, Inc. in Blacksburg, Virginia, has just announced it has succeeded in making baboons live as long as eighty-one days with sugar-free pig kidneys.

One worry with pig xenotransplantation is the possibility of transmitting
55 viruses. In fact, we catch lots of viruses including the **flu** from pigs and other animals. Still, organ transplants should always be disease-free. One study did show that porcine endogenous retroviruses (PERVs), which are integrated into pig genes, replicated in mice that had severely weakened immune systems. Fortunately, PERVs have not been shown to cause
60 disease. Further, "There are no known viruses in the pig genome that have caused disease in man," according to Khazal Paradis, the director of clinical research at Imutran Ltd. in Britain.

But the potential for such viral **spread** hasn't been ruled out. Happily, for every biotech problem somebody always comes up with a solution.
65 Indeed, Immerge Biotherapeutics has now bred miniature pigs that don't produce PERV capable of replicating in human cells, even though it also found that its inbred miniature swine do not transmit PERV viruses to human cells.

But pity the poor dog. Pigs may soon become man's best friend.

(739 words)

flu respiratory infection

spread transmission

Reading Comprehension

■ Respond to each of the questions below.

The answer to question 1 is false because the Russian boy was saved "in the nick of time."

1. The author begins his article with a frightening anecdote about a young Russian boy who was killed for his body parts.   TRUE ☐ FALSE ☑

2. The author has been personally touched by the issue of human organ donation.   TRUE ☑ FALSE ☐

3. What is a "pig patch"?
   a freeze-dried pig intestinal lining
   _____

4. List three uses of a pig patch.

   a) close sores _____

   b) re-grow cartilage in knees _____

   c) reinforce the abdominal wall during hernia operations _____

5. What problem is associated with the transplantation of whole organs? How can this problem be solved?

Organ rejection is the main problem: rejection is quick and untreatable. Rejection can be solved by

biotechnology: human genetic material is inserted into animals, inciting the body to recognize the foreign

organ as its own.

6. Why do scientists consider pigs to be the best potential donors?

Pigs' organs are the right size for humans and the supply is cheap and accessible (pigs are easy to breed).

_____

7. Which of the following statements is true?

   a) Pig organs are immediately rejected when transplanted into non human primates.

   b) GGTA1 is the pig gene responsible for organ rejection.

   c) Pigs have been genetically modified to eliminate the GGTA1 gene.

   (d) All of the above

8. Animals can transmit viruses to humans.   TRUE ☑ FALSE ☐

9. The author is optimistic that science can solve the problem of cross-species viral transmission.   TRUE ☑ FALSE ☐

Question 10 tests the student's ability to identify the main idea of the text.

10. In general, the author believes that

   a) human organ trafficking must be stopped.

   b) the problem of pig organ rejection can be solved.

   c) xenotransplantation is too risky to pursue.

   (d) until science comes up with a better alternative, xenotransplantation is society's best hope for overcoming the shortage of human organs.

Discussion

Answers will vary. For an explanation of *speciesist* (question 3), see the Additional Notes in the Teacher Section of the companion website.

■ **In small groups, discuss your answers to each of the questions below.**

■ **Be prepared to share your group's ideas with the rest of the class.**

1. How do you feel about animal experimentation?

2. How do you feel about xenotransplantation?

3. Are you a "speciesist"? That is, do you treat your species better than other species? Explain.

VOCABULARY TIP
The word *species* is the same in the singular as it is in the plural—"one species," "two species," etc.

Word Work

In the article, ten terms are defined for you:

Adjectives	Adverb	Expression	Nouns
1. foreign 2. grisly 3. whole	4. tremendously	5. in the nick of time	6. ~~breed~~ 7. flu 8. sore 9. spread 10. swine

■ **In the text below, there are ten terms in italics. Replace each of the terms with one of the words from the list above. Pluralize nouns as required. The first one has been done for you as an example.**

Every day, some *types of animals* (1. ___breeds___) are disappearing. In fact, *complete* (2. ___whole___) species are "going the way of the dodo bird"! While there is no concern for chickens, cows or *pigs* (3. ___swine___), there is a great deal of concern for African wild dogs, Chinese pandas and North American swift foxes. Many species recently added to the world's endangered species list are entirely *unknown* (4. ___foreign___) to most Canadians. Extinction can almost always be blamed on the world's most "unendangered" species—humankind. The human species commits *horrible* (5. ___grisly___) acts of "animalcide" every day. These acts must stop, or the human species may one day find itself on the endangered list. Species are *enormously* (6. ___tremendously___) inter-dependent; when one dies, the others risk death too. There is evidence that seemingly insignificant plant species could be of vital importance to human health. Plant extracts can treat *skin infections* (7. ___sores___) and can shorten *respiratory infections* (8. ___flu___). Who knows? Maybe some plant extracts could one day be used in the treatment of more serious diseases like cancer and AIDS. Disease and the *transmission* (9. ___spread___) of disease are serious problems for humanity. Humanity can stop species extinction *just in time* (10. ___in the nick of time___). It's not too late!

Have You Heard?

For additional listening practice, visit the companion website.

insulin hormone that regulates blood sugar

In the second part of this exercise, students are asked to work in pairs and write ten sentences, one for each of the terms defined. Model sentences are included in the Additional Notes in the Teacher Section of the companion website.

Bob McDonald, host of the CBC radio program *Quirks and Quarks*, interviewed Dr. David White about a controversial study conducted on twelve Mexican teenagers with Juvenile (or Type 1) Diabetes. The program segment aired on September 7, 2002. The study was controversial because the diabetic teenagers were injected with **insulin**-producing islet cells from pigs. Listen in as Mr. McDonald interviews Dr. White about the study.

Pre-Listening Vocabulary

▬ Match each word with its definition. The first one has been done for you as an example.

Terms		Definitions
1. daily	_g_	a) collect
2. harm	_e_	b) disagreeable
3. harvest	_a_	c) not accept
4. monitor	_j_	d) small chance
5. nasty	_b_	e) damage
6. obvious	_h_	f) experiment
7. reject	_c_	g) ~~done every day~~
8. remote risk	_d_	h) evident
9. trial	_f_	i) trouble
10. worry	_i_	j) observe

▬ After verifying your answers with your teacher, find a partner and correctly use the above terms in ten sentences of your own. Each partner is responsible for writing five sentences that demonstrate the correct usage of the terms.

While Listening

You will hear the interview twice.

- **The first time you listen, try to identify the general idea.**
- **The second time you listen, pay attention to the details of what Dr. White has to say, taking point-form notes to help you remember the information.**

Listening Comprehension

- **Referring to your notes, respond to each of the questions below.**

1. Pig insulin has been used to treat diabetes for many years.   TRUE ☑ FALSE ☐

2. Fill in the blank. The islets are the insulin-producing cells. Therefore, it is an _____obvious_____ step, instead of actually injecting the insulin, to transplant the pig islets themselves into the patients.

3. Why did the human-to-human islet transplant study conducted in Edmonton at the University of Alberta only transplant thirty-seven patients over three years?
   There was a lack of human donors to provide the pancreas from which the islet cells are harvested.

Sertoli Italian physiologist who first described certain cells

4. According to Dr. White, rejection is less likely in non-human-to-human islet transplants than in human-to-human islet transplants since pig islets are transplanted along with **Sertoli** cells.   TRUE ☑ FALSE ☐

white cells protect the body from infection (also known as leukocytes)

5. Sertoli cells destroy **white cells** in a process known as **apoptosis**.   TRUE ☑ FALSE ☐

apoptosis cell death

6. The small twelve-patient trial was a complete success.   TRUE ☐ FALSE ☑

The answer to question 6 is false because the success rate was only 50 percent. (In six of the twelve trials, there is evidence that the pig islets are functioning.)

7. How can a non-human-to-human transplant actually be made safer than a human-to-human transplant?
   Pigs can be raised in a bio-secure environment; in this way, they won't acquire any diseases that will be passed on to the recipient. On the other hand, human-to-human transplants offer doctors a limited time frame in which to do the transplant (accident victims, etc.); hence, there is a potential that certain diseases in the donor organ will not be identified and will therefore be passed on to the recipient.

retrovirus virus whose genetic information is contained in Ribonucleic Acid (RNA)

The answer to question 8 is false because Dr. White indicates that pig retroviruses do no harm to humans and human retroviruses do no harm to pigs.

8. Porcine endogenous **retroviruses** and human endogenous retroviruses are extremely dangerous for their hosts.   TRUE ☐ FALSE ☑

9. There is a great deal of evidence for cross-species retroviral infection.   TRUE ☐ FALSE ☑
   The answer to question 9 is false because Dr. White indicates that there is no evidence of cross-species retroviral infection. For additional comments, see the Additional Notes in the Teacher Section of the companion website.

10. In general, is Dr. David White for or against the use of xenotransplantation to treat Type I Diabetes?

He is for the use of xenotransplantation to treat Type I Diabetes.

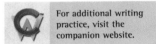

Would You Write That Down?

Your teacher may ask you to complete one or more of the writing assignments below.

> **WRITING SUGGESTION**
> First impressions count. When submitting a written assignment, make sure that it is easy to read. For in-class assignments, if your handwriting isn't legible, print. Use a word processor for assignments that you can prepare at home. Leave enough room for your teacher to correct and comment; double space and leave a 2.5 cm margin. Before handing in a written assignment, ask yourself what kind of first impression it makes. The first impression will surely count when you get your grade!

Free-form Writing

- **Write 75 to 100 words in response to one of the following questions:**

1. Society frequently discusses racism and sexism, so why is "speciesism" so rarely mentioned?

2. Explain why you are—or are not—a vegetarian.

3. Is xenotransplantation a risky science? Justify your answer.

Essay Writing

- **Write a 300- to 400-word essay using one of the thesis statements below.**
- **Do some research on the Internet to find evidence that supports your chosen thesis statement. (See Appendix A to review the structure of a persuasive essay.)**

1. Humans need (or do not need) to eat animals to be healthy.

2. Humans and animals are (or are not) of equal value.

3. Animal experimentation is (or is not) necessary.

4. Xenotransplantation is (or is not) a good solution to the human organ shortage.

5. Xenotransplantation is (or is not) worth the risk.

Would You Speak Up?

For additional speaking practice, visit the companion website.

Answers will vary.

Answers will vary. Discourse structure is outlined in "Appendix B: Discourse and Debate" (p. 192). Given the polemic nature of *Parallels: Taking a Stand in English*, a persuasive discourse structure is recommended. The suggested speaking time is five minutes; you may wish to increase or decrease the required speaking time. As indicated in the Speaking Suggestion above, encourage students to tell the audience why what they have to say is important!

Answers will vary. Debate structure is outlined in "Appendix B: Discourse and Debate" (pp. 192–194). Arguments "for" and "against" the proposal are listed on page 100. For more information on running small group or whole class debates, refer to the Additional Notes in the Teacher Section of the companion website.

Your teacher may ask you to participate in one or more of the speaking activities below.

Discussion

- In small groups, consider one (or more) of the following questions.
- Be prepared to share your thoughts with other groups in the class.

1. How do you feel about the speed at which biotechnology is advancing?

2. Is the scientific community out of touch with the general population? Justify your answer.

3. Do you think that xenotransplantation will create more problems than it will solve? Why or why not?

4. Is one human life worth more than one animal life, ten animal lives, one hundred animal lives, one thousand animal lives? Justify your response.

5. In his article (p. 102), Michael Fumento refers to the expression "to cast (or throw) pearls before swine" (line 46). What does this expression mean? Can you describe a context in which this expression could be used?

Discourse

- Prepare a structured, five-minute speech on one of the thesis statements below. (See Appendix B for suggested speaking structure.)
- Do some research to find evidence that supports your chosen thesis statement. Make sure your speech has an introduction, a development and a conclusion.

1. Eating animals is (or is not) wrong.

2. Society should (or should not) allow the genetic modification of animals.

3. Xenotransplantation is (or is not) necessary.

4. The human species is (or is not) more important than other species.

5. Xenotransplantation exploits (or does not exploit) animals.

Debate

- Debate the following proposal: Xenotransplantation is wrong. (See Appendix B for the rules of debate.)

What's That Word Mean Again?

In the reading and listening sections, we focused on twenty terms—ten from each section. The activity below is designed to help you review this vocabulary.

Hangman

Do you remember playing the language game Hangman in primary school? Play a few games with a partner to review key vocabulary.

Required
- A pen or pencil
- Five sheets of blank paper
- A bit of luck!

Instructions

1. With a partner, review the twenty terms presented in the reading and listening sections of this part of Unit 4.

2. Set up a Hangman game as indicated in the illustration.

3. Student A secretly chooses a word from the list and draws a blank for each letter in the word.

4. Student B guesses a letter. If Student B guesses correctly, Student A writes the letter on the appropriate blank. If Student B guesses incorrectly, Student A draws part of the hangman.

5. A point is awarded when Student B guesses the word **or** when Student A completes the hangman before the word is guessed.

6. Change roles and start a new game.

7. Play the best three out of five.

Remember: Don't look at the word list while you are actually playing the game.

Would You Like to Work Together?

In this section, you will work with another student on a joint writing and speaking project.

Answers will vary. This paired project encourages cooperative learning.

Project Overview

In the "Did You Know?" section of this part of the unit, you read an overview article about xenotransplantation (pp. 99–100). One way to summarize an article and assimilate information is to write information questions, the answers to which are found in the article you are reading. Take for example the first sentence of the "Did You Know?" article, "According to Health Canada, xenotransplantation (or cross-species transplantation) is the transfer of living cells, tissues or organs from one species to another." A question you could write based on the information contained in this sentence would be, "What is xenotransplantation?" Working with a partner, you will create five information questions based on the "Did You Know?" article and five information questions based on an Internet article about xenotransplantation. You and your partner will then ask these ten questions to another team of two in the class.

Required

• A computer with Internet access
• A grammar textbook

Procedure

This activity is carried out in two parts.

Part A

1. Working with your chosen (or assigned) partner, create five information questions based on the "Did You Know?" article. Then go to the English version of the Wikipedia website and type "xenotransplantation" into the search engine located in the left-hand menu; create five information questions based on this online article.
   (Base your questions only on the information contained in this article and not on the information contained in the links included in this article.) Use at least four different tenses when writing your questions. To review question formation, see *Parallels: Taking a Stand in English—English Grammar*, Units 2 to 6. After each question, name the tense used (simple present, present continuous, simple past, past continuous, present perfect, etc.).

2. Double-check your question formation and submit your list of information questions to your teacher for verification.

Part B

3. With your partner, challenge another team of two to respond correctly to your teacher-verified list of information questions. Note: You must read (not show) your questions to the opposing team and neither team may look back at the original articles.

4. Give one point for each correct answer and no points for each incorrect answer.

5. If you're unsure about the answer, ask your teacher to act as "referee."

6. Alternate asking and answering questions with the other team.

7. The team with the highest score wins!

Variation: Your teacher may increase the difficulty of this project by selecting two new (and longer) articles on xenotransplantation and giving copies of the articles to all teams of two. All teams read both articles. Half the teams write questions based on Article A and half the teams write questions based on Article B. The "challenge" is then carried out as described in Part B above, pairing Article A teams with Article B teams.

Can We Come and Go as We Please?

Have you ever heard the expression: "It is a matter of life and death"? It is used to indicate that something is very important. In this unit, we will literally deal with matters of life and death. We will consider whether all people should have the right to end their lives—and whether some people should not have the right to begin their lives.

SECTION A

Voluntary Active Euthanasia

Examines whether individuals should have the right to assisted suicide.

SECTION B

Wrongful Life

Examines whether genetically defective or diseased fetuses should be eliminated.

Voluntary Active Euthanasia

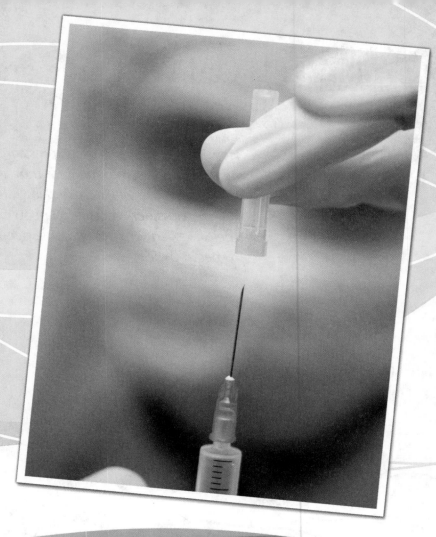

Did You Know?

If you intend to assign the cooperative learning project outlined in the "Would You Like to Work Together?" section of this unit (p. 127), you must assign it *before* starting this unit.

The term *euthanasia* is derived from the Greek words *eu*, meaning "good," and *thanatos*, meaning "death." It can be defined as the act of ending the life of a person suffering from a terminal or incurable disease.

Euthanasia can be divided into two categories:

1. Voluntary euthanasia

2. Non-voluntary euthanasia

In voluntary euthanasia, the person gives consent to his or her own death. In non-voluntary euthanasia, also referred to as "mercy killing," the person is unable to give consent to his or her own death.

There are two basic types of euthanasia:

1. Passive euthanasia

2. Active euthanasia

In passive euthanasia, an action *not* taken results in death; for example, the person isn't hooked up to a respirator. In active euthanasia, an action taken results in death; for example, the person is given a lethal injection.

In Canada, the distinction between passive and active euthanasia is important: active euthanasia is treated as a criminal act, while passive euthanasia is not.

In this unit, we will focus our attention on voluntary active euthanasia, also referred to as assisted suicide. You will be asked to consider whether mentally competent people suffering from incurable diseases should have the right to ask someone to help them end their lives *when* and *how* they choose.

It isn't an easy issue.

While the word *euthanasia* literally means "good death," you will soon see that not everyone agrees that such a death is, in fact, good.

Let's examine the arguments.

Assisted suicide is right because it	Assisted suicide is wrong because it
1. ends physical and psychological suffering.	1. ends lives.
2. eliminates a number of unwanted and expensive medical treatments.	2. diminishes the dying process.
3. affirms people's right to control their bodies and their lives.	3. can be abused.

Who owns your life? Who owns your body? Are your answers to these questions the same? If you were asked to describe your life, would you start talking about your arms, legs, heart and lungs? Or would you talk about your friends, family and activities? These are some of the challenging questions that you will be asked to consider in this section of Unit 5.

What's the Buzz?

On page 116, you will find three case studies.

■ **In teams of three or four, read each of the case studies and respond to the questions.**

■ **Respond from a moral and not a legal standpoint; that is, don't say you wouldn't do something "because it is illegal." Be prepared to share your answers with the rest of the class.**

Case Study 1: Stephanie Martin

Stephanie Martin is a thirty-four-year-old single mother of fourteen-year-old twin boys. When she was thirty-two years old, Stephanie consulted a doctor, complaining of nausea, vomiting and headaches. The cause of Stephanie's symptoms was quickly discovered: she had an inoperable brain tumour located in her frontal lobe. Patients with frontal lobe tumours may experience behavioural and emotional changes, memory loss and impaired judgment. At first, Stephanie was determined to fight the disease; however, her thinking has recently changed. She asks you, her doctor, to put an end to her suffering with an overdose of morphine. Do you agree to her request? Why? Why not?

_____

_____

_____

_____

Case Study 2: John Moreno

After a routine check-up, eighteen-year-old John Moreno was informed that he had acquired the Human Immunodeficiency Virus (HIV). John lives with his parents and his older sister, who don't know that John is gay. Antiviral therapy can be very effective in the treatment of HIV-infected patients. However, John doesn't want to pursue this therapy, as the required regimen of medication would be impossible to hide from his family. John is so upset about the possibility of his family finding out that he is gay that he refuses all future treatment. He says that he will "let nature take its course" and that he will contact the Right to Die Society of Canada when "the time is right." You are his best friend. What do you do?

_____

_____

_____

_____

Case Study 3: Mark Hampton

Mark Hampton is a seventy-eight-year-old retired university professor living alone. He was recently diagnosed with mild Alzheimer's disease, the first stage of the degenerative illness. In the mild stage, which typically lasts from two to four years, patients repeat themselves, forget names and lose things. Mark knows that eventually he won't be able to understand language, recognize his friends and family members or care for himself. A proud man, Mr. Hampton decides that this isn't how he wishes his life to end and asks you, his doctor, to give him a dignified death. Do you agree to his request? Why? Why not?

_____

_____

_____

_____

GRAMMAR TIP
Which is a relative pronoun used to relate non-essential information about things: Dr. Smith's lecture, which lasted more than an hour, was quite boring. *That* is a relative pronoun used to relate essential information about things: Did you attend the lecture that Dr. Smith gave? For more information on relative pronouns, see Unit 10 in the companion volume *Parallels: Taking a Stand in English—English Grammar.*

For additional reading practice, visit the companion website.

On October 24, 1993, Saskatchewan farmer Robert Latimer killed his twelve-year-old daughter, Tracy, a forty-pound quadriplegic suffering from a severe form of cerebral palsy. Mr. Latimer was convicted of second-degree murder in 1994 and given a life sentence with no chance of parole for ten years. Mr. Latimer's conviction was appealed and upheld by the Supreme Court of Canada on January 18, 2001. In March 2008, Mr. Latimer was granted parole. Tom Koch is an author, researcher and lecturer who expressed his opinion on the Supreme Court's decision and the debate surrounding non-voluntary euthanasia. His article appeared in the *Vancouver Sun* on February 7, 2001.

Before Reading

Don't forget to skim and scan.

- Read the defined words and comprehension questions before reading the article.

> **READING STRATEGY**
> How would you describe where you are sitting right now? Would you say that your location is favourable to reading comprehension? Are you in a quiet room with adequate lighting? Do you have a pen or pencil, a highlighter and a dictionary close by? If not, you may want to consider changing your environment for one that will work with you—and not against you.

While Reading

From the title of Mr. Koch's article, you can probably guess how he feels about non-voluntary euthanasia (or mercy killing). Notice, however, that Mr. Koch presents the other side of the issue first (lines 1 to 4). Why do you think he begins this way? How does presenting the other side first reinforce his argument?

Students are asked why the author of "Disabled Are Not Dogs" begins his essay with a viewpoint in opposition to his own. The author does so to appear more "open-minded." In such a situation, the reader assumes that the author has considered "both sides of the issue" and opted for the better (more logical) of the two.

harsh severe

DISABLED ARE NOT DOGS

BY TOM KOCH

Many Canadians believe Robert Latimer's ten-year sentence for the murder of his daughter, Tracy, was too **harsh**, and that "mercy killing" is an idea whose time is now. In British Columbia, MP [Member of Parliament] Sven Robinson and *Vancouver Sun* columnist Stan Persky have taken this position.

5 Others insist a mercy killing law, or a royal pardon for Latimer, would endorse non-care for the fragile. Working through the Supreme Court's judgment, they're probably right.

Latimer supporters justify Tracy's murder because she had untreatable pain. This isn't true, however. "There was evidence that Tracy could have
10 been fed with a feeding tube into her stomach, an option that would have improved her nutrition and health," the justices wrote. This, they continued, "might also have allowed for more effective pain medication to be administered, but the accused and his wife [Laura] rejected this option."

"Had the Latimers not rejected the option of relying on a feeding tube," in
15 short, the pain that drove Latimer to murder might have been managed.

instead in its place

Similarly, doctors said surgery removing Tracy's "upper thigh bone" would relieve the physical pain resulting from her hip dislocation, a complication resulting from her disease. But Latimer saw this as "mutilation," and killed his daughter **instead**.

20 A pardon for Latimer would say death is better than treatments like tube feeding and amputation, even when they save lives, relieve pain and improve health.

relieve reduce or diminish

In the same vein, two years before Tracy's murder, the *Journal of the American Medical Association* reported on a new procedure to **relieve** the
25 "spasticity" of patients like Tracy. It involved using an "intrathical pump" to deliver controlled doses of medication directly into the spinal fluid. We know, too, it was in use in Vancouver in 1993.

mercy compassion
messy complicated

We don't know if anyone suggested this approach in the Latimer case—or if Robert Latimer would have accepted it—because it is easier to talk
30 about **mercy**, and mercy killing, than it is to deal with the **messy** details of patient care.

cope deal with
something successfully

Finally, the month before Tracy was killed, her parents decided not to place her in a group home where she could have received the care she needed. Provinces fund such institutions not only for patients, but for families who can't **cope**.
35 Pardoning Latimer says, "Better to be gassed than to enter a skilled care facility." Tell that to Granny when she thinks about a retirement home.

But the Senate select committee on euthanasia advocated a lesser charge than murder in difficult cases, Latimer supporters argue.

They forget the committee also said that was to be considered only after
40 first-rate palliative (pain management) treatment and care have been exhausted. They weren't here. Latimer rejected them.

Those who seek mercy for Latimer and minimal penalties for others like him sometimes argue: "Hey, we put down our beloved pets. Why not our loved ones as well?"

45 The answer is Canadians value their relatives and neighbours more than their pets. We therefore protect our citizens more carefully than the lives of cats, dogs and parakeets. One reason we have a national health care system is to ensure everyone gets the treatment they need to live the best life they can.

50 Still, some say Tracy wasn't worth saving. Persky, for example, argues she was "without any prospect of a meaningful future." She was physically restricted and had the mental level of a four-year-old. This is supposed to make her murder OK.

meaningless without significance

meaningful with significance

To say Tracy Latimer's murder wasn't important because her life was
55 **meaningless** is to say the lives of the different are no lives at all. Unless one believes everyone who is developmentally and physically challenged has a meaningless future, who is to say her future was without merit? Can you draw the line that will say these lives are **meaningful** and those are not? I can't.

60 Finally, some argue Latimer shouldn't be treated like a common murderer because his motives were good. Since he's unlikely to kill again, what purpose is served by his incarceration?

The answer is simple. "Mercy" for Bob Latimer would give other relatives permission to kill their dependents without undue concern for the conse-
65 quences. Arguing Latimer's sentence is "cruel and unusual" would say there is indeed little difference between putting down the fragile child (or parent, or spouse) and the family pet.

spouse husband or wife
sibling brother or sister

Latimer's ten-year sentence says parents, **spouses** and **siblings** don't have life-and-death powers over dependent persons. Offer Latimer
70 "mercy" and you withdraw it from the fragile, whose lives may be forfeited as a result.

To pardon him would be to say anyone can put down a son, daughter or spouse just as you would arthritic, half-blind, old Fido.

794 Words

Reading Comprehension

- Indicate whether each of the following statements is true or false.
- If a statement is false, explain why it is false. The first one has been done for you as an example.

1. Mr. Koch's article is about voluntary active euthanasia. TRUE ☐ FALSE ✓

   Mr. Koch's article is about non-voluntary active euthanasia: Tracy Latimer was unable to give consent to her death, as she functioned at the level of a four-year-old.

2. According to the author, Tracy Latimer had untreatable pain. TRUE ☐ FALSE ✓

   The author claims that Tracy was not in untreatable pain, citing Supreme Court justices to support his position. (Latimer supporters claimed Tracy was in untreatable pain, not the author.)

3. Mr. Latimer viewed amputation as mutilation. TRUE ✓ FALSE ☐

   _____

   _____

4. The author believes that Tracy's pain could have been better managed. TRUE ☑ FALSE ☐

_____

_____

5. Mr. Latimer refused to have Tracy hooked up to an intrathical pump to control her pain. TRUE ☐ FALSE ☑

The author indicates that he is unsure as to whether Mr. Latimer was aware of this option.

_____

6. Tracy's parents wanted to place her in a group home. TRUE ☐ FALSE ☑

Tracy's parents decided *not* to place her in a group home.

_____

7. The author is unable to decide whose lives are meaningful and whose lives are not. TRUE ☑ FALSE ☐

_____

_____

8. The author believes that Mr. Latimer's motives were good. TRUE ☐ FALSE ☑

Latimer supporters claim that his motives were good; the author makes no such claim.

_____

9. The author argues that if mercy is shown to Mr. Latimer, others will be encouraged to follow his example and kill their relatives. TRUE ☑ FALSE ☐

_____

_____

Question 10 tests the student's ability to identify the main idea of the text.

10. In general, the author believes that pardoning Mr. Latimer is wrong because it would send the message that people and animals are of equal value. TRUE ☑ FALSE ☐

_____

_____

Discussion

Answers will vary.

▬ **In pairs or small groups, discuss and then write down your answers to each of the following questions.**

▬ **Be prepared to share your answers with the rest of the class.**

1. The focus of this part of the unit is on voluntary active euthanasia, or assisted suicide; however, the article selected for your reading comprehension exercise deals with non-voluntary active euthanasia, or mercy killing.

Some opponents of assisted suicide claim that if society legalizes assisted suicide, the next step will be the legalization of mercy killing—and eventually even murder! This type of argument is called a "slippery slope" argument. Do you feel such an argument has any merit? Can you think of a situation in which the legalization of one behaviour led to the legalization of another?

2. The author seems to be arguing that in situations where pain can be controlled, mercy killing (and presumably assisted suicide) is wrong. What do you think? Is physical pain the only justifiable motivation for mercy killing and assisted suicide?

3. Are all lives meaningful, or are some lives meaningless? Justify your point of view.

Word Work

In the article, ten terms are defined for you:

Adjectives	Adverb	Nouns	Verbs
1. harsh 2. meaningful 3. meaningless 4. messy	5. instead	6. mercy 7. sibling 8. spouse	9. ~~cope~~ 10. relieve

■ In the text below, fill in the blanks with one of the terms listed above. You can only use each term once.

Every day, people 1. _____*cope*_____ with 2. _____harsh_____ realities: a job is lost; a 3. _____spouse_____ asks for a divorce; a 4. _____sibling_____ dies; a foe shows no 5. _____mercy_____. Life is 6. _____messy_____. However, there's always a good side to the difficulties that people face.

You don't believe me?

Take a moment to ask yourself when you grew the most as a person—during the good times or during the bad times 7. _____instead_____? Very likely your life was most 8. _____meaningful_____ when times were tough. Think about people who say they have it all, and yet find their lives 9. _____meaningless_____. They waste their lives in harmful activities designed to fill the void and 10. _____relieve_____ their pain. It's rather ironic, don't you think?

Pain may well be a part of life, but suffering is entirely optional.

For additional listening practice, visit the companion website.

On November 21, 2004, the CBC radio program *Sunday Edition* broadcast host Michael Enright's essay on euthanasia. Mr. Enright is an eloquent speaker, and his essay is both thoughtful and thought provoking.

VOCABULARY TIP
A collocation is a group of words that are frequently used together to express an idea.

Answers will vary for inferred meanings. For teacher's feedback (dictionary definitions), see the Additional Notes in the Teacher Section of the companion website.

Pre-Listening Vocabulary

Below, you will find a chart containing ten collocations taken from the radio excerpt. To understand a collocation, you must understand the meaning of the group of words—and not just the individual words themselves.

- Examine each of the collocations below and try to infer the meaning of each one by using a dictionary to look up any individual words that you may not know.
- Then verify your inferences by asking your teacher for feedback.

Collocations	Inferred Meanings	Teacher's Feedback
1. ease the burden		
2. frame the question		
3. hardened criminal		
4. heart-wrenching plea		
5. moral monster		
6. pain management		
7. painful decision		
8. palliative care		
9. shift the focus		
10. tangle of emotions		

While Listening

You will hear the interview twice.

- The first time you listen, try to understand the speaker's position on the euthanasia debate.
- The second time you listen, pay attention to the details of what the speaker has to say, taking brief point-form notes to help you remember the information.

Listening Comprehension

▬ **Referring to your notes, respond to each of the questions below.**

1. At the beginning of the radio segment, Mr. Enright wonders what his doctor's reaction would be if he asked his doctor to kill him. He also wonders how he would ask his doctor to kill him.　　TRUE ☑　FALSE ☐

2. What prompted Mr. Enright to start thinking about his doctor and his death?
   Two recent criminal cases involving assisted suicides: a) a seventy-four-year-old great-grandmother in Vancouver, Evelyn Martins, who was acquitted of assisting in the suicides of two British Columbia women; and b) a Montreal woman, Marielle Houle, who was charged with helping her thirty-six-year-old son with muscular dystrophy to die.

3. It is against the law to assist in someone's death in Canada.　　TRUE ☑　FALSE ☐

4. Irwin Cotler[1] has called for a renewed debate on assisted death in the Canadian House of Commons. Mr. Enright defines four types of assisted deaths to be discussed.

▬ **Match each type with its correct definition in the chart below.**

Types of Assisted Death	Definitions
1. voluntary euthanasia ___d___ 2. involuntary euthanasia ___c___ 3. active euthanasia ___b___ 4. passive euthanasia ___a___	a) Life support is withdrawn and the patient dies of dehydration or starvation. b) A doctor or assistant does something to help promote death. c) A patient is unable to give consent. d) A sick person declares that he or she wants to die.

5. According to Mr. Enright, which kind of assisted death is the most contentious?
   A context in which the wishes and the consent of the patient are unknown: involuntary euthanasia

6. Mr. Enright believes that we have calm, reflective debates in this country.　　TRUE ☐　FALSE ☑

7. Fill in the blanks. "In Holland, where assisted suicide has been allowed for many years, the debate still rages on. Opponents say that doctors have dispatched patients who are not sick, but merely ___old___ or ___depressed___."

8. In Holland, opponents of assisted suicide mention "problems of completion." What exactly is a problem of completion?
   A "problem of completion" occurs when the death medicine doesn't work, and people die wretchedly.

   1. Minister of Justice at the time of the original broadcast.

9. According to Mr. Enright, a debate on assisted suicide must include a discussion of pain management and palliative care.

TRUE ☑   FALSE ☐

Question 10 test the student's ability to identify the main idea of the segment.

10. In general, Mr. Enright believes that
a) Canadians need a fair debate on the legalization of euthanasia.
b) Canadians have debated the legalization of euthanasia for too long.
c) euthanasia shouldn't be legalized.
d) euthanasia should be legalized.

Would You Write That Down?

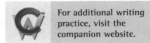

For additional writing practice, visit the companion website.

Two types of writing assignments are included below. Your teacher will tell you which assignment(s) you should complete.

> **WRITING SUGGESTION**
> Increase your credibility as a writer by directly referring to experts who have written on the subject of your essay. Name the experts and paraphrase or quote their opinions. Remember to reference correctly—or you will lose your credibility. (See Appendix A for more information about referencing.)

Answers will vary. In free-form writing, no specific structure is required; however, the student is asked to write 75 to 100 words. You may wish to increase or decrease the number of words required. The free-form writing assignments are great for "sampling" student writing ability.

Free-form Writing

▬ **Write 75 to 100 words in response to one of the following questions:**

1. Do you think that euthanasia is a "good death"? Why or why not?

2. Briefly describe a situation in which suffering changed you for the better.

3. Are your life and your body one in the same, or are they different? Explain.

Answers will vary. The recommended essay format for *Parallels: Taking a Stand in English* is the persuasive essay (see "Appendix A: The Persuasive Essay" on page 182), but you may opt for another essay structure. The student is asked to write 300 to 400 words. You may also wish to increase or decrease the number of words required.

Essay Writing

▬ **Write a 300- to 400-word essay using one of the thesis statements below.**

▬ **Do some research on the Internet to find evidence that supports your chosen thesis statement. (See Appendix A to review the structure of a persuasive essay.)**

1. People should (or should not) have the right to end their lives.

2. Keeping a person artificially alive is (or is not) a misuse of public money.

3. All life (or not all life) has value.

4. Good palliative care makes (or does not make) euthanasia unnecessary.

5. Mercy killing should (or should not) be legalized.

Would You Speak Up?

You may be asked to participate in one or more of the speaking activities below.

> **SPEAKING SUGGESTION**
> Who hasn't had the misfortune of listening to someone read an entire speech from beginning to end? To make sure you don't fall into this trap, only have a brief outline with you when speaking in public. Write down your main points and any names, facts, figures or quotes that you are unlikely to remember. Remember to refer—not read.

Answers will vary. In question 1, students are asked to explain the expression *no pain, no gain*. This expression means that one achieves nothing of value without experiencing difficulty. See the Additional Notes in the Teacher Section of the companion website for a comment on question 4.

WORD CULTURE
The expression *no pain, no gain* was popularized by actress Jane Fonda in a series of aerobics workout videos from the 1980s. Eighteenth-century variants on the expression include *pain is forgotten where gain follows* and Benjamin Franklin's axiom *God helps those who help themselves.*

Discussion

- **In small groups, consider one (or more) of the following questions.**
- **Be prepared to share your thoughts with other groups in the class.**

1. "No pain, no gain" is a fairly common expression. Explain this expression. What can an individual gain from pain?

2. A couple of generations ago, most people died at home. Today, the majority of people die in hospitals. Is "institutionalized death" good for society? Justify your response.

3. Do we live in a society that devalues the sick? Explain.

4. Other than compassion, what could motivate a family member to help a loved one die?

5. Why do you think many older people don't support assisted suicide?

Answers will vary. Discourse structure is outlined in "Appendix B: Discourse and Debate" (p. 192). Given the polemic nature of *Parallels: Taking a Stand in English*, a persuasive discourse structure is recommended. The suggested speaking time is five minutes; you may wish to increase or decrease the required speaking time. As indicated in the Speaking Suggestion above, encourage students to write down the main points and to refer to their notes instead of reading the entire speech when speaking in public.

Discourse

- **Prepare a structured, five-minute speech on one of the thesis statements below. (See Appendix B for a suggested speaking structure.)**
- **Do some research to find evidence that supports your chosen thesis statement. Make sure your speech has an introduction, a development and a conclusion.**

1. Legalizing doctor-assisted suicide is (or is not) dangerous for society.

2. People who commit a mercy killing should (or should not) go to jail.

3. Disease and disability have (or do not have) value.

4. Canadians should (or should not) "deinstitutionalize" death.

5. Mercy killing devalues (or does not devalue) the lives of the disabled.

Answers will vary. Debate structure is outlined in "Appendix B: Discourse and Debate" (pp. 194–198). Arguments "for" and "against" the proposal are listed on page 115. For more information on running small group or whole class debates, refer to the Additional Notes in the Teacher Section of the companion website.

Debate

- **Debate the following proposal: Assisted suicide is wrong. (See Appendix B for the rules of debate.)**

What's That Word Mean Again?

In the reading and listening sections, we focused on twenty terms—ten from each section. Try to complete the activity below without reviewing the terms in advance.

Answers will vary. This game-like activity is a supplementary activity appropriate to some, but not all, academic contexts.

Crossword Puzzle

Do you enjoy the challenge of a crossword puzzle in your first language? Why not take up the challenge in English?

Required
A pen or pencil

Instructions
Read the clues and fill in the corresponding blanks.

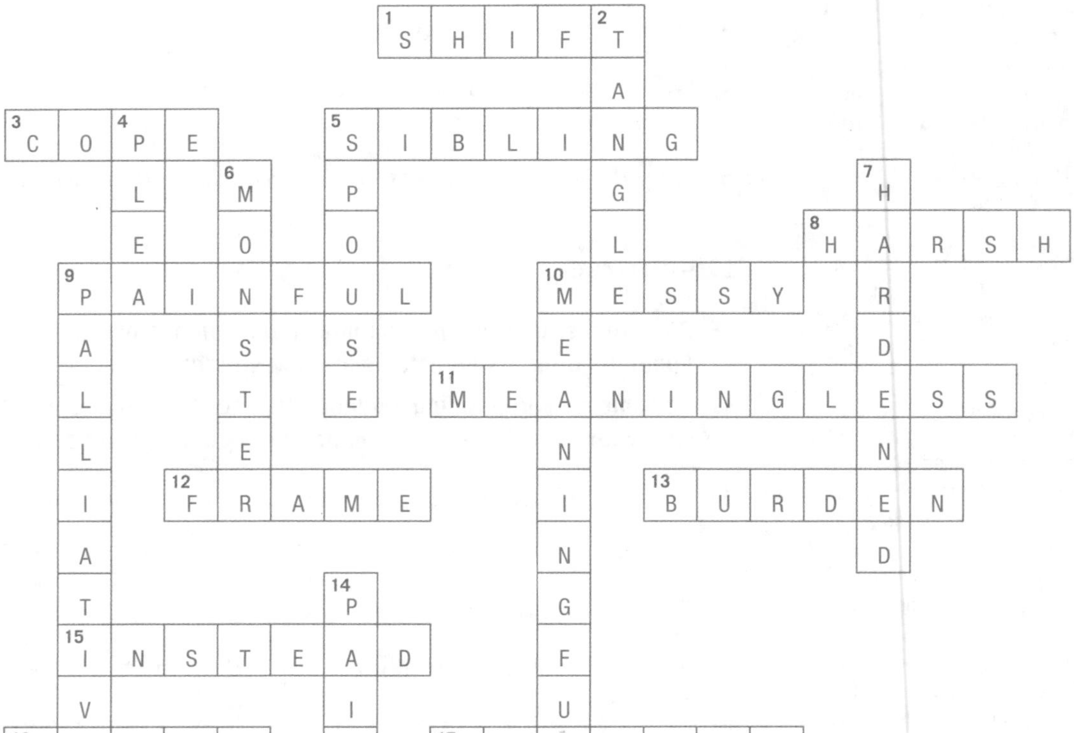

1 SHIFT
2 TANGLE
3 COPE
4 PLEA
5 SIBLING
5 SPOUSE
6 MONSTER
7 HARDENED
8 HARSH
9 PAINFUL
9 PALLIATIVE
10 MESSY
10 MEANINGFUL
11 MEANINGLESS
12 FRAME
13 BURDEN
14 PAIN
15 INSTEAD
16 MERCY
17 RELIEVE

Across	**Down**
1. _____ the focus (collocation)	2. _____ of emotions (collocation)
3. deal with or handle something successfully	4. heart-wrenching _____ (collocation)
5. brother or sister	5. husband or wife
8. severe	6. moral _____ (collocation)
9. _____ decision (collocation)	7. _____ criminal (collocation)
10. complicated	9. _____ care (collocation)
11. without significance	10. with significance
12. _____ the question (collocation)	14. _____ management (collocation)
13. ease the _____ (collocation)	
15. in its place	
16. compassion	
17. reduce or diminish	

Would You Like to Work Together?

In this section, you will work with another student on a joint writing and speaking project.

This project must be assigned *before* students start Unit 5, Section A. It may be adapted to any topic covered in this textbook.

Answers will vary. This paired project encourages cooperative learning.

Should students have difficulty generating five questions due to limited knowledge on the subject, allow them to do some research on the Internet.

Project Overview
You and your partner will construct, complete and present a K-W-L chart. A K-W-L chart is a chart in which you outline what you know about a topic, what you want to know about a topic and what you have learned about a topic. Take the topic of music downloading (Section A in Unit 2 of this textbook) as an example (see page 128).

This project will be assigned *before* you begin Unit 5, Section 2, "Voluntary Active Euthanasia" and will be evaluated by your teacher *after* you complete this section.

Required
• A computer and word processor
• Internet access

Topic: Music Downloading		
A. What We Know	**B. What We Want to Know**	**C. What We Have Learned**
1. Music downloading is a controversial issue.	1. Is it illegal to download music in Canada?	1. No, it is not illegal to download music in Canada. In 2004, a Canadian judge ruled that music downloading and music swapping do not violate Canadian copyright law.
2. Most famous artists are opposed to music downloading.		
3. Many unknown artists like downloading for the exposure it gives them.	2. Can Internet Service Providers (ISPs) be forced to reveal the identity of Canadian clients who download music?	2. No, ISPs cannot be forced to reveal the identity of clients who download music.
4. Most teenagers prefer MP3s to CDs.	3. Has anyone been sued for swapping music files?	3. Yes, people have been sued— particularly in the U.S.
5. An MP3 is more environmentally-friendly than a CD.	4. What is PureTracks?	4. PureTracks is a Canadian service for music downloads.
	5. Can technology stop music file sharing?	5. Yes, downloads are sometimes encoded to prevent buyers from making copies.

Procedure

1. Working together, construct a K-W-L chart on the topic of voluntary active euthanasia using the chart above as a model.

2. In Part A, write five complete sentences indicating what you know about voluntary active euthanasia. Number your sentences. In Part B, write five questions indicating what you would like to learn about voluntary active euthanasia. Number your questions.

3. Orally present Parts A and B to your teacher and classmates.

4. *After* you, your teacher and your classmates have completed Unit 5, Section A, "Voluntary Active Euthanasia," respond in Part C to the questions you raised in Part B. Number your responses. Note: If, by the end of the unit, you have not learned the answers to all of your questions, do some research on the Internet to find the answers.

5. Orally present Part C to your teacher and your classmates.

6. Submit your completed K-W-L chart to your teacher for evaluation.

Wrongful Life

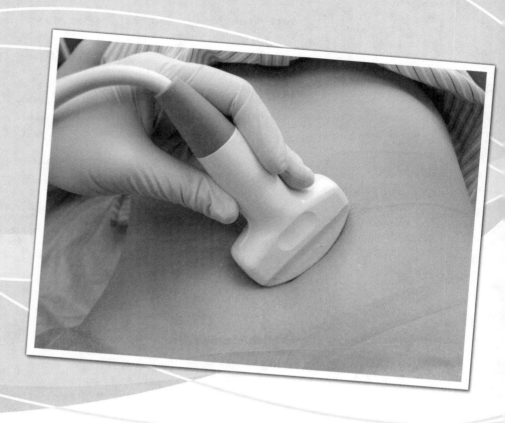

Did You Know?

If you intend to assign the cooperative learning project outlined in the "Would You Like to Work Together?" section of this unit (p. 143), you must assign it *before* starting this unit.

carrier transmitter of genetic defect

Through genetic testing, it is possible to prevent the conception of embryos likely to develop into children with genetic diseases, such as Huntington's (a hereditary brain disorder) and cystic fibrosis (a fatal genetic disease affecting the lungs and digestive system). Through prenatal testing techniques, such as ultrasound and amniocentesis, it is possible to detect fetal abnormalities, such as Down syndrome (a condition caused by the presence of an extra chromosome) or spina bifida (a condition in which the spine doesn't form properly).

Parents who are **carriers** of certain genetic diseases may decide not to have children, and expectant mothers who are carrying abnormal fetuses may decide to abort.

Sometimes parents or expectant mothers are uninformed of—or misinformed about—genetic diseases or congenital abnormalities, and their children are born sick or disabled.

In such situations, some parents sue their healthcare professionals for "wrongful birth," and some children sue their mothers' healthcare professionals for "wrongful life." In the first instance, the parents want compensation for the increased costs associated with raising diseased or disabled children. In the second instance, the children want compensation for lost income as well as the pain and suffering associated with being disabled.

In this unit, our focus will be on the concept of wrongful life, which is based on the assumption that those with genetic diseases or disabilities shouldn't be born, in other words, that their lives are "not worth living."

Here is the question you will be asked to answer: Should genetically diseased or disabled fetuses be eliminated?

Let's examine the arguments.

The elimination of genetically diseased or disabled fetuses is right because it	The elimination of genetically diseased or disabled fetuses is wrong because it
1. eradicates physical and psychological suffering.	1. devalues human life.
2. reduces health care costs.	2. devalues the disabled.
3. is always better to prevent than to cure.	3. devalues diversity.

The debate focuses on the value of human life. Is all human life—irrespective of its form—valuable? The question is far from simple.

What's the Buzz?

Below you will find three case studies.

- In teams of three or four, read each of the case studies and respond to the questions.
- Be prepared to share your answers with the rest of the class.

Case Study 1: Alison Anderson

Alison Anderson is a thirty-nine-year-old single woman expecting her first child. As women over the age of thirty-five are at greater risk of having a child with Down syndrome, Alison's doctor recommends that Alison undergo an amniocentesis. The results of the test indicate that Alison's fetus has the syndrome, and she is informed that babies with Down syndrome suffer from physical problems as well as some form of mental retardation. Alison is distressed, and she asks her doctor for advice. If you were Alison's doctor, what would you advise?

Answers will vary. For additional comments, see the Additional Notes in the Teacher Section of the

companion website.

Case Study 2: Linda and Steve Adams

During a routine physical examination, Linda Adams mentions to her family doctor that she and her husband are trying to get pregnant. Linda and Steve are a healthy couple in their mid-twenties, and Linda's doctor gives her a few brochures on pregnancy. Linda becomes pregnant, but contracts **rubella** during the first trimester of her pregnancy; she is informed that her fetus has a 25 percent chance of having mental retardation as well as eye, ear and/or heart defects. Linda decides to continue with the pregnancy, and her child is born blind. A simple blood test could have determined that Linda wasn't immune to rubella, and she could have been vaccinated before becoming pregnant. While this information was included in one of the brochures she received, Linda didn't take the time to read it. Linda blames her doctor for her child's blindness; she feels that he should have given her this information during her physical examination. Do you think Linda should sue her doctor?

rubella contagious viral infection

_____

_____

_____

Case Study 3: Cynthia Carson

Cynthia Carson grew up in a dysfunctional family; her parents drank, and she was physically and psychologically abused. Cynthia started drinking at the age of ten. Cynthia is now an alcoholic, and she is pregnant. Although Cynthia tries to stop drinking during her pregnancy, she simply can't help herself. Cynthia's baby boy is born with Fetal Alcohol Syndrome (FAS), and he is mentally retarded. Is Cynthia guilty of child abuse?

_____

_____

_____

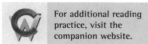

For additional reading practice, visit the companion website.

In France recently, a series of controversial wrongful life court decisions against medical practitioners shook the world's medical community. Practitioners were successfully sued by children (or their representatives) who claimed that ultrasound testing had failed, allowing them to be born with genetic abnormalities or physical defects. Subsequent to these court decisions, the French parliament passed legislation prohibiting wrongful life cases. Anne Marie Owens is a journalist who wrote about the reliability of ultrasound technology and wrongful life court cases. Her article appeared in the *National Post* on January 12, 2002.

Before Reading

Don't forget to skim and scan.

■ **Read the defined words and comprehension questions before reading the article.**

> **READING STRATEGY**
> How would you describe where you are sitting right now? Would you say that your location is favourable to reading comprehension? Are you in a quiet room with adequate lighting? Do you have a pen or pencil, a highlighter and a dictionary close by? If not, you may want to consider changing your environment for one that will work with you—and not against you.

While Reading

Remember that not all parts of a text need to be read in order to understand it. While reading the text below, skim over lines 68 to 82. You will see for yourself that you don't have to read all to understand all.

LIABILITY ISSUES BESET ULTRASOUND TECHNOLOGY

BY ANNE MARIE OWENS

For most expectant parents, the ultrasound scan is the first baby picture: a grainy image in fluid motion, incontrovertible evidence of new life.

But increasingly, when the baby does not turn out quite as expected, parents are blaming ultrasound technology for **letting them down**.

5 Long regarded as a helpful scientific tool for ferreting out some birth defects, determining pregnancy dates, monitoring the baby's development and revealing its sex, the ultrasound has become a powerful legal weapon.

In France last week, **physicians** stopped performing ultrasound scans on pregnant women to protest court rulings that have blamed unwanted
10 children on **unreliable** ultrasounds.

This technological walkout, which forced legislators to pass a bill prohibiting any **further** lawsuits of this kind, is the most dramatic response yet to a judgment by France's highest court entitling disabled children to significant damages if their pregnant mothers were not given the chance to
15 abort them.

This highly controversial "wrongful life" decision in effect establishes a child's legal right to never have been born. It has been decried around the world for implying the child would be better off dead.

Most troubling for those who routinely perform ultrasounds on pregnant
20 women is the implication that this standard prenatal screening tool is somehow infallible and that someone got it wrong.

let somebody down disappoint somebody

physician doctor

unreliable undependable

further additional

What the French case points to, and what practitioners are trying to combat in Canada, is the illusion of control in an area that, even with the most advanced technological tools, is still largely uncontrollable.

25 "There are no guarantees here," warns Dr. Dorothy Shaw, a clinical professor at the University of British Columbia and diagnostic director at BC Women's Hospital.

An ultrasound, of course, is simply a snapshot that is only as good as the sonographer carrying out the scan, and, beyond that, as the person 30 analyzing the results.

enhance improve or make better

Advances in technology, which have dramatically **enhanced** the quality of an image from a shape-shifting blur to a clear three-dimensional picture, have helped create this illusion of certainty.

"People need to be very aware that even in the best hands, an ultrasound 35 doesn't guarantee you a normal baby," said Dr. Shaw. "It is common for women to arrive with a misunderstanding that the ultrasound will reassure them that this pregnancy is normal."

The reality is that an ultrasound, taken at about eighteen weeks into the pregnancy, will only detect about half of the babies with chromosomal 40 abnormalities. It does a better job of detecting visible bodily abnormalities, but even then, studies show accuracy levels ranging anywhere from 20 percent to 90 percent for finding such things as a **defect** in the abdominal wall.

defect imperfection

When it comes to detecting the sex of the fetus, the anecdotal evidence of 45 distress among people preparing for a little Johnny, only to welcome a little Jane into their lives, is legion. "What people forget is that the fetus is evolving," said Dr. Shaw. "It can look one way at one point, but it can look quite different a few weeks later."

She points to the example of brain abnormalities, which could develop 50 after eighteen weeks, after the standard ultrasound.

guideline official recommendation

In Canada, the emerging politics of ultrasounds are more nuanced than in France. There have been back-room debates by hospital committees about whether or not to reveal the sex of a fetus, strict **guidelines** over who can reveal the information gleaned from scans, and a campaign to 55 have a standardized registry of licensed sonographers.

Standard practice, as dictated by the Society of Obstetricians and Gynecologists of Canada, is to offer ultrasounds, optimally at about the eighteenth or nineteenth week of gestation. "Ultrasound examinations have the potential to be happy experiences, but a real or mistaken diagnosis 60 of fetal abnormality can lead to psychological devastation," say clinical guidelines.

"The biggest risk of ultrasound is over-interpretation or missed diagnosis ... The patient should be informed that not all anomalies can be detected."

The guidelines also say the sex of the fetus should not be revealed, except in 65 cases where it is deemed medically necessary because of genetic concerns affecting a particular gender. The practice, however, differs drastically from clinic to clinic.

→

Students are instructed to skim over lines 68 to 82: none of the reading comprehension questions which follow the article is based on information contained within these four paragraphs.

Dr. David Vickar, of the Canadian Society of Diagnostic Medical Sonographers, says most doctors in Alberta routinely refused scans to determine gender because it was an unnecessary cost. That changed three years ago, when parents protested to the College of Physicians and Surgeons, arguing it was their right to know.

BC Women's Hospital will reveal the baby's gender after twenty-four weeks gestation, with the timeline in place to guard against parents of cultures that prefer boys opting to terminate pregnancies of girls.

In Halifax, IWK-Grace Hospital, which had for years offered fetal sex information as part of prenatal screening, decided to halt the practice last year as a cutback to services deemed medically unnecessary.

Standards of practice that vary with every clinic and laboratory mean that some patients will be told the results of their ultrasound by the technician conducting the scan, while others will be referred to the overseeing physician.

Normand Laberge, spokesman for the Canadian Association of Radiologists, said the ultrasound has become such an accepted medical procedure that an illusion of simplicity has developed around it.

"The ultrasound is not something simple. It's not a modern stethoscope," he said. "There is a considerable amount of skill required in operating and reading it."

mishap unfortunate accident

He said the French case could simply be "a **mishap** of the court," but the liability chill that it evokes is already felt around the world.

In the French case, a boy born with Down syndrome was awarded damages because an abnormality was not detected from an ultrasound scan in pregnancy. The mother said she would have had an abortion if she had known the boy, known as Lionel, would be born disabled.

warn caution or notify

A similar decision a year before awarded damages to Nicolas Perruche, a severely disabled child whose mother was not **warned** of the dangers of rubella during pregnancy. Nicolas was born with a weak heart and no ability to hear or speak.

In Canada, there have been relatively few of these cases, and the courts have so far rejected the "wrongful life" premise.

An example is the case of Sarah Mickle, born in 1991 with CHILD syndrome, a congenital disorder affecting her right side. She has severely reddened skin on that side, no right hip, shortened right limbs, and a paddle-like right hand. Her life expectancy is normal and her intellectual abilities unharmed.

limb arm or leg

Because only one of Sarah's **limbs** was examined during an obstetrical ultrasound, her parents argued the Salvation Army Grace Hospital in Windsor deprived them of their right to choose an abortion.

The presiding Ontario Court judge argued that a reasonable woman, informed of the physical defects, would not necessarily have chosen abortion. "To characterize Sarah's existence as a form of harm would be an extraordinary denigration to the value of her life," he ruled.

To begin to judge otherwise, as happened in the French cases, is what concerns the people who carry out ultrasound scans.

115 "It is very frightening," said Mr. Laberge, of the radiologists' association. "This is not France, thank goodness ... But it is a step in a direction that is worrisome for all of us."

1196 words

Reading Comprehension

■ Indicate whether each of the following statements is true or false.

■ If a statement is false, explain why it is false. The first one has been done for you as an example.

1. Ultrasound scans produce clear images of the fetus.   TRUE ☐ FALSE ✓
   Ultrasound images are grainy or unclear.

2. Ultrasounds can determine the fetus's sex and how the fetus is developing.   TRUE ✓ FALSE ☐

_____

_____

3. Ultrasounds are completely reliable.   TRUE ☐ FALSE ✓
   Ultrasounds can be unreliable.

_____

4. Throughout the world, there is great support for France's wrongful life decisions.   TRUE ☐ FALSE ✓
   These decisions have been decried (or criticized) throughout the world.

_____

5. Ultrasounds today produce three-dimensional images of the fetus.   TRUE ✓ FALSE ☐

_____

_____

6. Ultrasounds are typically performed during the first trimester (the first twelve weeks) of the pregnancy.   TRUE ☐ FALSE ✓
   Ultrasounds are performed during the second trimester, approximately eighteen weeks into the pregnancy.

_____

7. Ultrasounds can detect all anomalies if properly done by qualified personnel.   TRUE ☐ FALSE ✓
   Ultrasounds do not detect all anomalies.

_____

8. Canadian medical guidelines state that in general, the sex of the fetus shouldn't be revealed.

TRUE ☑ FALSE ☐

_____

_____

9. The ultrasound isn't a simple procedure.

TRUE ☑ FALSE ☐

_____

_____

Question 10 tests the student's ability to identify the main idea of the text.

10. In general, this article is about the difficulties and the consequences of using ultrasound technology in controversial wrongful life lawsuits.

TRUE ☑ FALSE ☐

_____

_____

Discussion

Answers will vary. With respect to the second question, India and China are two countries in which female infanticide and "gendercide" (selected female fetal abortions) are practised.

- In pairs or small groups, discuss and then write down your answers to each of the questions below.
- Be prepared to share your answers with the rest of the class.

1. Can you think of a situation in which a person is "better off dead"? Explain.

2. Ultrasounds can usually determine the sex of the fetus and whether it is developing normally. In some cultures, female fetuses are aborted because they are the "wrong" sex. Is it wrong to abort a fetus because it is female? Justify your response.

3. In Canada, 88 percent of fetuses with Down syndrome are aborted. Does this percentage take your breath away? Why or why not?

WORD CULTURE
The mid-nineteenth-century expression *take one's breath away* means "to surprise one greatly." The expression is an exaggeration: one is so surprised that one stops breathing. The adjective *breathtaking* communicates the same meaning.

Word Work

In the article, ten terms are defined for you:

Adjectives	Expression	Nouns	Verbs
1. further 2. unreliable	3. be let down	4. defect 5. guideline 6. limb 7. mishap 8. ~~physician~~	9. enhance 10. warn

- In the text below, fill in the blanks with one of the terms listed above. You can only use each term once.
- Correctly conjugate all verbs in the simple present tense.

I think it's possible to trust your 1. _____*physician*_____ too much. Remember that doctors make mistakes too. Every day there is a medical 2. _____mishap_____; either the diagnostic equipment used was 3. _____unreliable_____, or the doctor should have performed 4. _____further_____ tests. Either way, the patient 5. _____is let down_____ by the doctor—and by the doctor's profession.

Patients 6. _____warn_____ other patients all the time about the importance of taking control of their medical treatment. It's important to heed this warning; in fact, for some, it might even be a matter of life and death. If nothing else, taking control of one's medical treatment 7. _____enhances_____ the doctor/patient relationship as the patient is an active participant in his or her treatment.

If I can offer one 8. _____guideline_____, it's to ask questions—a lot of questions—before accepting any medical treatment. Whether it's as simple as a broken 9. _____limb_____ or as complicated as a heart 10. _____defect_____, you can never ask too many questions.

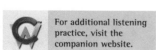

For additional listening practice, visit the companion website.

On March 11, 2002, the CBC news program *The National* ran a feature entitled "Measuring Up" by reporter Alison Smith, with guests Adele and Linda Warner, Gregor Wolbring, Katrina Howell, Dr. Lap Chi Tsoy and Tom Koch. This video segment is about eugenics, the practice of eliminating undesirable genetic traits from the human genome through genetic and prenatal testing and the elimination of "undesirable" fetuses.

Note: Tom Koch, a guest in this interview, is the author of the article in Section A of this unit.

Pre-Watching Vocabulary

Below you will find a chart containing ten collocations taken from the video segment. To understand a collocation, you must understand the meaning of the group of words—and not just the individual words themselves.

VOCABULARY TIP
A collocation is a group of words that are frequently used together to express an idea.

■ Examine each of the collocations below and try to infer the meaning of each by using a dictionary to look up any individual words that you may not know. Then verify your inferences by asking your teacher for feedback.

Collocations	Inferred Meanings	Teacher's Feedback
1. extended family		
2. gene pool		
3. genetic defect		
4. genetic makeup		
5. grieving process		
6. in one's wildest dreams		
7. litmus test		
8. people of difference		
9. soap opera		
10. special-needs child		

While Watching

You will watch the video segment twice.

■ The first time you watch, try to understand the various speakers' points of view.

■ The second time you watch, pay attention to the details of what each speaker has to say, taking brief point-form notes to help you remember the information.

Watching Comprehension

■ Referring to your notes, respond to each of the following questions.

1. Gary and Linda Warner's daughter Adele has Down syndrome.   TRUE ☑ FALSE ☐

2. What does Linda Warner mean when she says, "You kind of have to play the hand you're dealt"?

   She uses this expression in reference to her daughter Adele. At first, Mrs. Warner was upset that her

   daughter Adele had Down syndrome: she describes the first year as a "grieving process." She didn't get

   the "perfect child" she had wanted. She realized it's important to "accept the things you cannot change."

3. Genetic testing for Down syndrome is a recent development.   TRUE ☐ FALSE ☑

4. Fill in the blanks. "The more we learn about our ___genetic makeup___, the human genome, the more choices will confront us. Some scientists say that within ten years some ___10,000___ genetic diseases and conditions will be identified. How are we going to use that ___knowledge___ in a world where some notion of perfection is within our ___grasp___ and under our control?"

5. According to Gregor Wolbring, scientist at the University of Calgary, how are sexism, ableism and racism similar?

All three are social justice concepts.

6. According to Mr. Wolbring, "normal" is a lack of variation.   TRUE ☑ FALSE ☐

7. Explain why Katrina Howell made an appointment for an abortion and then cancelled it.

Katrina and her husband Chris are both carriers of cystic fibrosis. They already had one son with CF, and they didn't want another child with the fatal disease. In the 11th week of her pregnancy, Katrina's fetus was tested and found not to have CF. Katrina cancelled the abortion.

8. Is ethicist Tom Koch for or against eugenics?

He is against eugenics. He claims that "all diseases are part of the diversity of the human race."

9. Down syndrome is usually hereditary.   TRUE ☐ FALSE ☑

The answer to question 9 is false because Down syndrome occurs at random; it may sometimes be hereditary, but usually it's not.

Question 10 tests the student's ability to identify the main idea of the segment.

10. In general, Alison Smith's documentary
  a) is for eugenics.
  b) is against eugenics.
  c) presents positions both for and against eugenics.
  d) is about Down syndrome.

Would You Write That Down?

For additional writing practice, visit the companion website.

Two types of writing assignments are included below. Your teacher will tell you which assignment(s) you should complete.

WRITING SUGGESTION
Increase your credibility as a writer by directly referring to experts who have written on the subject of your essay. Name the experts and paraphrase or quote their opinions. Remember to reference correctly—or you will lose your credibility. (See Appendix A for more information about referencing.)

Free-form Writing

- Write 75 to 100 words in response to one of the following questions:

1. Briefly describe how knowing a disabled person has affected your life.

2. How would you feel about having a child with Down syndrome?

3. Would you want to know the gender of your child before it was born? Why or why not?

Essay Writing

- Write a 300- to 400-word essay using one of the thesis statements below.
- Do some research on the Internet to find evidence that supports your chosen thesis statement. (See Appendix A to review the structure of a persuasive essay.)

1. The elimination of disabled fetuses is (or is not) "genetic genocide."

2. It is (or is not) wrong to abort a fetus because of gender.

3. Society values (or does not value) diversity.

4. Everyone should (or should not) have the right to be born.

5. Prenatal testing is (or is not) risky.

Would You Speak Up?

You may be asked to participate in one or more of the speaking activities below.

> ### SPEAKING SUGGESTION
> Who hasn't had the misfortune of listening to someone read an entire speech from beginning to end? To make sure you don't fall into this trap, only have a brief outline with you when speaking in public. Write down your main points and any names, facts, figures or quotes that you are unlikely to remember. Remember to refer—not read.

Discussion

- In small groups, consider one (or more) of the following questions.
- Be prepared to share your thoughts with other groups in the class.

1. Is it self*less* or self*ish* to abort a diseased or disabled fetus?

2. Since World War II, eugenics has been viewed with disfavour. Should society reconsider its stand on eugenics?

3. In the video segment "Measuring Up," Linda Warner (the mother of Adele, a child with Down syndrome) says, "It's not a perfect world. You know, you just can't throw away what you don't want or what doesn't please you, or what you don't like." Do you agree or disagree with her statement?

4. What can children with Down syndrome teach our society?

5. Does our society discriminate against the disabled? Explain.

Discourse

- **Prepare a structured, five-minute speech on one of the thesis statements below. (See Appendix B for a suggested speaking structure.)**
- **Do some research to find evidence that supports your chosen thesis statement. Make sure your speech has an introduction, a development and a conclusion.**

1. Physicians should (or should not) reveal the gender of the fetus.

2. A eugenics program should (or should not) be implemented in Canada.

3. Genetic testing should (or should not) be banned.

4. Society values (or does not value) the disabled.

5. Prenatal testing should (or should not) be obligatory.

Debate

- **Debate the following proposal: The elimination of genetically diseased or disabled fetuses is wrong. (See Appendix B for the rules of debate.)**

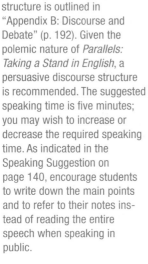

What's That Word Mean Again?

In the reading and listening sections, we focused on twenty terms—ten from each section. Try to complete the activity below without reviewing the terms in advance.

Crossword Puzzle

Do you enjoy the challenge of a crossword puzzle in your first language? Why not take up the challenge in English?

Required
A pen or pencil

Instructions
Read the clues and fill in the corresponding blanks.

Across

1. imperfection
3. _____ opera (collocation)
8. in one's _____ dreams (collocation)
9. _____ process (collocation)
10. people of _____ (collocation)
11. caution or notify
12. doctor
15. improve or make better
16. additional
17. genetic _____ (collocation, missing word a synonym of "flaw")
18. _____ test (collocation)
19. unfortunate accident

Down

2. _____ family (collocation)
4. gene _____ (collocation, four letters)
5. undependable
6. let somebody _____ (expression)
7. official recommendation
13. special-_____ child (collocation)
14. genetic _____ (collocation meaning "the way genes are arranged or combined")
18. arm or leg

Would You Like to Work Together?

In this section, you will work with another student on a joint writing and speaking project.

Project Overview

You and your partner will construct, complete and present a K-W-L chart. A K-W-L chart is a chart in which you outline what you know about a topic, what you want to know about a topic and what you have learned about a topic. Take the topic of human reproductive cloning (Section B in Unit 2 of this textbook) as an example.

This project will be assigned *before* you begin Unit 5, Section B, "Wrongful Life" and will be evaluated by your teacher *after* you complete this unit.

Required
- A computer and word processor
- Internet access

Topic: Human Reproductive Cloning		
A. What We Know	**B. What We Want to Know**	**C. What We Have Learned**
1. Human reproductive cloning is a controversial issue.	1. Is human reproductive cloning legal in Canada?	1. No, human reproductive cloning is illegal in Canada.
2. Cloning is a method of asexual reproduction.	2. What is the success rate for cloning mammals?	2. The success rate for cloning mammals is less than three percent.
3. No scientist has ever cloned a human being.	3. Do mammals reproduced by cloning age at the same rate as mammals reproduced naturally?	3. No. Mammals reproduced by cloning age more quickly than mammals reproduced naturally.
4. Scientists have cloned goats, pigs and dogs.	4. What is recombinant DNA technology?	4. Recombinant DNA technology is a synonym of DNA or gene cloning.
5. Clones occur naturally.	5. What was the first cloned animal?	5. The first cloned animal was a sheep named Dolly.

Procedure

1. Working together, construct a K-W-L chart on the topic of wrongful life using the chart on page 143 as a model.

2. In Part A, write five complete sentences indicating what you know about wrongful life. Number your sentences. In Part B, write five questions indicating what you would like to learn about wrongful life. Number your questions.

3. Orally present Sections A and B to your teacher and classmates.

4. *After* you, your teacher and your classmates have completed Unit 5, Section B, "Human Reproductive Cloning," respond in Part C to the questions you raised in Section B. Number your responses. Note: If, by the end of the unit, you have not learned the answers to all of your questions, do some research on the Internet to find the answers.

5. Orally present Part C to your teacher and your classmates.

6. Submit your completed K-W-L chart to your teacher for evaluation.

More than 400 years ago, English author and philosopher Sir Francis Bacon stated that "knowledge is power." In our modern technological age, this statement has never been more relevant as humanity possesses more knowledge now than ever before. Modern technology has given us the power to acquire and record vast amounts of information. However, does everyone have the right to know everything? Are there some things that people shouldn't know? Are there some things that people should pay to know? Who knows? By the end of this unit, you will!

SECTION A
Electronic Surveillance

Examines whether recording visual images should be permitted in public and private places.

SECTION B
Human Gene Patenting

Examines whether researchers have the right to own specific human gene sequences.

Electronic Surveillance

Did You Know?

Do you ever get the feeling that you are being watched? If so, don't panic! You are not paranoid—you are simply perceptive. The truth is you *are* being watched. You are being watched when you

- log on to your computer;
- turn on your cellphone;
- walk into a store;
- fill up your car;
- access an Automatic Teller Machine (ATM);
- use your credit card;
- enter your school or workplace.

Your actions are constantly being caught on videotape or digitally recorded for future reference. While some people are unconcerned by such surveillance, other people find it quite disturbing. The latter group is demanding restrictions on surveillance in daily life in order to protect personal privacy.

In Section A of this unit, we will focus on the use of video surveillance in public and private places.

Is video surveillance right or wrong? Let's examine the arguments.

Video surveillance is right because it	Video surveillance is wrong because it
1. helps prosecute shoplifters and other thieves.	1. threatens personal privacy.
2. reduces the incidence of child and elder abuse.	2. cultivates a society of mistrust.
3. is an effective defence against terrorism.	3. can be abused by the government.

Notice that there are strong pragmatic arguments in support of video surveillance and equally strong idealistic arguments against it. Are you a pragmatist or an idealist? Let's find out!

What's the Buzz?

■ **In pairs or small groups, respond to each of the questions below. Be prepared to share your answers with the class.**

Answers will vary. Answers are neither right nor wrong. Students must simply support their points of view.

1. A husband and wife hire a nanny to take care of their baby. The nanny has great references, but the husband and wife are anxious about leaving their child with a stranger. Should they buy a hidden camera to monitor the nanny's interactions with their child? Why or why not?

   _____

   _____

2. After six months of surveillance, the nanny referred to in the previous question is found to be competent and caring. Should the husband and wife remove the spy camera from their home? Should they inform the nanny that her actions were being recorded? Explain.

   _____

   _____

3. A local high school has recently been experiencing a great deal of vandalism, particularly in the restrooms. School authorities are considering installing video surveillance equipment inside the restrooms (in public areas only). Should they install the surveillance equipment? Justify your answer.

   _____

   _____

4. A husband suspects that his wife is cheating on him. Should he hire a private detective to film his wife's comings and goings? Why or why not?

_____

_____

hoods head coverings attached to coats

5. Recent fashion trends have made **hoods** very popular among British teenagers—but not among British storeowners. Video surveillance can't easily identify hooded teens, and some merchants want to ban teens with hoods from their stores. Should a storeowner be allowed to ban teenage customers because of their clothes? Explain your point of view.

_____

_____

Have You Read?

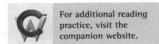

For additional reading practice, visit the companion website.

George Orwell's novel *1984* was first published in 1949. In his work, Orwell condemns totalitarianism, recounting a frightening tale of life under the constant surveillance of "Big Brother." In the article that you are about to read, journalist Richard Foot recounts a day in the life of Canadian privacy lawyer David Fraser. As you will soon discover, Big Brother isn't merely science fiction; it is science *reality*. Mr. Foot's article appeared in the *Windsor Star* on December 31, 2004.

Before Reading

Remember to skim and scan.

- Scan the headings, defined words and comprehension questions before reading the article.

While Reading

Mr. Foot recounts the events that occurred as David Fraser went about his business on a typical morning.

- Draw a timeline of these events on a separate piece of paper to help you remember them. You will see how each event is linked to a form of surveillance technology.

> READING STRATEGY
> Have you ever had a difficult time understanding a text? Sometimes viewing information graphically can help your understanding. For example, organizing information in a chart or diagram can help you see the relationship between the ideas in the text—and ultimately grasp the content.

BUSINESS OR BIG BROTHER?

BY RICHARD FOOT

David Fraser walks out his front door on a midwinter morning bound for work. His movements and activities are under surveillance, tracked by networks of people and distant computers in his own city and around the planet.

spy secret agent

5 Fraser isn't a wanted man, nor is he a foreign **spy**.

He's an ordinary Canadian inhabiting a world so wired by ubiquitous technology that almost everything he does is monitored and measured in breathtaking detail.

Fraser, a Halifax privacy lawyer, isn't concerned about the surveillance
10 itself. What worries him is that most Canadians simply don't know their lives are so closely watched by the silent eyes of business and government. Like federal privacy commissioner Jennifer Stoddart, he calls public ignorance about the vast, daily exchange of personal information the greatest threat to privacy in Canada today.

15 "The critical thing is that people must be aware of it," Fraser says. "Yet most people simply don't understand how much private information they leave behind them each day, during their ordinary routines."

trail trace

Fraser's own daily data **trail** begins after he gets up each morning, when he turns on his home computer and logs on to his e-mail, alerting his
20 Internet service provider that he's awake and online. The ISP stores copies of his e-mails and tracks the websites he surfs.

Cellphone, a Homing Signal

An hour later, he and his two boys are driving in rush-hour traffic, with his cellphone transmitting signals to a local radio tower, telling his cellular
25 company precisely where he is in the city.

Fraser doesn't need to use the phone for it to track his whereabouts; cellphones transmit signals every few seconds once they're turned on. Many

store put something away for use in the future

cellular companies **store** tracking records for years, in order to manage network capacity.

30 But police can obtain records of cellphone calls and locations with less trouble than it takes them to get a wiretap on a regular land line.

After taking his sons to school, Fraser stops at a hardware store to buy paint for a weekend renovation project at his neighbourhood church.

Two sets of video surveillance cameras watch and record his movements
35 inside the store. He pays for the paint using the church's in-store account, which means his name, and by inference his religious affiliation, are entered into the store's computer records.

He stops at a gas station, where more video cameras watch him buy a tank of gas while also recording the licence plate number on his Honda Accord.
40 He pays at the pump with his Visa card, and also uses his Aeroplan card to earn points on the purchase. The gas company, Visa and Aeroplan now each have records of his visit.

At the bank, another camera records him walking into the building toward an automatic teller. A hidden camera inside the ATM also records his visit to the machine.

The ATM sends Fraser's withdrawal request to a bank-networking company—a faraway **hub** of computers—which contacts the computers at his bank. Details of the transaction will be stored for several years on both computer databases.

It's shortly after 9 a.m. when Fraser arrives at his office building. A swipe card that opens the parking garage records on a digital **log** that he has entered the building.

He rides an elevator upstairs, watched by a **tiny** video camera inside the elevator compartment.

He turns on his computer and **logs on** to his office e-mail, alerting the corporate law firm where he works that he's arrived at his desk.

Although he enjoys the privilege of a private office, his workplace e-mails are far from private. Like most Canadian workers, the messages he sends and receives are stored on the company database, where a copy is kept on file even after Fraser erases the message from his e-mail delete box.

Some companies archive employee e-mail records every month, and store the data for several years. Others use Internet tracking software that monitors every website an employee surfs on their workplace computers, what chat-groups they visit and what discussions they have there.

Even if his own company isn't observing his Internet use, a **slew** of outside organizations are. As he begins his morning tour through various online newspaper sites, the websites themselves—and the advertisers that place ads on the sites—plant "cookies," "spyware" or other invasive software on his computer, surreptitiously transmitting information about who is visiting the particular web page.

By the time he's run his morning **errands**, arrived at work, perused the web and answered his e-mail messages, Fraser's personal activities have already been tracked by a handful of people he's never met, plus a dozen video surveillance cameras and several dozen databases around the world.

It's only 10 a.m. The day is just beginning. When he flies to Calgary on business, Fraser will also spread his digital DNA across the country.

Video cameras will watch and record his presence at airports; before he even walks through airport security, various agencies of the federal government will have received notice of his reservation on Air Canada.

Trail of Personal Data

His cellphone will register his presence in Calgary. From there, his Calgary hotel will send details of his booking to his credit card company; the Internet service provider for the hotel will record the e-mail messages he sends from his laptop inside his room; even the hotel itself—if it uses digital key cards—will have a record of when he leaves and enters his room.

---

hub centre

log journal or record

tiny minuscule

log on access a computer system

slew large number or amount

errand task or small job

"So much of this information that's collected on us is staggeringly **trivial**," says Fraser. "But if you put it all together, it can be used to create profiles
90   of people, which allows inferences about them."

944 Words

Reading Comprehension

— Respond to each of the questions below.

1. In line 6, the author uses the term *ubiquitous*. What does this term mean? Rephrase and simplify the sentence in which this term is used.

Ubiquitous means "present everywhere at the same time." Simplified rephrasing: He's an average guy living

in a world where technology is everywhere; everything he does is monitored and recorded.

2. Mr. Fraser is concerned about surveillance itself.   TRUE ☐ FALSE ☑

3. What does the acronym "ISP" stand for?

The acronym ISP stands for Internet Service Provider.

4. Which of the following statements is incorrect?
  a) ISPs store copies of users' e-mails.
  (b) Cellular companies know the location of their clients whether the cell-phone is on or off.
  c) Gas stations record their clients' licence plate numbers.
  d) ATMs are equipped with hidden cameras.

5. Details of banking transactions done on ATMs are stored for several years.   TRUE ☑ FALSE ☐

6. What is a swipe card?

a "key card" used to open doors

7. Which of the following statements is incorrect?
  a) Copies of employee e-mail messages may be stored in company data-bases.
  b) Employee e-mail messages may be archived by the employer.
  c) Websites visited by employees may be monitored by the employer.
  (d) None of the above

8. In line 69, the author uses the term *surreptitiously*. What does this term mean? Rephrase and simplify the sentence in which this term is used.

Surreptitiously means "furtively or secretly." Simplified rephrasing: By the time Fraser completes his errands,

his activities have secretly been recorded by unknown individuals throughout the world.

9. At the gas station, David Fraser was videotaped. Name four other places where David Fraser's movements were recorded on video.

  a) in a hardware store   **c)** in an elevator at his office

  b) at the bank (and/or the ATM)   **d)** in airports

10. The main idea of the article is to inform the reader about the amount of surveillance that exists today.　　TRUE ☑　FALSE ☐

Discussion

■ **In pairs or small groups, discuss your answers to each of the questions below. Be prepared to share your thoughts with the class.**

1. Lawyer David Fraser claims that Canadians are unaware that they are being watched. Were you unaware of any of the surveillance practices mentioned in the article? If so, which one(s)?

2. Stores videotape customers in order to discourage, reduce and prosecute theft. Do you believe that clothing stores should be allowed to videotape customers in change rooms? Explain your answer.

3. Do you think that the government knows too much about you and therefore has too much power over you? Does the situation concern you?

Word Work

In the article, ten terms are defined for you:

Adjectives	Nouns	Verbs
1. tiny 2. trivial	3. errand 4. hub 5. log 6. slew 7. spy 8. ~~trail~~	9. log on 10. store

■ **Each of the sentences below contains a term in italics. Choose a term from the list above that could replace the italicized term without changing the meaning of the sentence. Pluralize nouns and conjugate verbs as required.**

■ **Try doing the exercise without referring to the definitions provided in the reading section.**

1. Did the thief leave a *trace* behind for the police?　　　　_trail_

2. How many times a day do you *access* your computer?　　　_log on_

3. I have a few *small jobs* to do: buy groceries, go to the bank and fill up the car.　　　　_errands_

4. I have a *large amount* of homework to do.　　　　_slew_

5. In the spring, I *put away* my winter clothes.　　　　_store_

6. My employer keeps a *record* of all employee e-mails.　　　_log_

7. My grandmother's kitchen was the *centre* of all household activity.　　　_hub_

GRAMMAR TIP
The verb *dream* has two past tense forms: *dreamed* and *dreamt*. While most verbs have either regular past tense forms **or** irregular past tense forms, some verbs have both. For lists of common regular and irregular verbs, see the companion volume *Parallels: Taking a Stand in English—English Grammar.*

8. She wastes her time worrying about *unimportant* matters. _____ trivial

9. There is a *minuscule* camera hidden in the artificial plant. _____ tiny

10. When I was a child, I dreamed of becoming a *secret agent*. _____ spy

For additional listening practice, visit the companion website.

WORD CULTURE
The expression *turn the table on someone* originates from the custom of reversing the table or board in games like chess and checkers so that the opponents' relative positions are switched. A similar expression is *turnabout is fair play*.

People snoop. It is a fact of life. For example, many parents snoop on their children, looking through their children's dresser drawers, closets and diaries. With today's technology, snooping has become highly sophisticated, enabling some parents to become highly sophisticated snoopers. Listen in on a report about parents who spy on their children in an interview conducted by Suhana Meharchand of the CBC television program *News Morning Weekend Edition*. Ms. Meharchand interviews two guests: Sean Dodds, who runs a store called Spy Depot in Toronto, and parenting expert Kathy Lynn. The segment, entitled "Spying on Kids," aired on January 23, 2005.

Pre-Watching Vocabulary

Below you will find ten idiomatic expressions, phrasal verbs and collocations.

▬ **Match each expression with its correct explanation. The first one has been done for you as an example.**

Expressions		Explanations
1. back and forth	_g_	a) investigate someone's actions
2. be a happy median	_i_	b) watch someone carefully
3. catch someone doing something	_e_	c) invent something
4. check up on somebody	_a_	d) have difficulty with something
5. dream something up	_c_	e) see someone doing something wrong
6. growing number	_j_	f) reverse the situation between two people
7. keep an eye on someone	_b_	g) first in one direction and then in the other
8. struggle with something	_d_	h) use something to make something else happen
9. turn the table on someone	_f_	i) be an acceptable situation or compromise
10. use something as a springboard for something else	_h_	j) more and more (people or things)

After matching expressions with explanations, students are asked to pair up and write ten sentences that demonstrate correct usage. For model sentences, see the Additional Notes in the Teacher Section of the companion website.

While Watching

You will watch the video clip twice.

■ **The first time you watch, try to understand the speakers' positions on using spy equipment in the home.**

■ **The second time you watch, pay attention to the details of what each speaker has to say, taking brief point-form notes to help you remember the information.**

Watching Comprehension

■ **While you are watching, respond to each of the questions below.**

1. Sean Dodds thinks that spy gadgets have a place in the home. TRUE ☑ FALSE ☐

2. The software program eBlaster tracks
   a) keystrokes.   b) participation in chat-groups.
   c) e-mails.   (d) All of the above

3. Which of the following places does Sean Dodds *not* mention as a possible hiding place for cameras?
   (a) books
   b) pagers
   c) **fanny packs**
   d) air fresheners
   e) speakers
   f) fake plants
   g) microwave ovens

4. Sean Dodds says that spy cameras have increased in popularity because people see them everywhere, including on television shows. He mentions two other reasons. What are they?
   a) Spy cameras are "much more friendly to the user" (i.e., they're more "user-friendly").
   b) They're much cheaper.

5. Parenting expert Kathy Lynn believes that if parents use spy cameras on their children, their relationship with them will be largely unaffected. TRUE ☐ FALSE ☑

6. Fill in the blanks. According to Ms. Lynn, "If our kids know we don't trust them, then they may act in ways that are _____untrustworthy_____ because they're doing what they think we expect. Or they may just shut down. Or they may become _____sneakier_____. But what they're not going to become is friendlier, happier or more open because they're getting a message that we're spying."

LISTENING STRATEGY
Before listening for information, consider what you already know about the subject. In this case, what do you know about spy equipment? What jargon (or specialized language) do you think will be used—*camera, wires, alarm systems*? Putting yourself in the right context is a springboard to understanding.

fanny pack small bag worn on a belt

The answer to question 5 is false because Kathy Lynn believes that the relationship will be ruined.

7. Ms. Lynn doesn't support the use of spy gadgets in any situation. How does she feel about blocking Internet sites for children?

Ms. Lynn supports buying Internet equipment to block sites "ahead of time."

8. Ms. Lynn believes that we are buying more spy gadgets than before because we think we have the right to know everything all the time, and because we are becoming extremely paranoid.

TRUE ☑ FALSE ☐

9. Fill in the blanks. "Life is not harder, more dangerous than it was. It's more complex, for sure. But it's still teenagers being teenagers, and we need to be _____parenting_____ them, not _____spying_____ on them."

10. The video segment is a presentation of both sides of the controversial issue of using spy equipment in the home.

TRUE ☑ FALSE ☐

Would You Write That Down?

Your teacher may ask you to complete one or more of the following writing activities.

Free-form Writing

■ **Write 75 to 100 words in response to one of the following questions:**

1. Have you ever spied on anyone (or been spied on)? If so, write a brief description of the event. Write about the event itself as well as your feelings about it.

2. In previous generations, people didn't even lock their front doors. Nowadays, not only do they lock their front doors, they also install peepholes, alarm systems and video surveillance cameras. Do you think this generation is paranoid, or is it right to be fearful of others?

3. In this section of Unit 6, we have seen how technology threatens personal privacy. However, some technologies, such as call display and digital encryption, actually protect personal privacy. In your opinion, is technology a friend or foe of personal privacy?

WRITING SUGGESTION
Good writers carefully choose the order in which they present their main points. They never begin or end with their weakest point—they hide it in the middle of their text. If you want to leave a good impression, create a strong first and last impression.

Essay Writing

- Write a 300- to 400-word essay using one of the thesis statements below.

- Do some research on the Internet to find evidence that supports your chosen thesis statement. (See Appendix A to review the structure of a persuasive essay.)

1. Personal privacy does (or does not) exist in today's technological world.

2. Video surveillance in the school or workplace is (or is not) acceptable.

3. Parents should (or should not) use hidden video surveillance to monitor their children's behaviour.

4. Storeowners should have (or should not have) the right to ban hooded teens from their stores.

5. Electronic surveillance promotes (or does not promote) good social conduct.

Would You Speak Up?

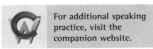

For additional speaking practice, visit the companion website.

Your teacher may ask you to participate in one or more of the following speaking activities.

Discussion

Answers will vary.

eavesdrop listen secretly

- In pairs or small groups, consider one (or more) of the following questions. Be prepared to share your thoughts with the class.

1. Why do people **eavesdrop**? Think of a situation in which you eavesdropped and explain why you did it.

2. Look up the word *privacy* in a dictionary. Does privacy exist in today's society? Justify your response.

SPEAKING SUGGESTION
When ordering your points in a presentation, use the same strategy suggested for writing persuasive essays—hide your weakest point in the middle of your presentation.

3. Should police be allowed to use photo radar, a system in which a computerized radar gun takes a picture of a speeding car, reads the licence plate number from the picture and mails a ticket to the owner of the car? Why or why not? (Note: Photo radar can't identify the driver of the car.)

4. Can you think of any situation in which you would use spy equipment on a friend, boyfriend/girlfriend or family member? Explain.

5. In the video segment, parenting expert Kathy Lynn claims that parental use of spy equipment on children would "totally ruin the relationship." Do you agree with this statement?

Discourse

- Prepare a structured, five-minute speech on one of the thesis statements below. (See Appendix B for suggested speaking structure.)
- Do some research to find evidence that supports your chosen thesis statement. Make sure your speech has an introduction, a development and a conclusion.

1. Government agencies should (or should not) have the right to monitor personal communication (phone calls, e-mails, Internet browsing, etc.).

2. Identity theft is (or is not) a serious public concern.

3. Canadian privacy rights are (or are not) threatened.

4. Eavesdropping is (or is not) wrong.

5. Canadian anti-terrorism laws are (or are not) adequate.

Debate

- Debate the following proposal: Video surveillance is wrong. (See Appendix B for the rules of a debate.)

What's That Word Mean Again?

In this section of Unit 6, we have focused on twenty terms—ten from the reading section and ten from the listening section. Review these terms by completing the activity below.

Word Memory Game

Have you ever played "Memory"? Memory is a card game in which cards are placed face down on a flat surface. Players must turn over two cards at a time, trying to make a *match*. A match occurs when two identical cards are turned over or—in the case of a word memory game—when a word and its definition are turned over. If a match isn't made, the cards must be turned face down again, and the next player takes his or her turn. If a match is made, the two cards are removed and the player takes another turn. The winner is the player with the most cards.

Materials
- One to three partners
- Forty blank index cards
- A pen or pencil
- A dictionary
- A good memory!

Instructions

1. Review the twenty terms and their explanations.

2. Write down each term and its explanation (you can use a synonym, a definition or a translation) on two separate index cards (twenty terms + twenty explanations = forty index cards).

3. Shuffle the cards.

4. Lay the cards face down on a flat surface.

5. Begin the game.

Alternate Version: You may make the game more challenging by insisting that the player who makes the match use the word in a sentence. If the player can't use the word correctly, the cards are turned faced down again and the next player takes his or her turn.

Would You Like to Work Together?

In this section, you will work with another student on a joint writing and speaking project.

Project Overview

You and your partner will do a written summary of an article on electronic surveillance and give a verbal response.

A summary should be no longer than four sentences:

1. In the first sentence, identify the title, the author and the main idea of the article.

2. In the remaining three sentences, enumerate three pieces of evidence that support the main idea. (Note: There will likely be more than three pieces of evidence; choose <u>any</u> three.)

On pages 6 and 7 of this textbook you will find an article by Susan Schwartz entitled "The Truth Is, I've Been Guilty of Lying." An example summary of this article would be as follows:

In "The Truth Is, I've Been Guilty of Lying," Susan Schwartz claims that it is surprising how dishonest "decent" people can be.

    1. The author believes that she is a "decent" person, but admits that she frequently tells lies.

    2. An expert indicates that totally honest people are not liked by others.

    3. An online poll suggests that a majority of people claim it is possible to be "too honest."

A verbal response requires that you respect the following guidelines:

1. Identify the author's main idea.

2. Agree <u>or</u> disagree with the author's idea.

3. Provide three supporting ideas (statistics, expert opinion or example) to support your opinion. (Note: Do not "reuse" the author's supporting ideas. Do some research on the Internet to find three supporting ideas of your own.)

Required
- This textbook
- A dictionary and a grammar book
- A computer with Internet access

Procedure
This activity is carried out in two parts.

Part A: The Summary
1. Working individually, read the article "We've All Been in the Camera's Eye for a Long Time" by Michael Geist (pp. 178–179). Use a dictionary to help you understand any difficult terms.

2. Working together, summarize the article using the example summary above as a model. Verify your spelling and grammar.

3. Submit your summary to your teacher for evaluation.

Part B: The Verbal Response
4. Working together, read your teacher's evaluation of your summary. Decide whether you agree or disagree with the author's main idea. (Note: The two of you must share the same opinion.)

5. Conduct research on the Internet, looking for three ideas that support your opinion. (Remember: Search for statistics, expert opinion and/or examples.)

6. Meet with your teacher and give a verbal response using the guidelines provided above. During your meeting, your teacher will evaluate your response by asking you a series of questions: be prepared!

Human Gene Patenting

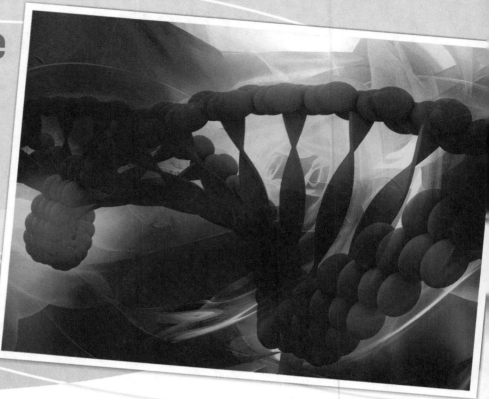

Did You Know?

A patent is basically a contract between an inventor and society. On the one hand, the inventor agrees to invest time and money in the invention and to share the invention with society. On the other hand, society agrees to grant the inventor exclusive rights to the invention, typically for a twenty-year period. If the invention is successful, the inventor's exclusive rights (or monopoly) could make him or her very rich. If the invention is unsuccessful, the inventor's time and money are lost.

In 1980, the inventors of a genetically modified bacterium were granted a patent, opening the door to the patenting of specific gene sequences, genetic tests and therapies. By 2003, more than 30,000 human gene patents had been granted.

While human gene patenting is obviously big business, not everyone is convinced that it is good business. You can argue that human gene patenting encourages biopharmaceutical companies to develop genetic tests and therapies. However, you can also argue that human gene patenting allows the biopharmaceutical companies to charge exorbitant prices for the tests and therapies being developed. For the patient unable to afford the price, the consequence is obvious: no money, no test; no test, no therapy; no therapy, no patient!

Human gene patenting is an important societal issue. Let's examine the arguments.

Human gene patenting is right because it	Human gene patenting is wrong because it
1. provides adequate compensation for biopharmaceutical companies.	1. overcompensates biopharmaceutical companies.
2. promotes the development of genetic tests and therapies for society.	2. makes genetic tests and therapies available only to the wealthy.
3. encourages healthy competition in the field of genetic research.	3. discourages cooperation among researchers.

Money is at the heart of the conflict surrounding human gene patenting. While money is "the root of all evil," it also "makes the world go round." In this debate, you will have to decide how much is too much and where compensation ends and exploitation begins.

What's the Buzz?

■ In pairs or small groups, respond to each of the following questions. Be prepared to share your answers with the class.

Answers will vary. Answers are neither right nor wrong. Students must simply support their points of view.

1. You run a pharmaceutical company that makes medication to treat Acquired Immune Deficiency Syndrome (AIDS). In Canada, your company charges $15,000 for a year's supply of medication while in Sub-Saharan Africa, your company only charges $600 for the same amount of medication. There are tens of millions of people living with AIDS in Sub-Saharan Africa where the average salary is about a dollar a day. Should your company simply provide the AIDS medication for free to this impoverished region? Why? Why not?

_____

_____

2. Between 1997 and 2001, the cost of patented prescription drugs increased by 68.3 percent in Canada (Brown). You are the prime minister and you are about to call an election. Do you reduce patent protection from twenty to ten years and risk antagonizing the powerful biopharmaceutical industry? Why? Why not?

_____

_____

3. More than 80 percent of Canadians over the age of sixty-five take prescription drugs (Canadian Pensioners Concerned) and many of them live on fixed incomes. You are the prime minister of Canada. Should your government increase taxes and use the revenue generated to provide free medication to senior citizens? Why? Why not?

_____

_____

4. You are a geneticist researching Type-1 diabetes. Some of your research has been funded by the Canadian government. You believe that you have discovered the mechanism that protects the human body from this disease. Do you apply for a patent before sharing your knowledge with the scientific community? Explain.

_____

_____

5. Early onset Alzheimer's disease (afflicting people under the age of sixty) may be caused by gene mutations that can be identified by genetic testing. Would you want to be tested for the gene mutation even though there is currently no cure for the disease? Explain your answer.

_____

_____

Have You Read?

For additional reading practice, visit the companion website.

The next article was co-authored by Timothy Caulfield and Richard Gold. Professor Caulfield's research focuses on genetics, ethics and the law. Professor Gold's research focuses on the relationship between technology, commerce and ethics. Their article is about a conflict concerning the patenting of a breast cancer gene. On one side of the conflict, we have the Canadian healthcare system; on the other side, we have Myriad Genetics, an American biopharmaceutical company. Their article appeared in the *Ottawa Citizen* on Wednesday, November 21, 2001.

READING STRATEGY
Have you ever had a difficult time understanding a text? Sometimes viewing information graphically can help your understanding. For example, organizing information in a chart or diagram can help you see the relationship between the ideas in the text—and ultimately grasp the content.

Before Reading

Remember to skim and scan.

- **Read the defined words and comprehension questions before reading the article.**

While Reading

Professors Caulfield and Gold present the arguments and the people and organizations on both sides of the debate.

On pages 180–181, you will find another article by Timothy Caulfield on the subject of human gene patenting. Students are directed to this article in the "Would You Like to Work Together?" section of this unit (pp. 172–173).

 As you are reading, chart the arguments for and against gene patenting as well as the people and organizations for and against it. By the end of the article, you will have a clearer picture of the debate.

> **VOCABULARY TIP**
> In this article, you will find many variations of the word *patent*. *Patent* and *patenting* can be used as nouns or as adjectives to modify other nouns (e.g., *patent protection* and *patenting process*). We can speak about discoveries being *patentable* (adjective) or we can argue about their *patentability* (noun) when they are *patently* (adverb) silly. In addition, if a person is granted a patent, he or she can be referred to as a *patentee* (noun).

THE DARK SIDE OF GENE PATENTING

BY TIMOTHY CAULFIELD AND RICHARD GOLD

Should we be able to patent human genes? Recent events in Canada have given a practical spin to this controversial and philosophically complex question.

enforce make people obey

5 U.S.-based Myriad Genetics, which owns the patent on a gene that predisposes women to breast cancer, has decided to **enforce** its rights by insisting that all diagnostic tests involving the gene be done through Myriad. At more than $3,000 for a test, a number of provincial governments have said the cost is prohibitive. In Ontario, the Harris government said it will challenge the patent.

mixed blessing something good and bad at the same time
breakthrough discovery

10 Gene patents clearly present a **mixed blessing**. On the one hand, we want patents to encourage industry to find new health **breakthroughs**; on the other, we fear the ethical and health policy implications of them doing so. Around the world, thousands and thousands of patents have already been issued for human genetic material. Patenting a gene is considered by

WORD CULTURE
The expression *a mixed blessing* is a modern one, dating to the first half of the twentieth century.

15 industry, and much of the research community, as an essential and logical part of the gene discovery process. But, as **highlighted** by the Myriad issue, gene patenting has always had a dark side: patents can be used to block access to the medical procedures we had hoped the genetic era would bring.

highlight emphasize

20 Despite the "where-did-this-come-from?" attitude that provincial governments are displaying around the Myriad problem, the human gene patent issue has received intense **scrutiny** for more than a decade. Professional bodies, such as the American College of Medical Genetics, have **cautioned** against what they perceive to be an overly liberal application of patent

scrutiny examination
caution warn

25 law in the context of human genetic material. UNESCO's 1997 Universal Declaration on the Human Genome and Human Rights says the "human genome in its natural state shall not give rise to financial gains." And in March 2000, just before the announcement that a **rough draft** of the human genome had been achieved, Tony Blair and Bill Clinton issued a

rough draft first version

30 joint statement calling for open access to the genome.

Given all this cautionary commentary, how did we end up with the Myriad controversy?

First, through the lens of the law, there has never really been any doubt that human genetic material is patentable. Since the key U.S. Supreme Court case of Diamond vs. Chakrabarty in 1980, in which an oil-eating bacterium was found to be patentable, there has been little that has not been viewed as potentially worthy of patent protection, providing the "invention" contained an element of human ingenuity. In fact, recent Canadian case law has been leaning toward a more inclusive view of patentability, as highlighted by last year's Federal Court of Appeal decision allowing patenting over a genetically modified mouse.

award accord

Second, there are justifications for allowing patents in this context. Patents are meant to encourage innovation by **awarding** a twenty-year monopoly to the "inventor." Because big profits can often be decades removed from an actual biomedical discovery, biotechnology is a risky and capital-intensive business. Patents give investors a sense of security that they will see a return on their investment.

More importantly, however, universities and the federal and provincial governments have also bought into the patenting game. Policy-makers are understandably excited about the economic potential of biotechnology: it is currently the fastest growing sector of the Canadian economy.

bit player unimportant participant

Finally, the developed world has openly embraced gene patents. Not only the United States, but Europe and Japan, the major economic powers in the health-care field, have accepted patents for human genetic material. Canada is just a **bit player** in this world context. Even if Canada wanted to eliminate gene patents, it may not have the option. Under international trade agreements, Canada is probably obliged to grant patents on human genes.

We are entering an era when more and more gene-based tests, drugs and therapies will be moving from the laboratory and into clinics. Although the Myriad dilemma is the tip of a very big iceberg, now is not the time to cast blame. Myriad is doing exactly what one would expect any commercial enterprise to do: make money using all its legal rights.

craft construct

The Canadian government should use the Myriad controversy as a stimulus to work with the international community to **craft** long-term strategies to mediate the concerns. Given the complex history of gene patents and the various and often conflicting social goals at play, this would undoubtedly be a long and frustrating process. But reform is essential.

750 words

Reading Comprehension

▬ **Respond to each of the questions below.**

1. In line 2, the authors use the term *spin*. What does this term mean? Rephrase and simplify the sentence in which the term is used.

The word *spin* is a synonym of *interpretation*. Simplified rephrasing: The issue of human gene patenting should be examined or interpreted from a practical (and not philosophical) viewpoint.

2. Myriad Genetics' patent on a gene that predisposes women to breast cancer gives the company exclusive rights to expensive genetic testing.   TRUE ☑ FALSE ☐

3. Why are gene patents a "mixed blessing"?

    On the positive side, gene patents encourage genetic discoveries; on the negative side, gene patents raise

    ethical (and health policy) questions (and/or gene patents block access to medical treatment—some

    patients can't afford the tests and therapies).

4. Which of the following statements is correct?
    a) The issue of human gene patenting hasn't been around for very long.
    b) The American College of Medical Genetics is an enthusiastic supporter of human gene patenting.
    c) United Nations Educational, Scientific and Cultural Organization (UNESCO) supports human gene patenting.
    d) British Prime Minister Tony Blair and American President Bill Clinton believe that knowledge of the human genome shouldn't be restricted.

The answer to question 5 is false because U.S. and Canadian law (strongly) support the patenting of genetic material.

5. The legality of human gene patents is questionable.   TRUE ☐ FALSE ☑

6. What is the justification of offering a twenty-year patent monopoly?

    Patents encourage investment in companies that may have to wait a very long time to generate any

    profit—if any profit is generated. Inventing has its risks, and these risks should be compensated.

7. Which of the following statements is incorrect?
    a) Biotechnology has great economic potential for the Canadian economy.
    b) Human gene patents are only recognized in the United States and Canada.
    c) International law requires Canada to recognize and honour human gene patents.
    d) None of the above

8. In the second last paragraph, the authors write that "… the Myriad dilemma is the tip of a very big iceberg …" What does this statement suggest?

    This statement suggests that many other companies will follow Myriad's example and enforce their

    patent rights on their genetic tests and therapies.

The answer to question 9 is false because the authors state that the objective of any business is to make money. Myriad is a business like any other.

9. The authors criticize Myriad for making money.   TRUE ☐ FALSE ☑

Question 10 tests the student's ability to identify the main idea of the text.

10. In general, the authors support human gene patent reform.   TRUE ☑ FALSE ☐

Discussion

Answers will vary.

■ **In pairs or small groups, discuss your answers to each of the following questions. Be prepared to share your thoughts with the class.**

1. "A genome is an organism's complete set of deoxyribonucleic acid (DNA), a chemical compound that contains the genetic instructions needed to develop and direct the activities of every organism." (National Human Genome Research Institute). On April 14, 2003, a complete map of the human genome was finally completed after thirteen years of work and international cooperation. Medical law specialist Maureen McTeer has described the human genome as "… a public treasure, and not a private treasure trove." What does she mean by this statement? Do you agree with her?

2. In your opinion, should science sell or share its knowledge with society? Explain.

3. Should a person be refused genetic testing and therapy because he or she doesn't have enough money to pay for them?

Word Work

In the article, ten terms are defined for you:

Collocations	Nouns	Verbs
1. a bit player 2. a mixed blessing 3. rough draft	4. breakthrough 5. scrutiny	6. award 7. caution 8. craft 9. enforce 10. highlight

- Each of the sentences below contains a term in italics. Choose a term from the list above that could replace the italicized term without changing the meaning of the sentence. Pluralize nouns and conjugate verbs as required
- Try doing the exercise without referring to the definitions provided in the reading section.

1. A *first version* of the essay is due next class.   *rough draft*

2. Many are calling for intense *examination* of the Canada Patent Act.   scrutiny

3. The geneticist *emphasized* the contributions of all members of the research team.   highlighted

4. The judge *made the defendants obey* his ruling.   enforced

5. The lawyers carefully *constructed* their defence strategy.   crafted

6. The student was *accorded* first place for her ingenious research project.   awarded

7. The teacher *warned* the students not to plagiarize.   cautioned

8. The United States is definitely not *an unimportant participant* in world politics.   a bit player

9. This year, there has been an exciting new *discovery* in the field of cancer research.   breakthrough

10. Winning the lottery was *good and bad at the same time*; her life became easier in some ways and more difficult in others.

a mixed blessing

For additional listening practice, visit the companion website.

In Canada, approximately 20,000 new cases of breast cancer are diagnosed every year, and as many as 2,000 of these cases have a genetic risk factor. Women with abnormalities carried in BRCA1 and BRCA2 genes develop breast cancer more often than those without the abnormalities, and they develop it at a younger age (Canadian Cancer Society). As you learned in the reading, Myriad Genetics holds a patent on the BRCA1 and BRCA2 gene mutations as well as on the genetic test designed to identify them. In 2001, Myriad told Canadian provincial governments to stop genetic testing for BRCA1 and BRCA2 with alternate tests, stating that all such testing would have to be done at Myriad using Myriad's (more expensive) test. In a CBC radio interview from October 6, 2001, host Bob McDonald interviews medical ethicist Dr. Miriam Shuchman on the subject of human gene patenting.

After matching expressions with explanations, students are asked to pair up and write ten sentences that demonstrate correct usage. For model sentences, see the Additional Notes in the Teacher Section of the companion website.

Pre-Listening Vocabulary

Below you will find ten idiomatic expressions, phrasal verbs and collocations.

■ **Match each expression with its correct explanation. The first one has been done for you as an example.**

Expressions		Explanations
1. argue vociferously	*h*	a) provide or supply something
2. be able to afford something	j	b) contract between countries
3. be at the heart of something	i	c) legally protected original creation
4. big hoopla	e	d) find an answer to something
5. come up with something	a	e) much excitement about something
6. dump on someone	g	f) important consequences
7. far-reaching implications	f	g) criticize someone (slang)
8. intellectual property	c	h) argue loudly
9. international treaty	b	i) be at the centre of something
10. work something out	d	j) be able to buy something

■ After verifying your answers with your teacher, find a partner and use the expressions in ten sentences of your own. Each partner is responsible for writing five sentences that demonstrate the correct usage of the terms.

LISTENING STRATEGY
Before listening for information, consider what you already know about the subject. In this case, what do you know about human gene patenting? What jargon (or specialized language) do you think will be used— *biotechnology, cancer, sample*? Putting yourself in the right context is a springboard to understanding.

While Listening

You will hear the interview twice.

■ The first time you listen, try to identify the general idea of what Dr. Shuchman has to say.

■ The second time you listen, pay attention to the details of what Dr. Shuchman has to say, taking brief point-form notes to help you remember the information.

Listening Comprehension

■ While you are listening, respond to each of the questions below.

1. Women with a history of breast cancer in their families have an increased risk of possessing the genes for breast cancer. TRUE ☑ FALSE ☐

2. Fill in the blanks. "There was a _____hoopla_____ a few years ago when those were discovered. Absolutely. It was a very big deal because you could say, 'Look, at least some cases of breast cancer are going to be related to this gene.' We're going to be able to find out much earlier that someone's at risk for it and maybe do things that would _____prevent_____ it."

3. Which of the following statements is incorrect?
   a) Myriad owns the patents on BRCA1 and BRCA2.
   b) Myriad is one of the two biggest gene-sequencing companies in the United States.
   c) Myriad has only patented the breast cancer genes.
   d) Myriad was able to increase investment in their company due to their BRCA1 and BRCA2 patents.

4. Ontario says that genetically testing blood samples at Myriad in Utah using Myriad's test will cost much more than doing the testing in Ontario using alternate tests. How much more?
   Ontario says that testing at Myriad using Myriad's test will cost four times as much.

5. Because Myriad owns the patents on the breast cancer genes, the company also owns the patent on any test related to these genes. TRUE ☑ FALSE ☐

6. Ontario and Alberta are still testing for the breast cancer genes. British Columbia has stopped testing and will send blood samples to Myriad at the patient's expense. What is Quebec doing?
   Quebec is paying the price and sending the samples to Utah (Myriad) for testing.

7. At the moment, Myriad is the only company holding marketable gene patents.   TRUE ☐ FALSE ☑

8. Fill in the blanks. "So Myriad is going to keep coming out with these tests. Sooner or later, they're going to start coming out with ___therapies___. All these companies that own the rights to genes are going to do that. And ___healthcare___ systems are saying, 'Wait a second. There's no way we're going to be able to afford whatever gene-based tests or gene-based therapies you come up with.'"

9. Making the case against gene patenting, ethicists, the United Nations (UN) and the National Institutes of Health (NIH) have argued that there is a difference between patenting drugs and patenting genes. What is the basis of their argument?

Genes are found in nature; drugs are developed (i.e., invented) in the laboratory. It is wrong to patent what is found in nature.

10. The radio segment is a one-sided presentation of the controversial issue of patenting human gene sequences.   TRUE ☐ FALSE ☑

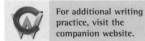

Would You Write That Down?

For additional writing practice, visit the companion website.

Your teacher may ask you to complete one or more of the following writing activities.

Free-form Writing

▬ **Write 75 to 100 words in response to one of the following questions:**

1. How would you feel if you were denied a genetic test for cancer because you couldn't afford to pay for it?

2. In your opinion, is the current twenty-year patent protection period too long? Why or why not?

3. Is patent protection exploitation or compensation? Justify your choice.

> **WRITING SUGGESTION**
> Good writers carefully choose the order in which they present their main points. They never begin or end with their weakest point—they hide it in the middle of their text. If you want to leave a good impression, create a strong first and last impression.

Essay Writing

- Write a 300- to 400-word essay using one of the thesis statements below.
- Do some research on the Internet to find evidence that supports your chosen thesis statement. (See Appendix A to review the structure of a persuasive essay.)

1. Canada's healthcare system can (or cannot) afford to respect patent rights.

2. Selling patented drugs to the Third World for profit is (or is not) immoral.

3. People who can't afford genetic testing and therapy must (or must not) manage without it.

4. Genetic testing for incurable diseases is (or is not) futile.

5. Canadian seniors are (or are not) overmedicated.

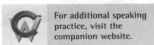

Would You Speak Up?

For additional speaking practice, visit the companion website.

Your teacher may ask you to participate in one or more of the following speaking activities.

Discussion

Answers will vary.

- In pairs or small groups, consider one (or more) of the following questions. Be prepared to share your thoughts with the class.

1. If you found a cure for AIDS, would you sell it or share it? Explain.

2. Do you think the developed world should freely share technology with the developing world? Why or why not?

3. Look up the words *wisdom* and *knowledge* in a dictionary. Explain the difference between the two terms. Was Myriad Genetics wise not to share its knowledge freely? Explain.

4. Modern society has more knowledge than all other previous societies combined. For all its knowledge, do you think it is a better society? Explain your answer.

5. Should science primarily be considered as a business? Why or why not?

SPEAKING SUGGESTION
When ordering your points in a presentation, use the same strategy suggested for writing persuasive essays—hide your weakest point in the middle of your presentation.

Discourse

- Prepare a structured, five-minute speech on one of the thesis statements below. (See Appendix B for a suggested speaking structure.)

- Do some research to find evidence that supports your chosen thesis statement. Make sure your speech has an introduction, a development and a conclusion.

1. AIDS medication should (or should not) be free.

2. Myriad Genetics' decision to enforce its patent rights was (or was not) wrong.

3. Canadian patent reform is (or is not) essential.

4. Granting patents on human gene sequences is (or is not) wise.

5. Scientific knowledge should (or should not) be freely shared.

Debate

- Debate the following proposal: Human gene patenting is wrong. (See Appendix B for the rules of a debate.)

What's That Word Mean Again?

In this section of Unit 6, we have focused on twenty terms—ten from the reading section and ten from the listening section. Review these terms by completing the activity below.

Word Memory Game

Have you ever played "Memory"? Memory is a card game in which cards are placed face down on a flat surface. Players must turn over two cards at a time, trying to make a *match*. A match occurs when two identical cards are turned over or—in the case of a word memory game—when a word and its definition are turned over. If a match isn't made, the cards must be turned face down again, and the next player takes his or her turn. If a match is made, the two cards are removed and the player takes another turn. The winner is the player with the most cards.

Materials
- One to three partners
- Forty blank index cards
- A pen or pencil
- A dictionary
- A good memory!

Instructions

1. Review the twenty terms and their explanations.

2. Write down each term and its explanation (you can use a synonym, a definition or a translation) on two separate index cards (twenty terms + twenty explanations = forty index cards).

3. Shuffle the cards.

4. Lay the cards face down on a flat surface.

5. Begin the game.

Alternate Version: You may make the game more challenging by insisting that the player who makes the match use the word in a sentence. If the player can't use the word correctly, the cards are turned faced down again and the next player takes his or her turn.

Would You Like to Work Together?

In this section, you will work with another student on a joint writing and speaking project.

Project Overview

You and your partner will do a written summary of an article on human gene patenting and give a verbal response.

A summary should be no longer than four sentences:
1. In the first sentence, identify the title, the author and the main idea of the article.
2. In the remaining three sentences, enumerate three pieces of evidence that support the main idea. (Note: There will likely be more than three pieces of evidence; choose <u>any</u> three.)

On pages 6 and 7 of this textbook, you will find an article by Susan Schwartz entitled "The Truth Is, I've Been Guilty of Lying." An example summary of this article would be as follows:

In "The Truth Is, I've Been Guilty of Lying," Susan Schwartz claims that it is surprising how dishonest "decent" people can be.
1. *The author believes that she is a "decent" person, but admits that she frequently tells lies.*
2. *An expert indicates that totally honest people are not liked by others.*
3. *An online poll suggests that a majority of people claim it is possible to be "too honest."*

A verbal response requires that you respect the following guidelines:
1. Identify the author's main idea.

2. Agree <u>or</u> disagree with the author's idea.

3. Provide three supporting ideas (statistics, expert opinion or example) to support your opinion. (Note: Do not "reuse" the author's supporting ideas. Do some research on the Internet to find three supporting ideas of your own.)

Required
- This textbook
- A dictionary and a grammar book
- Computer with Internet access

Procedure
This activity is carried out in two parts.

Part A: The Summary
1. Working individually, read the article "The Bioethics Debate" by Timothy Caulfield (pp. 180–181). Use a dictionary to help you understand any difficult terms.

2. Working together, summarize the article using the example summary above as a model. Verify your spelling and grammar.

3. Submit your summary to your teacher for evaluation.

Part B: The Verbal Response
4. Working together, read your teacher's evaluation of your summary. Decide whether you agree or disagree with the author's main idea. (Note: The two of you must share the same opinion.)

5. Conduct research on the Internet, looking for three ideas that support your opinion. (Remember: Search for statistics, expert opinion and/or examples.)

6. Meet with your teacher and give a verbal response using the guidelines provided above. During your meeting, your teacher will evaluate your response by asking you a series of questions: be prepared!

Why Fertility Should Not Be Commercialized

By Margaret Somerville

There is a concordance of interest among otherwise disparate groups—gay-rights advocates, the fertility industry, scientists and the government of Quebec—to change the social-ethical value that human life should not be commercialized, although they do so for very different purposes.

Selling sperm, ova or embryos, or paying a surrogate mother, is a crime in Canada punishable by 10 years imprisonment, thanks to the Assisted Human Reproduction Act of 2004. It governs "new reproductive technologies" in Canada, so-called NRTs.

Same-sex married couples argue that these prohibitions should be eliminated because they discriminate against them in exercising their right, which comes with marriage, to "found a family" as guaranteed under Article 16 of the United Nation's Universal Declaration of Human Rights.

The fertility industry (a $3-billion-a-year industry in the United States alone) also opposes these prohibitions because it finds them a major hurdle to getting on with business—payment is necessary to attract gamete "donors." For the same reason, it opposes prohibition of donor anonymity.

Some scientists want the prohibitions on payment and the act's prohibitions on cloning and the creation of human embryos for research repealed to facilitate research, particularly human embryo stem-cell research.

And the government of Quebec is in the Court of Appeal of Quebec challenging the constitutional validity of the AHR Act on the grounds that, because health is a provincial matter, the federal government had no authority to enact it.

[...]

So what are the arguments for and against the sale of gametes and embryos and payment of surrogate mothers, which values are at stake, and what messages would we send if we were to change the law to allow payment?

The Case for Legalization

Reports of gametes being sold and surrogate mothers paid in Canada, despite the legal prohibitions, are used to argue that if people are going to do that, we should legalize those transactions. Such a response means declaring ethical and moral bankruptcy. There will always be people and corporations that break laws, but we don't abandon those laws if they protect individuals and society from serious risks and harms or enshrine important fundamental values.

The language used to promote legalizing payment for ova donation describes desperate, childless couples and young women interested in helping them. The fertility industry heavily markets itself through the lens of altruism.

On the whole, however, women are not interested in "donating" unless they are paid and the majority, at least, do it to earn money they need. Desperate Canadian childless couples, going to the U.S. to buy gametes and embryos, have been described as cross-border shoppers. Should we be shopping for gametes and embryos?

We have always formed our most important shared societal values around the two landmark events in each and every human life, birth and death. Commercializing the passing on of human life to the next generation affects a radical change in the values created around birth. A child becomes a wanted product and the more exclusive the product the more it costs—the ova of tall, blond, blue-eyed, athletic, Ivy League graduates are being advertised for up to $50,000 U.S. each.

A next step is designer children—genetic interventions to further enhance embryos' "desirable" characteristics. That, too, will be good business for the fertility industry, especially because the potential market is larger than just infertile people.

Risks to ova donors are also a serious concern. Ovarian stimulation and ova retrieval involve a small risk of death or serious injury, including of future infertility, and considerable discomfort. A major concern is ensuring the fully informed consent of the donor. As a non-therapeutic procedure, legally, ova donation requires the fullest possible disclosure of harms and risks and free consent. Payment raises concerns about undue influence affecting consent.

Some advocates of payment draw an analogy between payment for abortion and payment for gametes, but the similarities are superficial, at best. Whatever our views on the morality and ethics of abortion, there is a major difference between paying a physician to carry out a procedure (as is the case in abortion) and paying people for parts of their bodies and, arguably, the most intimate and precious aspect of those bodies—their ability to pass on life to their children through their gametes. The same is true of paying a woman for the use of her body to gestate a child, as in surrogate motherhood. Likewise, there's a difference between poor people (or anyone) using their bodies to work for money, on the one hand, and selling their bodies, on the other. Calls for an open domestic market and the commercialization of human reproduction—as was the case with slavery—make human life and its transmission property to be bought and sold. And that affects all of us and our values, not just those who trade or are traded.

A Sacred Trust

As the French Civil Code puts it, human life and its transmission should be "hors de commerce" if we are to respect it as we should and hold it in trust. Human life and its transmission are not property to do with as we like. We implement this approach in prohibiting the sale of organs for transplantation. Gametes and embryos deserve at least equal respect.

Finally, and most important of all, in deciding whether payment for gametes and embryos is ethically acceptable, we must consider the impact commercializing human reproduction would have on the children who result and on others' respect for them.

The ethical doctrine of anticipated consent requires that when a person seriously affected by a decision cannot give his or her consent to that decision, we must ask ourselves whether we can reasonably anticipate that if they were present they would consent. If not, it's unethical to proceed. Many adults conceived through sperm donation have spoken out against paying donors, saying that it turns them and their lives into commodities. Indeed, as their ranks swell and they contact each other on the Internet, an increasing number of donor-conceived adults are speaking out against gamete donation itself.

(1,008 words)

It's No Holiday

By Leigh Turner

Researching overseas "transplant tourism" I find myself surfing the website of a company located in the Philippines. I scroll past the ads for cosmetic surgery and click the ad for a kidney transplant. The website asks me whether I want to add the kidney transplant package to my shopping cart, as if I were buying a book or DVD.

Organ brokers connect individuals wanting to buy kidneys to poor individuals desperate for cash. As organ sales—illegal in most countries—drop in India, China and Pakistan, brokers are shifting to the Philippines as their main source of kidneys.

One Australian company sells kidney transplants in the Philippines for $55,000 U.S. The price includes all hospital, broker and organ provider fees. A hospital in the Philippines offers two rates for kidney transplants. The five-star package costs $80,000. The three-star package costs $65,000. Both prices include $3,000 for a "charity donation" to the organ "donor." Liver4you, a business that sells liver and kidney transplants in the Philippines, advertises kidney transplants for $35,000 to $85,000.

Overseas Medical Services, a Canadian company advertising organ transplants in the Philippines, doesn't list prices. But the company website mentions that once organ recipients return to Canada the cost of post-transplant care is covered under provincial health plans. This means taxpayers pay the bill if diseases are transplanted with the organs.

Websites of organ brokers and medical tourism companies try to make buying kidneys seem like purchasing other consumer items. But human kidneys aren't the same as kidney beans. What organ brokers fail to disclose is how kidneys are bought and sold.

Philippine government officials periodically engage in public hand-wringing about the country's market in organs. But despite these theatrics, the government supports commercial organ transplantation. The Philippine Information Agency, a government body, advertises that kidney transplants in the Philippines can be purchased for as little as $25,000.

→

Government officials work with transplant physicians and hospital executives to increase the flow of international patients flying to the Philippines for kidney transplants. Doctors from the country's leading kidney transplant institute—a government hospital—are part of the medical tourism road show supported by the Philippine government. Government officials want to double the number of foreign patients buying kidney transplants at Philippine hospitals. They plan to make medical tourism an economic engine for the Philippines.

The Philippines' medical tourism industry faces many obstacles. India offers cheaper medical facilities. Singapore has better hospitals. The Philippines' major "competitive advantage" is that it has a significant number of citizens living in poverty as well as a government that permits organ sales.

Some economists and philosophers argue that individuals should be free to sell body parts. This emphasis on "autonomy" does not map onto the grim reality of how organs are solicited by brokers and sold by easily exploited and often desperate slum dwellers.

Individuals who sell organs are rarely told about the consequences of having a kidney removed. Dockyard workers and street vendors often discover only after selling a kidney that they can no longer perform demanding physical labour. They commonly have no access to health care after kidney removal. They cannot get treatment if they suffer complications.

Selling a kidney does not help poor individuals escape from poverty. Instead, they find themselves targeted by debt collectors and unable to keep the small sums they are paid for their kidneys. Individuals who sell a kidney are rarely paid what they were promised, and if they try to recover promised payments from local organ brokers, they can be threatened or beaten. When sellers are paid, they typically earn less than $2,000.

Just as poor individuals are harmed by selling a kidney, buyers are sometimes harmed by the very procedure that was supposed to improve their health. Purchased kidneys are often not properly screened or transplanted. The medical literature on transplant tourism describes the many dangers associated with buying organs in such countries as the Philippines and China.

Legislators, medical associations and patient groups wanting to promote organ donation rather than organ sales need to understand how easily organ trafficking crosses national borders. In most countries, legislation related to organ transplantation prohibits buying and selling of organs within national boundaries. However, commercial organ transplantation occurs across international networks.

We need laws and enforcement mechanisms capable of stopping Canadian citizens from buying organs from desperate individuals living in some of the poorest places on earth. Individuals considering buying an organ in the Philippines or elsewhere should understand that purchased organs are often inadequately screened, transmit infectious diseases, and are not transplanted according to international clinical standards. Little of the money they pay goes to the person who provides the organ. And finally, individuals selling kidneys are usually in poor health and live in extreme poverty.

Despite the many perils associated with buying human organs, Canadians are among the patients purchasing kidney transplants in the Philippines. They should be fully aware of what this entails.

(821 words)

Euthanasia: Dignified Death or Murder Masked as Compassion?

By Charles W. Moore for the *Times & Transcript*

"Dr. Death" Jack Kevorkian, 79, who claims to have participated in at least 130 assisted suicides, was released from prison in Michigan Friday after serving eight years of a 10- to 25-year sentence for second-degree murder, having earned time off for good behaviour.

I hoped Kevorkian would spend the rest of his life behind bars, but at least he'll be prohibited from facilitating any more "mercy killings" or providing care for anyone who is older than 62 or is disabled during his pitifully-short two-year parole.

However, Kevorkian's release is sure to reignite the public controversy over physician-assisted suicide.

Currently, euthanasia and doctor-assisted suicide are not terms acknowledged in Canadian law. Most provinces permit doctors to withdraw artificial life support at the patient's request, but not to hasten death. Some radical euthanasia advocates demand outright legalization—a protected "right to death," but larger numbers call for Canada to adopt a policy mirroring that of the Netherlands, where physician-assisted suicide and euthanasia have been tolerated since the early 1980s and formally legalized in 2002 within certain guidelines.

It has also been legal in Belgium since 2002, and is legally tolerated to a degree in Switzerland when the "recipient" takes an active role in the killing, and Japan with the patient's consent under certain guidelines.

As with other contentious moral/ethical issues like abortion and homosexuality, euthanasia tends to polarize people. The religious orthodox of most faiths oppose mercy killing as being always morally wrong, and for faithful Christians, euthanasia is a non-starter. The Catholic Catechism summarizes the Christian standard, noting that "an act or omission which, of itself or by intention, causes death in order to eliminate suffering constitutes a murder gravely contrary to the dignity of the human person and to the respect due to the living God . . . . We are stewards, not owners, of the life God has entrusted to us. It is not ours to dispose of."

On the other hand, liberals and leftists tend to advocate what they characterize as "the individual's right to die with dignity."

Informed public debate is crucial to our society coming to terms with this difficult issue. Unfortunately, many people's perspectives regarding mercy killing are based on popular misconceptions.

Studies in the Netherlands and the U.S. indicate that only a minority of those requesting euthanasia or doctor-assisted suicide do so because of extreme pain. The 1991 Dutch Remmelink Report found pain to be a factor in only 32 percent of euthanasia requests, and the sole reason in none.

Some suggest that medical technology advances have created a need for euthanasia by making it possible to keep patients alive who would have certainly died twenty years ago.

This is simply not so. No patient is obliged to submit to heroic medical intervention, or to any treatment at all for that matter. Persons inclined to let nature take its course are not impeded by medical technology.

The most common reason for requesting euthanasia identified by the Remmelink Report was perceived loss of dignity. A Washington State study cited by Dr. Emanuel in a March 1997 *Atlantic Monthly* article found the leading reasons for requested euthanasia were "fear of a loss of control or dignity, of being a burden, and of being dependent." Among AIDS patients surveyed in New York, the leading causes were depression, hopelessness, and lack of family or social support.

Euthanasia opponents predict that legalization will ultimately lead to a "slippery-slope" descent into routine legalized murder. The Remmelink Report documented that more than half of Dutch physicians had participated in mercy killings, and 90 percent of GPs and 84 percent of specialists expressed willingness to do so.

→

A 650-member pro-life physicians' group called the Nederlands Artsenverbond (NAV) condemns euthanasia, which it claims is out of control in Holland, maintaining that close to 16,000 people in Holland die from mercy killing each year, more than four times the official body count. Medical inspector Dr. Gerrit van der Wal was cited saying that in these cases the doctor's acted out of "paternalism . . . thinking it was best for the patient."

NAV spokesmen concur that almost all Dutch doctors who perform mercy killings do so out of compassion, but contend that "Once you accept killing as a solution for one problem, you soon find 100 problems for which killing can be regarded as a solution."

Euthanasia opponents argue that legalizing euthanasia increases pressure on patients who require ongoing total care to ease the financial, physical, and psychological burden on their families, and demands on the health care system by agreeing to a quick and painless death, and makes lingering terminally ill patients seem perversely responsible for their own suffering.

A "right to die" too easily morphs into an obligation to die.

(801 words)

We've All Been in Camera's Eye for a Long Time

By Michael Geist

Before there was YouTube, the Internet video phenomenon that is currently streaming more than 100 million videos each day, there was George Holliday.

Holliday was a mere bystander on a Los Angeles street in 1992 when he captured amateur video of police officers beating Rodney King. The incident, which sparked riots and national outrage about police brutality, would likely never have come to light without the Holliday video.

Over the past few decades, there have been other instances of amateur video or surveillance cameras capturing major moments.

Many cameras captured the collapse of the twin towers in 2001; however, there was only one clear amateur video of the first plane hitting the north tower.

Similarly, there are numerous news clips of the aftermath of the Kennedy assassination, but Abraham Zapruder's infamous film is the only known video of the assassination itself.

These incidents are not limited to North America. In Britain, the grainy shopping centre surveillance camera footage of two 10-year-old boys abducting two-year old James Bulger in 1993 shocked an entire country.

What makes these videos noteworthy is not only the indelible connection they have with the events themselves, but also how serendipitous they are, since until recently many potentially controversial events have gone unrecorded and therefore unnoticed.

Indeed, most news reporting is not unexpected—news conferences, staged photo opportunities and even hidden cameras are all designed to capture specific images that typically offer few surprises.

Many observers have anointed 2006 as the year of Internet video, yet it is also the year that unexpected video has suddenly become expected.

While much of the attention lavished on YouTube has focused on its impact on the entertainment industry, the bigger story may ultimately be how Internet video, in combination with ubiquitous video cameras embedded in millions of cellphones, has dramatically increased the likelihood that someone, somewhere will capture video evidence of once-hidden events that can be made instantly available to the world.

Consider several events from the past two weeks:

• U.S. army officials were forced to respond to concerns arising from a YouTube-posted amateur video that displayed several male soldiers duct-taping a female soldier to a pole in Iraq;

• The University of California at Los Angeles, California's largest university, was rocked by a video showing school police repeatedly using a taser gun on a student after they demanded that the student, who did not have the requisite identification, leave a campus library.

The video, captured by an unidentified person in the library with a cellphone, has been viewed more than one million times on YouTube alone;

• Michael Richards, the actor who played Kramer on the hit television series *Seinfeld*, was captured on film barking a stream of racist and offensive comments at a Los Angeles comedy club.

As thousands watched the amateur video on the Internet, Richards appeared within hours on the Late Show with David Letterman to issue a public apology (the clip of Richards's appearance has also been viewed hundreds of thousands of times on Internet video sites).

These high profile incidents are just the tip of the video iceberg as the cameras are now always rolling.

Internet video sites receive thousands of new videos every hour, with sites such as YouTube hosting une-dited footage of Canadian soldiers in Afghanistan, clips that appear to show police brutality and videos from universities and academic conferences featu-ring violent confrontations between students and teachers.

While there are some obvious benefits that arise from the transparency and potential accountability that can come from video evidence of controversial events, the emergence of an always-on video society raises some difficult questions about the appropriate privacy-transparency balance, the ethics of posting private moments to a global audience, and the res-ponsibility of websites that facilitate Internet video distribution.

Those questions crystallized this month at a Gatineau school, after two 13-year-old students pos-ted classroom video taken with a cellphone of their teacher yelling at a fellow student on YouTube. News reports indicate the video may have been staged, with students inducing the teacher into the shouting match specifically so that it could be captured on video. Although the video has since been removed from YouTube, the teacher is currently on stress leave, the two students have been suspended, and the school has banned personal electronic devices from the classroom.

As technology continues to evolve, it is unlikely that such measures will prove successful.

With built-in video cameras on laptop computers, hundreds of tiny video-capable devices, an incredible array of video-ready cellphones, and widespread Internet access, the clip culture is rapidly morphing from bits of favourite television shows to videos of our friends, neighbours and even ourselves.

Rather than banning the technology, we must ins-tead begin to grapple with the implications of these changes by considering the boundaries between transparency and privacy.

As our expectations of the availability of video change, so too must our sense of the video rules of the road.

(825 words)

The Bioethics Debate

By Timothy Caulfield

Bioethics gets a lot of attention. Whenever there is a big new medical breakthrough, health care controversy or cutting-edge research development, news reports will usually include the voice of someone described as an "ethicist."

Many movies, such as *The Island*, *Gattaca* and *Million Dollar Baby*, have bioethics themes. Michael Crichton's latest book, *Next*, is built around bioethics, particularly the concerns associated with gene patents. Political leaders increasingly refer to bioethics issues as important national concerns.

But measured against most academic areas, bioethics is just a baby. Despite its ubiquitous nature, it hasn't been around all that long. Most would agree that bioethics—if you define it as the study of the social, ethical and legal issues associated with the life sciences and health-care practices—took off in the '60s and '70s, largely as a result of specific research ethics controversies and biomedical development (such as new transplantation techniques). In the '80s and '90s, the social concerns associated with large scientific initiatives such as the Human Genome Project, and with the morally complex areas of stem cell and cloning research, gave the field more profile and momentum.

In this relatively short time, bioethics has become a well established and politically influential field of study. There are an increasing number of scholars and health-care professionals throughout the world whose entire careers are devoted to bioethics. Big science projects almost always include an ethics component (in fact, it is sometimes mandated by the funding agency).

Many health-care facilities have onsite bioethics experts and committees, there are numerous national and international bioethics policy entities, and U.S. presidents have created their own advisory groups. In Canada, bioethics experts play an important role in a wide variety of health and research policy issues, from new reproductive technologies to health-care reform.

In general, all of this is a good thing. As science and technology become an increasingly prominent part of our lives, economy and health-care practices, an exploration of the bioethical issues seems absolutely essential.

But here is the rub. Some of the biggest policy responses to all this bioethics activity have been less than ideal. There is a saying that ethics is always to the rear of science, and limping a little. I'm not sure that is always true. In our understandable desire to respond to bioethics issues, we may be sprinting ahead of what the evidence tells us about the true nature and degree of the social problem.

Let's look at two of the highest-profile bioethics concerns from biotechnology, which is my field of study: Gene patents and genetic discrimination.

Concern about gene patenting has been a dominant ethics topic for decades and has included a diverse number of complex questions. Should we be able to patent "life"? Do patents hurt access to useful technologies? And do patents impede research and innovation?

It is the last concern that has generated the most policy attention, primarily because patents are meant to stimulate, not slow, innovation. As such, this issue has led to numerous national and international policy reports and recommendations—including a number in Canada. In the United States, there is a bill before Congress asking for a ban on gene patents because the practice "hinders the discovery of medical breakthroughs that could save lives."

There is little evidence that this is the case. Despite the fact that more than 20 percent of the human genome is patented, all available research, such as our own work and a 2007 international study by the American Association for the Advancement of Science, found no clear evidence that patents hurt biomedical research.

Admittedly, the evidence is not robust, but do we really want to change the law in response to an issue that may not exist?

What about genetic discrimination? Again, this has long been a topic of debate in the field of bioethics—specifically, fear that all the new genetic tests will lead to a novel, and socially inappropriate, form of discrimination. This concern has led to the enactment of legislation throughout the world. In the U.S., for example, almost every state has some kind of anti-genetic discrimination law and the federal government just passed a national one.

But, as noted by Hank Greely, in *The New England Journal of Medicine*: "Studies have shown that although there is widespread concern about genetic discrimination, there are few examples of it—and no evidence that it is common."

I am not saying that there aren't challenging social issues associated with gene patents and genetic testing. Obviously, there are—and some are conceptually complex and not necessarily amenable to empirical analysis.

But much of the policy-making has been centred on specific, potentially measurable, harms (e.g., genetic discrimination is happening and must be stopped; patents hurt research.) Many other bioethics concerns, such as in the areas of cloning and stem cell research, could also face this "where's-the-evidence?" dilemma.

Good policy is founded on good evidence. Without this foundation, we hurt the trust in, and legitimacy of, the bioethics commentary, waste policy-making energy (and there ain't a lot out there), and potentially end up with policies that don't address the real social issues.

Of course, the above discussion triggers questions about how much evidence should be required to justify policy change. Is speculation enough? Perhaps, if the stakes are high and the speculation is sound. But, in general, good, sustainable, policy is built on solid evidence.

Bioethics has profile and influence. With that, there will be increased expectations and scrutiny. Is bioethics ready for the challenge? I hope so.

(925 words)

The Persuasive Essay

In a persuasive essay, the writer attempts to persuade readers that his or her opinion on a controversial issue is the right one. The writer presents one side of the issue and supports his or her opinion with arguments backed up by statistics, examples and expert opinions. In short essays (300 to 400 words), five paragraphs is the standard format.

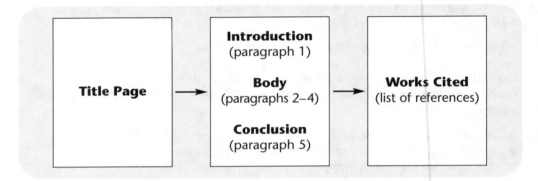

Introduction

The first paragraph of a persuasive essay is called the introduction.

The introduction begins with a "grabber"—a technique used to grab the reader's attention. Effective grabber techniques for essays include:

1. **Quotations**
   Sue Rodriguez asked, "… whose body is this? Who owns my life?"

2. **Definitions**
   "Euthanasia" is the act of killing someone to relieve pain and suffering.

3. **Facts**
   On February 12, 1994, Sue Rodriguez defied Canadian law and, with the help of an unidentified physician, ended her life.

The introduction ends with a thesis statement, an affirmative sentence that expresses the writer's opinion about the subject of the essay.

Euthanasia should not be legalized.

Body Paragraphs

The second, third and fourth paragraphs make up the body of the essay.

In each of these paragraphs, the first sentence begins with a transition term (*First, Second, Third / To begin, To continue, To finish*) followed by an argument in support of the thesis statement. The first sentence, also called the topic sentence, must be backed up with some form of evidence.

There are three types of evidence:

1. **Statistics**
   Facts: *Euthanasia became legal in the Netherlands on April 1, 2002.*
   Figures: *Approximately 85 percent of Dutch people support active euthanasia.*

2. **Expert Opinion**
   Quote: *Sue Rodriguez once asked, "I want to ask you gentlemen, if I cannot give consent to my own death, then whose body is this? Who owns my life?"*
   Paraphrase: *Sue Rodriguez asked the court to tell her who owned her body and her life.*

3. **Example**
   The story of Sue Rodriguez, a young woman diagnosed with Amyotrophic Lateral Sclerosis (ALS), demonstrates the need to legalize assisted suicide.

Ideally, at least two types of evidence are used in the body of the essay.

Conclusion

The fifth paragraph is called the conclusion.

The conclusion begins with a transition term (*In summary, To conclude*) and a summary in which the thesis and the three arguments are restated.

The essay ends with a "clincher"—a technique used to encourage the reader to think about the essay. Clincher techniques include:

1. **Connecting with the Introduction**
   An example of connecting with the grabber (see Introduction above) would be: *The response to both of Sue Rodriguez's questions is the same: she does!*

2. **Asking a Rhetorical Question**
   Should euthanasia be legalized? Without a doubt!

3. **Offering a Suggestion**
   Euthanasia should be a choice in the same way that abortion is a choice—and for the same reason: the body belongs to the individual, not the state.

Citation Style

Before writing a persuasive essay, you must do some research. Any research referred to in your essay must be correctly cited.

When you quote (use somebody's exact words), paraphrase (rephrase somebody's words) or refer to another writer's work, you must reference the writer to avoid being accused of plagiarism.

There are many different citation styles. The style suggested in this textbook is based on the *Modern Language Association (MLA) Citation Style*.

Basically, a citation includes two interrelated parts:

1. **Parenthetical Reference**

2. **Works-Cited List**

The parenthetical reference occurs in the body of the essay and the Works-Cited list appears at the end of the essay.

Parenthetical Reference

Parenthetical references are essential for quotes and paraphrases. Print sources (newspapers, books, etc.) and Internet sources are cited differently.

If the author of your quote or paraphrase is cited in someone else's work, use the phrase "as cited in," for example, "Fletcher, as cited in Manning 47." In this case, a complete reference to Manning should appear in the Works-Cited list.

Source	Author's Name Mentioned in the Reference	Author's Name Not Mentioned in the Reference
Print	Parenthetical references should include the **page number.** *Dr. Michael Manning writes, "In my opinion, the evidence overwhelmingly supports the proposal that we maintain our stringent prohibitions against legalized euthanasia and physician-assisted suicide in America." (85)*	Parenthetical references should include the **author's last name** and the **page number**. *One expert writes, "In my opinion, the evidence overwhelmingly supports the proposal that we maintain our stringent prohibitions against legalized euthanasia and physician-assisted suicide in America." (Manning 85)*
Internet	No parenthetical reference is required. *In a book review, Paul Tuns beautifully summarizes Manning's position by stating that "... Manning illustrates how if one exception is made to the rule against doctors killing their patients, soon the rule will fall apart."*	Parenthetical references should include the **author's last name**. *One reviewer beautifully summarizes Manning's position by stating that "... Manning illustrates how if one exception is made to the rule against doctors killing their patients, soon the rule will fall apart." (Tuns)*

Works Cited

On a separate page at the end of your essay, you must list all sources paraphrased or quoted in your essay. Follow these guidelines:

- The sources are listed in alphabetical order by last name (or by organization or title if no author has been identified).
- *Italicize* or underline all titles of complete works (newspapers, books, TV series, etc.).
- Use quotation marks for titles of works contained in another work (articles, book chapters, TV episodes, etc.).
- Capitalize all important words in a title.
- If citing an Internet source, indicate the date accessed using the phrase, "Retrieved: day/month/year."
- Make sure all entries are double-spaced, and the second, third and fourth lines of each entry are indented.

The following section lists common types of sources accompanied by examples. In particular, notice how Manning's and Tuns's works (see Parenthetical Reference examples above) are cited.

Type of Source	Example
1. Book with one author	Manning, Michael. *Euthanasia and Physician-Assisted Suicide: Killing or Caring?* New York: Paulist Press, 1998.
2. Article in a newspaper or magazine	Koch, Tom. "Disabled Are Not Dogs." *Vancouver Sun.* 7 February 2001: A-15.
3. Article on a website	Tuns, Paul. "Book on Euthanasia a 'Clarion Call'." The Interim: Canada's Pro-Life, Pro-Family Newspaper Online. Retrieved: 29 July 2005. http://www.theinterim.com/dec98/21euthanasia.html
4. Website	The John Donne Society. Ed. Mathews, John. "Meditations." Retrieved: 20 October 2004. http://www.johndonnesociety.org

The Title Page

An academic institution often has its own unique title page requirements. In general, a title page should contain the following elements:

1. **Essay Title**
   An abbreviated thesis statement is often a good title.

2. **Student's Name**
   Include your first and last names.

3. **Teacher's Name**
   Don't forget to include courtesy titles such as Mr., Mrs., Ms. or Dr.

4. **Course Title**
   Indicate the course code (if any).

5. **Academic Institution**
   Include the complete name of your school.

6. **Date Submitted**
   Indicate the date that you submitted the essay.

In some cases, the instructor may also want you to indicate your essay's total word count. If this is the case, don't count words in quotations.

Notice that in the example title page (p. 187), the first four elements are centred in the top third of the page and the last two elements are centred in the bottom third of the page.

The title page—and the entire essay—should be double-spaced with 2.54 cm margins to allow room for corrections.

Example Persuasive Essay

Read the annotated persuasive essay below on the legalization of active euthanasia. Following the essay, you will find information on persuasive strategies and language structures. **Note:** Double-space essays and indent the developing and concluding paragraphs.

A Time to Be Born and a Time to Die

By
(Student's name)

Presented to
(Teacher's name)

For the course
(Course name and code)

(Academic institution)

(Date submitted)

Grabber
(Quotation)

Sue Rodriguez asked, "… whose body is this? Who owns my life?" (as cited in conservativeforum.org). These two questions are at the heart of the debate surrounding the legalization of active euthanasia. To these questions, the proponents of legalization respond that their bodies and their lives belong to them. While such a response may at first appear reasonable, careful reflection reveals the opposite to be true: an individual's life is not his (or hers) alone and as such, active euthanasia should not be legalized.

Thesis statement
(Opinion on active euthanasia)

First transition term and argument
(Topic sentence 1)

First, the words "life" and "body" are not synonymous. The term "life" refers to a person's experiences while the term "body" refers to a person's anatomy. When people are asked about their lives, they talk about their friends and their families, not about their lungs and their livers. As the metaphysical poet John Donne wrote, "No man is an island, entire of itself … Any man's death diminishes me, because I am involved in mankind …" In other words, life is a collective—not an individual experience—and the death of one affects all.

Evidence
(Expert opinion)

Second transition term and argument
(Topic sentence 2)

Second, those who claim they have the right to choose their own deaths need to be reminded that they did not in fact choose their own births. Individuals must take full advantage of life and live each moment as if it were their last. As the philosopher George Santayana wisely stated, "There is no cure for birth and death save to enjoy the interval."

Evidence
(Expert opinion)

Third transition term and argument
(Topic sentence 3)

Evidence
(Statistic)

Transition term and summary

Clincher
(Suggestion)

Third, people cannot possess their "lives" or their "bodies" since neither should ever be considered as objects. Indeed, the objectification of the human body is behind many societal ills, prostitution being but one example. In Canada, it is estimated that female prostitutes have a mortality rate forty times higher than the national average (as cited in Menstuff). An object can be bought or sold and disposed of at will and as such, the body must never be perceived of—or treated as—a simple "object."

To conclude, the "my body/my life" argument is an inadequate rationale for the legalization of active euthanasia as the terms "life" and "body" do not have an identical meaning. People cannot choose when to be born, so they should not choose when to die. The objectification of the human body has negative consequences. As a result, those in favour of legalizing active euthanasia must come up with a stronger argument to support their cause if they wish society in general to adopt their point of view.

Works Cited

Conservativeforum.org. Ed. The Canadian Conservative Forum.

"Quotations: Sue Rodriquez." Retrieved: 19 July 2005.

http://conservativeforum.org/authquot.asp?ID=1068

Donne, John. "Devotions upon Emergent Occasions." Representative

Poetry Online. Retrieved: 22 July 2004.

http://eir.library.utoronto.ca/rpo/display/poet98.html

Menstuff: The National Men's Resource Center. Ed. Menstuff.

"Prostitution." Retrieved: 20 July 2004.

http://www.menstuff.org

Santayana, George. "War Shrines." Bartleby. The Columbia World of

Quotations. Retrieved: 22 July 2004.

http://www.bartleby.com/66/81/48181.html

Persuasive Strategies

There are four basic strategies to use when writing a persuasive essay:

1. **Don't use any first- or second-person pronouns** (*I, you, we, my, your, our,* etc.).
   By only using the third-person singular or plural (*he, she, it, they,* etc.), the essay appears impersonal and therefore rational.

2. **Don't use any contractions** (*he's, they're, we're,* etc.) **unless your teacher indicates otherwise.**
   Using a formal writing style will lend credibility to your essay.

3. **Place the weakest argument in the second paragraph of the body (paragraph 3).**
   By placing your weakest argument in the middle of the body paragraphs, the stronger two arguments hide the weakness of the argument. In other words, you begin and end strong.

4. **In the introduction, present the opposing viewpoint first, and then refute it in your thesis statement.**
   By presenting the opposing position and then refuting it, you appear open-minded; you indicate that you have considered both sides of the issue, opting for the better of the two. (See the introduction of the persuasive essay on page 182 for an example of this technique.)

Language Structures and Transition Terms

Some useful language structures to present and then refute an opinion are:

- *While proponents claim that …, it would appear the opposite is true.*
- *Some have asserted that …; nevertheless, …*
- *It could be argued that …; however, …*

Notice the words *nevertheless* and *however*. They are transition words and, like the terms *first, second* and *third*, they help the reader follow your train of thought.

Below is a list of commonly used transition terms and their functions.

Functions	Examples
To add an idea	*also, in addition (to), furthermore, moreover*
To emphasize an idea	*indeed, in fact*
To provide an example	*for example, for instance, to illustrate*
To show a result	*therefore, as a result*
To show a contrast	*however, nevertheless, otherwise, on the other hand*
To conclude	*to conclude, in conclusion, in summary, in brief, briefly*

Discourse and Debate

Discourse

A persuasive discourse is a formal speech intended to persuade the listeners that the speaker's opinion on an issue is the right one. Like the persuasive essay (see Appendix A), the speaker's opinion is supported with arguments backed up by statistics, examples and expert opinions. In short speeches (five to seven minutes), three arguments is the standard format.

The structure of a persuasive discourse is similar to that of a persuasive essay; an introduction, a body and a conclusion are required.

Introduction

Like the persuasive essay, the persuasive speech begins with a "grabber"—a technique used to grab the listener's attention. Effective grabber techniques for public speaking include:

1. **Rhetorical Questions**
   What are you having for supper tonight? Most of you will probably be having vegetables, rice and … meat.

2. **Provocative Statements**
   Eating animals is murder—plain and simple.

3. **Short Anecdotes**
   Picture it! It's a hot summer evening. You're having a barbecue. A couple of thick juicy steaks are cooking on the grill. All of a sudden …

At the end of the introduction, the speaker provides a preview statement, an affirmative sentence that expresses the speaker's opinion (the thesis statement) and enumerates the three arguments that the speaker will present to support his or her opinion.

Eating animals is wrong for three reasons. First, killing animals is murder. Second, raising animals for food is an inefficient use of farmland. And third, animals raised for food live in unbearable conditions.

Body

In the body of the speech, the speaker's three arguments are developed. Each argument is introduced with a transition term (*To begin, To continue, To finish*) and must be supported by **at least two** of the following types of evidence:

1. **Statistics**
   Do you know that if Americans reduced their meat consumption by 10 percent, sixty million people could be fed with the grain that would have been used to feed livestock?

2. **Expert Opinion**
   Suzanne Havala has written a book designed for the vegetarian teenager. Ms. Havala believes that …

3. **Example**
   Surprisingly, many vegetarian teens find friends and family to be less than supportive of their vegetarian lifestyle. In an article entitled "Hold Your Breath," nineteen-year-old vegetarian Nathalie McCabe recounts a story in which she is teased for not eating meat. She …

Conclusion

The conclusion begins with a transition term (*To conclude, In summary*) and a summary statement, a rephrased preview statement (see Introduction above). The speaker ends with a "clincher"—a technique used to encourage the listeners to think about what the speaker has said. Effective clincher techniques for public speaking include:

1. **Connecting with the Introduction**
   An example of connecting with the grabber (see Introduction, page 192) would be: *So what are you having for dinner tonight? Do yourself—and your arteries—a favour: eat some veggies, rice and tofu! Forget about the meat!*

2. **Demonstrating the importance of the thesis statement**
   If people realized the harm that is done by eating meat, they would change their diets and the current culture of killing would come to an end.

3. **Offering a Solution**
   The next time someone asks you to pass the steak, pass the salad instead!

Persuasive Strategies

There are four basic rules to keep in mind when giving a persuasive discourse:

1. **Keep it short and simple.**
   Your sentences should be short and your language should be simple.

2. **Repeat yourself.**
   While readers can go back and reread, an audience can't go back and "re-listen." Don't be afraid to repeat key pieces of information to help your listeners follow along.

3. Use transition terms.

Transition words, such as *first, second, third, to begin, to continue, to conclude*, are essential to help your listener follow your train of thought. (See page 198 for examples of common transition terms.)

4. Ask questions.

There are two types of questions that you should ask: rhetorical (ask and answer the question) and directed (select members of the audience and ask them questions). Never ask a question to a group of people. More often than not, no one will respond.

A Few Don'ts

Here are a few things not to do when giving a speech.

- Don't read your speech.
- Don't stand in one place.
- Don't talk to just one or two people in the audience.
- Don't avoid making eye contact.

Practise your speech ahead of time so that you don't feel the need to read it. It is a good idea to move around and connect with all members of the audience. As the saying goes, "You can't trust someone who doesn't look you in the eyes." Let your audience know they can trust you—and what you have to say!

Debate

A debate is a structured public discussion in which two teams take opposing positions on a controversial proposal. There are ten proposals suggested for debate in this textbook:

1. Music downloading is wrong. (Unit 2, Section A)

2. Human reproductive cloning is wrong. (Unit 2, Section B)

3. Same-sex adoption is wrong. (Unit 3, Section A)

4. Commercial surrogacy is wrong. (Unit 3, Section B)

5. The human organ trade is wrong. (Unit 4, Section A)

6. Xenotransplantation is wrong. (Unit 4, Section B)

7. Assisted suicide is wrong. (Unit 5, Section A)

8. The elimination of genetically diseased or disabled fetuses is wrong. (Unit 5, Section B)

9. Video surveillance is wrong. (Unit 6, Section A)

10. Human gene patenting is wrong. (Unit 6, Section B)

In the "Did You Know …?" sections of each unit, three arguments are suggested *for* and three arguments are suggested *against* each of these proposals.

The team for the proposal is referred to as the **affirmative team**, and the team against the proposal is referred to as the **negative team**. Each team is composed of two or three members, and there are three different types of speeches:

1. The First Speech

2. The Second Speech

3. Two Rebuttal Speeches

The affirmative team begins the debate, and the negative team ends the debate.

Overview of the Debate

The schema below shows the speaking order in a debate. The affirmative team begins, the negative team continues, the affirmative team responds and so on until the negative side ends the debate.

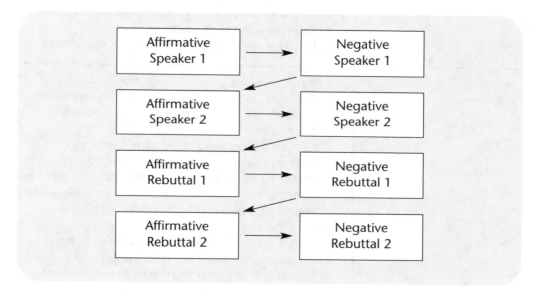

Overview of the Speeches

The first and second speeches are **one formal speech given by two people**. Like the five-paragraph persuasive essay, the speech is based on a thesis statement supported by three arguments. The first speaker delivers the introduction and presents the first argument. The second speaker presents the second and third arguments and delivers the conclusion.

The rebuttal speeches are **two informal speeches** given by each member of a two-member team or by the third member of a three-member team. The rebuttal speaker attacks the opposing team's arguments and defends his or her team's arguments. The rebuttal speaker must know his or her team's arguments well and prepare counter-arguments (arguments opposing the other team's arguments) **before** the debate. The rebuttal speech is organized while the debate is in progress.

> **DEBATING TIP**
> Rebuttal speakers should prepare a series of cue cards before the debate. On one side of each cue card, they should indicate a potential argument of the opposing team; on the other side, they should indicate a counter-argument.

Structure of the Affirmative Speeches

The debate is a highly structured oral presentation. Each speaker has certain tasks to perform in order to maintain the structure. The chart below outlines the tasks for each speaker.

Affirmative Speakers	Tasks
First	1. Introduces self and team and greets the audience. 2. Captures the audience's attention with an anecdote, a question, etc. 3. States the subject of the debate and the affirmative team's proposal. 4. Indicates the three arguments to be used to support the proposal and develops the first argument. 5. Uses transition words (see page 198). 6. Uses **at least two** of the following types of evidence to support the first argument: expert opinions, statistics and examples. 7. Summarizes the argument and reminds the audience of the two remaining arguments to be presented by the second speaker. 8. Uses a visual aid (blackboard, posters, handouts, etc.). 9. Refers to—but does not read—notes. 10. Respects speaking time (five to seven minutes).
Second	1. Introduces self. 2. Politely criticizes something the first negative speaker said or did. 3. Reminds the audience of the affirmative team's first argument and restates the two remaining arguments. 4. Uses transition words (see page 198). 5. Uses **at least two** of the following types of evidence to support the second and third arguments: expert opinions, statistics and examples. 6. Summarizes the affirmative team's position and reminds the audience of the team's proposal and three arguments. 7. Asks the audience to support the affirmative team's position. 8. Uses a visual aid (blackboard, posters, handouts, etc.). 9. Refers to—but does not read—notes. 10. Respects speaking time (five to seven minutes).
First Rebuttal	1. Introduces self. 2. Attacks the negative team's position. 3. Defends the affirmative team's position and asks the audience to support this position. 4. Uses **at least two** of the following types of evidence to attack and defend: expert opinions, statistics and examples. 5. Respects speaking time (three to four minutes).
Second Rebuttal	1. Introduces self. 2. Attacks the negative team's position. 3. Defends the affirmative team's position and asks the audience to support this position. 4. Uses **at least two** of the following types of evidence to attack and defend: expert opinions, statistics and examples. 5. Respects speaking time (three to four minutes).

Structure of the Negative Speeches

The debate is a highly structured oral presentation. Each speaker has certain tasks to perform in order to maintain the structure. The chart below outlines the tasks for each speaker.

Negative Speakers	Tasks
First	1. Introduces self and team and greets the audience. 2. Politely criticizes something the first affirmative speaker said or did. 3. States the negative team's opposition to the affirmative proposal. 4. Indicates the three arguments to be used to support the negative team's opposition. 5. Uses transition words (see next page). 6. Uses **at least two** of the following types of evidence to support the first argument: expert opinions, statistics and examples. 7. Summarizes the argument and reminds the audience of the two remaining arguments to be presented by the second speaker. 8. Uses a visual aid (blackboard, posters, handouts, etc.). 9. Refers to—but does not read—notes. 10. Respects speaking time (five to seven minutes).
Second	1. Introduces self. 2. Politely criticizes something the second affirmative speaker said or did. 3. Reminds the audience of the negative team's first argument and restates the two remaining arguments. 4. Uses transition words (see next page). 5. Uses **at least two** of the following types of evidence to support the second and third arguments: expert opinions, statistics and examples. 6. Summarizes the negative team's position and reminds the audience of the team's opposition and three arguments. 7. Asks the audience to support the negative team's position. 8. Uses a visual aid (blackboard, posters, handouts, etc.). 9. Refers to—but does not read—notes. 10. Respects speaking time (five to seven minutes).
First Rebuttal	1. Introduces self. 2. Attacks the affirmative team's position. 3. Defends the negative team's position and asks the audience to support this position. 4. Uses **at least two** of the following types of evidence to attack and defend: expert opinions, statistics and examples. 5. Respects speaking time (three to four minutes).
Second Rebuttal	1. Introduces self. 2. Attacks the affirmative team's position. 3. Defends the negative team's position and asks the audience to support this position. 4. Uses **at least two** of the following types of evidence to attack and defend: expert opinions, statistics and examples. 5. Respects speaking time (three to four minutes).

Transition Terms

The following is a list of common transition terms used in debating.

Functions	Examples
To add an idea	*also, what's more, in addition, to add to that*
To conclude	*to finish up, to wrap up, to conclude*
To emphasize an idea	*I repeat, I can't emphasize enough that …, as I said*
To provide an example	*for example, to illustrate, by way of illustration (or example)*
To sequence	*first, second, third*
To show a contrast	*on the one hand …, on the other hand …, on the contrary we …, notwithstanding*
To show a result	*because of this, owing to that, as a result*

Your PERFECT PARTNER to

Parallels

Second Edition

TAKING A STAND IN ENGLISH

LONGMAN

Active Study Dictionary

HELPS YOU BUILD YOUR VOCABULARY

Interactive CD-ROM

Now in colour

NEW EDITION

Longman

ISBN 978-1-405-86228-8

The *Longman Active Study Dictionary* is the most comprehensive intermediate dictionary. It offers an integrated thesaurus, full colour photographs and an interactive CD-ROM.

The best-selling dictionary in its category, the *Longman Active Study Dictionary* includes all the information students need to improve their English and increase their vocabulary.

PERFECT PARTNERS

PEARSON

Longman

Parallels

Second Edition

TAKING A STAND IN ENGLISH

Parallels: Taking a Stand in English, Second Edition, is an integrated skills course designed for intermediate to high intermediate college students.

- **Articles, radio excerpts and TV segments** dealing with controversial issues in the sciences and humanities increase Canadian cultural awareness.
- **Speaking and writing exercises** encourage informed expression.
- **Individual and paired vocabulary exercises** support vocabulary acquisition.
- **Grammar tips** help students avoid common pitfalls.
- **Etymological explanations** reinforce recall.
- **Strategies** and **suggestions** assist student success.
- **Additional articles** related to topics discussed in the book provide further reading practice.
- **Comprehensive appendices** structure written and oral productions.
- **Peer projects** encourage cooperative learning.

The *Parallels: Taking a Stand in English Companion Website* (www.longmanesl.ca/reid.cw) offers supplementary exercises.

Audio program (product 133096): Authentic audio texts from CBC radio.

Video program (product 133088): Authentic news reports from CTV and CBC television.

Student manual (product 133036)

RELATED COMPONENTS

Parallels: Taking a Stand in English — English Grammar, **Second Edition,** (product 133035) provides intermediate to high intermediate college students with meaningful practice in important areas of English grammar and usage.

Parallels: Taking a Stand in English — English Grammar Answer Key, **Second Edition** (product 133149)

Parallels: Taking a Stand in English — English Grammar — Teacher's Annotated Edition (product 133039)

COMBO PACKAGES

Parallels: Taking a Stand in English and *Parallels: Taking a Stand in English — English Grammar,* **Second Edition** (product 133105)

Parallels: Taking a Stand in English, Parallels: Taking a Stand in English — English Grammar, **Second Edition** and *Longman Active Study Dictionary* (product 133106)

082-BAC-127

PEARSON
Longman

ISBN 978-2-7613-3038

9 782761 330381

133038